# The Truth
# That Sticks

# The Truth
# That Sticks

## New Labour's
## Breach of Trust

*Martin Bell*

ICON BOOKS

Originally published in 2007 by Icon Books Ltd

This updated edition published in the UK in 2008
by Icon Books Ltd, The Old Dairy,
Brook Road, Thriplow,
Cambridge SG8 7RG
email: info@iconbooks.co.uk
www.iconbooks.co.uk

Sold in the UK, Europe, South Africa and Asia
by Faber & Faber Ltd, 3 Queen Square,
London WC1N 3AU or their agents

Distributed in the UK, Europe, South Africa and Asia
by TBS Ltd, TBS Distribution Centre, Colchester Road
Frating Green, Colchester CO7 7DW

This edition published in Australia in 2008
by Allen & Unwin Pty Ltd,
PO Box 8500, 83 Alexander Street,
Crows Nest, NSW 2065

This edition published in the USA in 2008
by Totem Books
Inquiries to Icon Books Ltd, The Old Dairy,
Brook Road, Thriplow, Cambridge SG8 7RG, UK

Distributed in Canada by
Penguin Books Canada,
90 Eglinton Avenue East, Suite 700,
Toronto, Ontario M4P 2YE

ISBN: 978-1840468-78-6

Typeset in 12 on 15pt ITC New Baskerville
by Hands Fotoset, Woodthorpe, Nottingham

Printed and bound in the UK by
J.H. Haynes & Co. Ltd

Martin Bell OBE is one of the best-known and most highly regarded names in British television journalism. As a BBC reporter he has covered foreign assignments in more than 80 countries and eleven wars including Vietnam, Nigeria, Angola, Nicaragua, The Gulf and Bosnia, where millions watched as he was nearly killed by shrapnel. In 1997 Martin became the first Independent MP to be elected to Parliament since 1950.

His previous books are *In Harm's Way* (Penguin, 1995), *An Accidental MP* (Viking, 2000) and *Through Gates of Fire* (Weidenfeld and Nicolson, 2003).

# CONTENTS

# LIST OF
# ILLUSTRATIONS

*Why is betrayal the only truth that sticks?*

Arthur Miller, *After the Fall*

*For Max, Natasha and Clementine*

# FOREWORD

This book began accidentally in the summer of 2006. The war in Iraq was then in its fourth year, with its casualties uncounted and its architects unpunished. In the Helmand province of southern Afghanistan, British troops were involved in their fiercest fighting since the Korean war. At home, the cash-for-peerages scandal was uncovering long-hidden layers of corruption in the geology of politics. The people's loss of trust in their leaders was more acute than during the relatively halcyon days, ten years earlier, of cash-for-questions.

I was at the literary festival in Dartington Hall in Devon. In the tent where books are sold I looked for one that would address these issues and ask 'How did we get into this mess, and how will we ever get out of it?' There was no such book. Then I remembered a saying of the French, that one is never so well served as by oneself. So I decided to write it myself; and to do it, as much as possible, from personal experience and reflection.

My thanks are due to many friends in the worlds of politics, diplomacy, soldiering and humanitarian assistance; to those truly honourable members of Parliament who are as concerned as I am about democracy's state of disrepair and wish to mend it; to the members of all parties and no party who have quietly helped me and given advice but would not wish to be named; to the parliamentary awkward squad past and present and especially Tam Dalyell, the former Father of the House of Commons; to Therese Lyras of Landmine Action; to Carne Ross, a brave and independent diplomat; to the Reverend Andrew Martlew and Imam Asim Hafiz of the Army Chaplains' Department; to Major Adam Jowett and Support Company of 3 Para; to Brigadier Bill Deller of the Suffolk Regiment; to General Lord Walker and the Pensioners of the Royal Hospital Chelsea; to the broken soldiers cared for by Combat Stress; to UNICEF for the inspiration of its people and programmes in Afghanistan; to Shima Islam of UNICEF for the pictures from there and Phil Pegum of the BBC for the pictures from Iraq; to Peter Cox who launched this project; and to Simon Flynn, Andrew Furlow and Duncan Heath of Icon Books who believed in it enough to make it happen.

No writer of fiction would have attempted a story like this. So much of what happened was unpredictable – and, in retrospect, unbelievable.

## CHAPTER ONE

# THE CONFIDENCE OF THE PEOPLE

*We will clean up politics ... The Conservatives are afflicted by sleaze and prosper from secret funds from foreign supporters. There is unquestionably a national crisis of confidence in our political system, to which Labour will respond in a measured and sensible way.*

Labour Party election manifesto,
general election 1997

In retrospect, the Labour Party victory of 1997 was a wholly predictable landslide. With 43 per cent of the vote (the Conservatives struggled barely to reach 30 per cent), at a stroke New Labour achieved total domination of the House of Commons.

The Conservative Party was routed as never before in living memory. The British electorate had passed harsh judgement on eighteen years of Tory rule, granting them a mere 165 seats to 418. It was a Labour landslide, and the land slid because of one issue above all others: sleaze.

'I want to renew faith in politics', proclaimed Tony Blair in his introduction to the Labour Party's election manifesto, 'through a government that will govern in the interest of the many, the broad majority of people who work hard, play by the rules, pay their dues and feel let down by a political system that gives the breaks to the few, to an elite at the top increasingly out of touch with the rest of us.'

These were heady words for a country that, at the time, seemed to be in danger of drowning in a tide of cheating, cronyism and corruption. Labour's simple but powerful campaign promise to 'end sleaze' was irresistible to millions, all the more so when delivered by their sincere and fresh-faced young leader who represented something other than politics as usual. He took office, as he said, amid 'a sense of hope beyond ordinary imagining'. That was not just how it seemed but how it was.

For me, the issue was of such great importance that I resigned from my reporting job with the BBC after 33 years, quitting a profession held low in public esteem – journalism – for another held even lower: politics.

Something about frying pans and fires came to mind. It was the most frightening time of my life, the war zones included.

In a dazed sort of way, I even had a walk-on role, in the early dawn of a government that claimed to offer not only new policies but new politics. I found myself unexpectedly, and even accidentally, elected to replace a Conservative MP, Neil Hamilton, who had come to seem symbolic of a party and government that had lost its moral compass. It was a popular insurrection against dodgy politics.

Tony Blair, the Labour Party leader for only three years, was as untested in government as most of his ministers. For eighteen years they had known nothing but opposition. But they represented a clean break with the past; and that was what won it for them. They were pledged by their manifesto to restore public trust in public life. So they would, wouldn't they? Or at least they would try. And if any words hung longer in the air than any others, it was these: 'We will clean up politics ...'

That promise may seem quaint now, in the light of all that has happened; but I and millions besides me believed it. According to their anthem at the time, things could only get better. They could hardly get worse, could they, than what had gone before? I was new to politics, and why should I not believe them? Indeed, my campaign was used – and I was aware of it at the time – to keep the 'sleaze' issue bubbling away at the top of the agenda. I had no problem with that and I still do not, except that it was treated as a kind of stage prop, to disappear when it had worked its magic at the touch of the conjuror's wand. And Tony Blair could conjure – oh, how he could conjure! – like no Prime Minister since Lloyd George, with whom he had other affinities, as we shall see.

Public trust in public life was as important an issue then as it is now; but as soon as the campaign was over, most of those who were elected on it seemed to shed it like yesterday's fashion accessory, no longer wanted on voyage. It had served its purpose and did not seem to matter to them any more. Sir Alistair Graham, chairman of the Committee on Standards in Public Life, was among those deemed surplus to requirements. On leaving office – or, more accurately, on being dismissed from it – he said: 'My greatest regret has been the apparent failure to persuade the government to place high ethical standards at the heart of its thinking and, most importantly, behaviour.'[1]

This book is about that failure. What happened to the dream of New Labour that we were sold? What happened to their commitment to honest and open government? Why this apparent nonchalance over patronage and the export of a faith-based foreign policy under the gun? Did the legality of their actions, whether in conferring a peerage or waging a war, appear on their radar at all? Why are the people who represent us *still* so unrepresentative of us? Why was the trust that we had in this lot – we who also believed in their new beginning – so totally lost as to seem irretrievable? Why were the civil servants and military chiefs unwilling to warn them, or even to express unpalatable opinions?

And what can we learn from these mistakes, so that our future governments should not repeat them?

These appear to be reasonable questions to be asking, and trying to answer, at the end of the most dazzling, disappointing and ultimately dangerous decade in modern politics.

\* \* \*

I had a front-row seat for four years not only on the floor of the House of Commons, but for most of that time on the Select Committee on Standards and Privileges. A parade of MPs, including some senior ministers, passed before us accused of having breached the MPs' code of conduct. Of the eleven MPs around the horseshoe table in Committee Room 13 – seven Labour, two Conservative, one Lib Dem and myself – I was the one at the centre of the horseshoe, neither on one side nor the other. It was instructive to see which MPs left their partisanship at the door and which did not, how they reacted when senior members of their party came before them, and how they dealt with the Parliamentary Commissioner for Standards, Elizabeth Filkin, whose zeal made them uncomfortable and who was eventually shown the door for doing her job too well.

The committee room's green carpet was probably an

interior decorator's mistake. It should have been ordinary domestic linoleum. Then it would have been easier to wipe the blood from the floor.

All this is part of the record of New Labour's years in office. Not all of it is discreditable. I have known worse governments among the dozen I have lived under. On the management of the economy, and in its commitment to aid in the developing world, I have known few better. It has promoted the peace process in Northern Ireland which has led to the voluntary disarmament of the IRA, the reconciliation of political opposites and an historic agreement which, if all goes well, will be its most enduring legacy. Both Clare Short and Hilary Benn at the Department for International Development have proved to be outstanding public servants. There has also been a generational shift of attitudes: under this government the country has become in some ways not only more prosperous, but more tolerant and in general more at ease with itself; but in other ways, more insular and nastier. Yet on the issue on which it was elected, public trust in public life, *its record was wholly, completely and unforgivably negative.* It traded in patronage. It squandered a unique opportunity to draw people in and reinvent the entire culture of politics. It even dodged the effects of its own reforms. I shall concentrate on this issue, which was the trigger of the Labour landslide, because it matters so much to me and to just about everyone else I talk to. It used to matter to New Labour too. This was the party that proclaimed: 'Our mission in politics is to rebuild this bond of trust between government and the people'; and which promised in the preamble to its manifesto: 'What follows is not the politics of 100 days that dazzles for a time, then fizzles out.'[2] On the issue of public trust, it fizzled out.

Edmund Burke got there first. In 1771 he wrote, in *Causes of the Present Discontents*: 'The great and only foundation of government is the confidence of the people.' It was true even then in a time of rotten boroughs and unrepresentative government. His words apply with even more force today, when we have the universal franchise but still, because of the voting system, an unrepresentative government. I shall tackle that issue too. The confidence of the people is what any government of any party, in good times or bad, should seek to win in the public interest, as well as its own, and do all it can to maintain. It is the hard currency of democracy. Confidence is not to be won by consulting the focus groups and telling people what they wish to hear. It may involve a willingness to take unpopular decisions and announce bad news in the 'blood, sweat and tears' tradition.

People like being told the truth, even if the truth is unpalatable. I take the view, which I shall seek to substantiate in what follows, that in its ten years in office the Labour government has, either deliberately or possibly in a fit of absence of mind, *arbitrarily, negligently and unnecessarily forfeited that confidence.* It has done so by double-counting its achievements, by massaging statistics, by burying bad news whenever possible and by confusing slick presentation with good governance. It has done so by crossing the line into media management and trying to write its own headlines. It has done so by exalting the black arts of spin into areas, like the analysis of military intelligence, where Downing Street's communications director has no business even to be present, let alone to be in any position of influence over the outcome. It has done so by sidelining the House of Commons and guillotining its debates. It has done so by asking the armed forces to do more with less, at an ever-

rising cost in human lives. It has done so by tearing the
Military Covenant to shreds. It has done so by a series of
foreign policy misjudgements; and by politicising the
diplomatic service. It has done so by the creeping accumu-
lation of power within 10 Downing Street. It has done so by
allowing the Prime Minister to be judge and jury on
allegations of ministerial misconduct. It has done so by a
disdainful attitude to the Committee on Standards in
Public Life; and it has done so most conspicuously, on
domestic affairs, in its exercise of the patronage of power.
The cash-for-peerages scandal will cast a permanent
shadow over New Labour's record and whatever reputation
for integrity it has left. The same applies to the Conservatives,
but they are not in power and did not campaign on an issue
of honest politics.

It is important not to be dewy-eyed about what governments can accomplish. All of them will disappoint some of
the people some of the time. Some of them may even
disappoint most of the people most of the time. There are
difficult choices to be made, limited resources to be
allocated and unpopular decisions to be taken. As the
Prime Minister himself liked to put it: 'To be in government
is to decide.' There is no new Jerusalem to be built or
shining city on the hill to be reached at the end of the road.
Man is not only the most destructive of animals but
probably the most discontented too. So the euphoria of
May 1997 was never going to last: the wonder was that it
lasted as long as it did. It was helped by the novelty of the
new regime, the weakness of the opposition, the soundness
of the economy, and the new Prime Minister's thespian
skills so deftly shown in his response, after three months in
office, to the death of Diana, Princess of Wales. This indeed
was a new kind of politics, branded and marketed in a new

kind of way. Cool Britannia ruled in 10 Downing Street. There was actually a Foreign Office committee formed to promote it, on which I (perhaps unwisely) agreed to serve. Even the furious *Daily Mail* was subdued, if not respectful, for a while. And Rupert Murdoch's News International, from *The Sun* to *The Times* to the *News of the World,* ate out of Labour's hand and it out of theirs.

What concerns me here is why the winners threw it away and sacrificed their greatest asset, which was the people's faith in their ability to do things differently and practise honest politics. Is there something about our democracy that makes this impossible? Does the electoral system reward and encourage the Shifty Tendency in politics? Does it underwrite untruths, licence lies and mandate mendacity? What sort of self-regulation was it – the system has changed now – that left the House of Commons the only institution in the country with the power to dismiss its regulator? In the interests of party discipline, are MPs obliged to go on voting for measures they don't believe in and against those that they favour? Even for a military adventure they know to be mistaken? What has happened to the calls of conscience and independent judgement? When our political parties are empty shells of the mass movements they used to be, why should they be bailed out by taxpayers who were once their supporters but have deserted them in droves? Is the connection between power and money so close and corrupt that honours have to be bought and sold to keep the parties in business? Or is there an alternative politics out there somewhere, a different idea of governing the country, awaiting ignition and lift-off?

These are the issues that I shall be addressing from the point of view of an Independent, a former member of the House of Commons club, a passionate and optimistic democrat – and someone with front-line experience of armed conflict. This has been the area of policy where the loss of trust has been most conspicuous and has had the most damaging consequences. From Vietnam to Bosnia I have seen at first hand the effects of man's inhumanity to man. From being an infantryman in Cyprus in the late 50s to visiting Darfur, the Democratic Republic of Congo and Afghanistan for UNICEF, I have completed half a century in the unquiet corners of the world. For that reason I shall pay particular attention to New Labour's expeditionary wars, especially those in Iraq and Afghanistan, and their role in widening the ever-growing gulf between politicians and people. The politicians' perceptions differ from the realities that the people can see for themselves. These wars were not policy options, to be plucked off the shelf like any others: they were matters of life and death. And the war in Iraq claimed hundreds of thousands of lives. The British and American lives were counted. The Iraqi lives were not, but could only be estimated. The highest estimate, extrapolated from local body counts, put the total at an astonishing 650,000, 1 in 40 of the population.[3] Iraq's own health ministry put it at between 100,000 and 150,000 – and rising every day.

\* \* \*

A case could be made that the government's honeymoon lasted as long as half-way through its second term. At some point in 2002 it committed itself to the worst miscalculation by any British government in memory – the decision to join the Americans in the invasion of Iraq in March 2003. The issue was one of trust because the case for war was argued on the grounds of Saddam Hussein's weapons of mass destruction, which turned out not to exist; and by dossiers

which were doctored to reach the pre-programmed conclusions. The proclaimed cause of war was a falsehood.
Only later was the regime change argument advanced to
take its place. *The people can be lied to, but they cannot be fooled.*
If a government could not be trusted to tell the truth on a
decision as important as sending the armed forces to war,
which is the most serious decision it ever takes, what else
could it not be trusted on? And when it asks us to move on,
why should we move on until it comes up with an answer,
an explanation or an apology? Or the full, impartial,
independent inquiry that it has so far refused?

The irony of it was that the Prime Minister was a most
gifted apologist. But he would apologise only for things
that he did not do, like the slave trade or the shooting of
army deserters. He was unwavering on the things that he
did, like trafficking in peerages or waging illegal wars.

Here was a man who sent the armed forces to war on the
basis of a grand self-deception; and whose answer to those
who didn't trust him was typically that it didn't matter
because he trusted himself – therefore he did not have to
plead for his reputation.

A consistent theme is the government's misuse of the
military; its fondness for pre-emptive warfare; its refusal to
heed the advice of those with experience of armed conflict,
not only in terms of casualties but in terms of outcomes –
what can be achieved by force and what can not; and its
photo-op mentality – the eagerness of ministers to be
pictured against a background of tanks and troops in the
field, usually in closely guarded camps, and a reluctance to
visit, or even pay tribute to, the repatriated hundreds of
wounded and shell-shocked veterans of its wars. At least in
Britain the dead were not brought home, unseen and
unhonoured, in the middle if the night, which was the

Americans' way of lessening the impact. But it might have given the government pause that its policies prompted something that had never happened before in a country with a centuries-old history of expeditionary warfare: the emergence of a group of bereaved families, whose sons had been killed in an unlawful war, as an active political force.

To the end of his premiership, Tony Blair retained his faith – not a soldier's faith but a civilian's – in the effectiveness of hard power. He never understood that the weapons of shock and awe, which cost so much in blood and treasure, more often frustrate than serve the purposes for which they are used. They recruit more than they kill. And military commanders are not magicians: they are the managers of organised violence.

The best witnesses of New Labour's wars are those who have fought in them; or, having military experience themselves, have thought about them and reached their own conclusions. The serving soldiers must remain anonymous. But the former soldiers, the old and the bold as the army calls them, have the freedom to speak out. I shall pay particular attention to the views of General Sir Rupert Smith, Britain's Clausewitz, who was the most experienced operational commander of his time. The government's fondness for the military option extended even to the imperial graveyard of Afghanistan. The commitment there was of a different order in terms of its legality, but was also launched on the basis of a falsehood: that its mission was pacification and reconstruction and that it might even end without a single shot being fired. That was the hope of the then Defence Secretary John Reid, whose only direct experience of soldiering was as a guest of the Armed Forces Parliamentary Scheme, an attempt by the forces, usually with mixed results, to educate MPs in the realities of service life. Many of them do it so they can write about it in their constituency newsletters.

I stood for Parliament in 1997 at the request of the Labour and Liberal Democrat parties. I have no particular axe to grind against them or any party. I have friends in all parties, and a handful of enemies in only one. (I do not include Neil Hamilton who, although a Tory MP, turned out not to be a member of the Conservative Party.) What follows is as truthful an account as I can manage, as someone who for a while was in the unusual and privileged position of being both an insider and an outsider, of the first ten years of New Labour. Not on all the accusations against it, even over Iraq and Afghanistan, was it guilty as charged. Or not quite as guilty. The truth was more complex, and I shall try to reflect it.

For instance, the involvement of British forces in both wars led to the government being accused of naivety: over Iraq, because it had believed in the presence of weapons of mass destruction that turned out not to exist; and over Afghanistan, because its Defence Secretary expressed the hope of the mission being so easily and cheaply accomplished. Then, when both these scenarios were proved to be tragically and spectacularly false, it was accused of mendacity: it must have known – so the charge sheet goes – that its prospectuses were bogus. And that its misjudgements would cost lives. Either it did not know what it should have known, or it did know and it lied.

I have an alternative thesis to offer, indeed a sort of triangulated 'middle way' so beloved of New Labour: the government did not deceive anyone else, neither the British public nor Parliament, by a fraction as much as it deceived itself. As people tend to do when they find themselves drifting in unfamiliar circumstances, all at sea without a compass or a chart, it clung to whatever flotsam floated by. It was promoting an ethical foreign policy and on a faith-driven mission to export democracy. On those mystery weapons of mass destruction, it was not ready to admit how little it knew. It wished to convince itself that the wars it embarked on were both justified and relatively cost-free. Its lack of military experience had the most serious consequences. A number of the witnesses testify to this. But it also made it easier for the government to believe what it wanted to believe and disregard the rest. *I only know what I believe* was the Prime Minister's fall-back position when all else failed.

As a schoolboy at Fettes, Tony Blair is said to have mocked those who joined the Cadet Force as 'toy soldiers', which casts an interesting light on his role in later events. But he wore the derided uniform at least once, in a school production, when he played Captain Stanhope in R.C. Sherriff's moving First World War play *Journey's End*; but its message of the futility of war seems to have been lost on him. A veteran Labour MP wrote to me: 'I think Blair likes war. Sorry, but I do. Pre-emptive or not.' A former Downing Street spin doctor, Lance Price, has written to the same effect, that the Prime Minister privately seemed to relish sending the troops to Iraq.

For the reasons behind the self-deception in military matters, it is useful to go back to the early years of the New Labour government and the NATO intervention in Kosovo in 1999. A week after it was over, in June 1999, Tony Blair, Alastair Campbell and others in the Downing Street entourage were greeted as saviours by the Kosovar Albanians in Pristina. It was a heady experience for a bunch of life-long civilians. A standing ovation at the Labour Party conference was as nothing compared to this. It intoxicated and to some extent may even have unhinged them. They never got over it. In an extraordinary speech to the Royal United Services Institute in London a month later, Campbell came out of the shadows and spoke of their reception as a 'magical moment' in his life. Nor did he miss an opportunity to attack the journalists reporting the war for a want of physical courage and professional judgement: they were deceived by 'the Serbian lie machine', they concentrated on NATO blunders as 'the only show in town', and they were reluctant to venture across the front-line minefields. 'The age of the dare-devil reporter seems to have died', remarked the Prime Minister's intrepid communications director, having flown in and out under close SAS protection.

And it was actually *during* the Kosovo conflict, in a speech in Chicago on 22 April 1999, that the Prime Minister himself set out the interventionist doctrine that was repeatedly invoked in the years to come: 'This is a just war, based not on any territorial ambitions but on values.' And three years ahead of President Bush, he identified his axis of evil: 'Many of our problems have been caused by two dangerous and ruthless men, Slobodan Milosevic and Saddam Hussein.' No one could accuse him of inconsistency.

It was the NATO action in Kosovo, and an early setback for its Brussels spin machine, that set off alarm bells in London and Washington and led to the establishment of the first Coalition Information Centre. Alastair Campbell rode to the rescue of Jamie Shea, the beleaguered NATO press secretary, impressing him greatly by installing a battery of 30 telephones within a matter of hours. This was not normal practice in the alliance's bureaucracy, known to its British critics as 'a hotbed of cold feet'. But it was how the real professionals did things. From that point on, Shea achieved a sort of media stardom and became the authoritative narrator of NATO's war. But it was an initiative with far-reaching consequences at home and abroad.

Abroad, it set a pattern of news management and generated the Coalition Information Centre in the Gulf state of Qatar – a mighty million-dollar sound stage of information and disinformation – to filter and control the news from the war in Iraq in 2003. This was the production company that created the fiction of the heroic rescue of Private Jessica Lynch; she later told a congressional committee: 'I'm still confused why they lied and tried to turn me into a legend.'[4]

At home, it led to the politicisation of news about the armed forces; the tactical subordination of the military to the political; the attempted silencing of the chiefs of staff; the downgrading of the 'one stars' (brigadiers and their equivalents) who used to manage the armed services' media relations quietly and professionally within the Ministry of Defence; and their replacement by political appointees not only in Whitehall but even closer to the front lines than any amateurs should be. The presence of a uniformed Downing Street operative in Kosovo, like a soldier without a rank, was a novelty at the time, but an ominous portent of things to come in deciding what would be embellished, and what suppressed, in the information war which, now more than ever, is an integral part of a real war. You don't win one without the other.

If the news could be managed so successfully there, then why not in Iraq and Afghanistan? This was where the self-deception took root. Such were the miscalculations that led the government to its later involvement in two countries which, more than any in the world, had a history of serial

British defeat over more than a century and a half. All it needed were armed interventions in Gallipoli and Singapore, and the government would have a full hand in revisiting the scenes of past disasters. The soldiers showed their usual steadiness under fire, but the politicians were all over the place, as their common sense went AWOL.

On his way out of the door of 10 Downing Street, Tony Blair likened the media, which he and his people had courted so assiduously, to a 'feral beast'. But even the press could not be blamed. No one else did this to New Labour.

They did it to themselves.

## CHAPTER TWO

# A HOUSE OF ILL REPUTE

*So are they all, all honourable men.*
William Shakespeare, *Julius Caesar*, Act III, scene 2

### 'WE WILL CLEAN UP POLITICS'

The New Labour project, which was presented as a mission to change the politics as well as the policies of government, was also compromised from the start by the big money needed to finance its ambitions. Labour was haunted by the memory of its 1992 election defeat – an election that it had really expected to win. It was beaten by the soap-box oratory of a decent man, John Major, who led a flawed, divided and in some ways corrupt political party, as the years that followed were so dramatically to show. It says something of the state that the Conservatives were in at the time that Neil Hamilton, MP for Tatton, was spoken of as a possible party leader and future Prime Minister. But Labour was also beaten by Big Money. It had sporting and showbusiness personalities on its side, to no effect, in Neil Kinnock's ill-fated 'victory rally' in Sheffield, but not enough millionaires. The wealthy voted Tory with their cheque books – and in the course of time, as these things happen and as cash translates into votes, some were duly recognised in the honours list for public and political services. No surprise there. The relationship between donation and reward was taken for granted. So the Labour Party, out in the wilderness for another five years, learned the bitter lesson of what worked and what did not. Never again would it be outspent or outmanoeuvred in the exercise of patronage. If money was what was needed, it would find the money. And when it became the governing party, which was only a matter of time the way things were going, it would have its hands on the levers of power and patronage, in a way that an opposition party can only dream of. The ghost of Lloyd George was still hovering.

This was not at all in the brochure. I remember well those early days of euphoria – indeed, I had a minor part to play in them in the traditionally Tory county of Cheshire. But I don't remember joining in the euphoria. It was bound not to last. I knew there would be setbacks and disappointments; and no doubt a fair share of scandals too. There is no such thing as scandal-free politics. Government MPs so far outnumbered opposition MPs that by the sheer law of averages some of them, and maybe even some ministers too, were bound to be accused of breaking the rules. What never occurred to me, however, in that new dawn – and Tony Blair's victory speech on the South Bank was delayed *until the dawn* because of its symbolism – was that Labour would be so careless on the issue that had swept it to power and moved more votes than any other. Its election manifesto had included a section that promised to clean up politics. The new government came into office committed to the 'reform of party funding to end sleaze'. Tony Blair told his still-euphoric MPs at their first post-election meeting: 'Remember, you are not here to enjoy the trappings of power, but to do a job and to uphold the highest standards in public life.' And six months into its first term, amid the first of a slew of scandals, he really did say 'we must be purer than pure'. It sounded like a promise. Maybe it was just an aspiration.

Now there are things that governments can do and things that they can't. They are constrained in so many ways, more than ever before, by circumstances and forces that they cannot fully control – inherited crises, sudden and unforeseeable emergencies, alliances, treaties, European and UN conventions and the general inter-dependence of things in the new world order. On restoring the confidence of the people in public life, alone among the issues facing them, the newcomers to power were not constrained by anything. They could do as they pleased. They could set an example of probity not known since the days of Gladstone. Or they could let things slide. They chose by default to let things slide, and on this crucial front of the battle for public opinion they fared even worse than their predecessors. The men (interestingly, there were few women) who brought the Tories into disrepute at the national level were, with a few exceptions like Jeffrey Archer and Jonathan Aitken, back-benchers and minor figures, well known for dodgy dealing and not much else. But the scandals that broke over New Labour, time after time, involved ministers of the crown and some of its principal movers, shakers and fundraisers. If such an instrument as a sleazometer existed, I believe that it would register the Labour scandals on a significantly higher scale than the Tory ones.

It was, however, much to Labour's credit that some of these scandals came to light as the result of reforms that the government itself had introduced, in its half-measures to clean up politics. These half-measures, especially the new limits on party funding, had the effect of lifting the stone and revealing the forms of life that flourished under it. The government was hoist with its own petard. But at least it had the distinction of making the petard. Cash-for-peerages was not an accident: it was a scandal just waiting to happen.

## CAST OF CHARACTERS

The list that follows is a catalogue of the main players in some of the more colourful episodes of the Labour years. It is by no means comprehensive. There are many others, both inside and outside government, with strong claims for inclusion. The outlines of the events qualifying each individual for the roll of honour are offered without comment, so that they can more eloquently speak for themselves. All but one are politicians and most are still serving Labour MPs. The Prime Minister himself is for the moment excluded. His time will come.

*Bernie Ecclestone.* The owner and impresario of Formula One donated £1 million to the Labour Party in 1997. In the run-up to the general election it was a timely and useful gift. After Labour came to power it announced a ban on the sponsorship of sporting events by tobacco companies. It then exempted Formula One motor racing from the ban. There was the obvious appearance of a *quid pro quo.* As Labour faced its first sleaze allegations, I asked the Prime Minister whether we had slain one dragon only to have another take its place with a red rose in its mouth. He denied any wrong-doing. Everyone who knew him, he said in an interview, knew that he was 'a pretty straight kind of guy'. The scandal subsided, but it raised a set of questions that were thought to belong to the past, not the present. The Labour Party returned the money to Mr Ecclestone.

*Ron Davies.* The Secretary of State for Wales and its 'architect of devolution' resigned in October 1998. He cited an 'error of judgement' when he was robbed at knifepoint by a man he met on Clapham Common, a well-known gay meeting place. He described it as his 'moment of madness'. He later stood down from the Welsh Assembly after a 'badger-watching' incident.

*Keith Vaz.* The MP for Leicester East and Europe Minister in Labour's first term came before the Committee on Standards and Privileges on a variety of matters including the alleged non-registration of interests. The Committee upheld a charge that he improperly recommended an associate for an honour. It concluded that he had obstructed the Commissioner and given her false information. He was suspended from the Commons for a month for a serious breach of the rules. He called it the Commissioner's 'last hurrah'.

*Geoffrey Robinson.* The MP for Coventry North West and former Paymaster General came to the attention of the Commissioner for Standards twice, mainly on issues of the alleged non-registration of interests. On the first occasion, in July 1998, he was found to have failed to register his interests but no penalty was imposed. On the second occasion, in May 2001, he was found to have misled the Commissioner and the Committee at his earlier appearance. He was later suspended from the House for three weeks for a 'serious breach of the rules'. His speech of apology lasted for just 54 seconds. He was also a central figure in one of the cases involving Peter Mandelson.

*Peter Mandelson (1).* The MP for Hartlepool and Secretary of State for Trade and Industry borrowed £373,000 from

Geoffrey Robinson MP to help finance a house purchase. At the same time his department was investigating the affairs of some of Mr Robinson's companies, although he distanced himself from the investigation. Mr Mandelson's application for a mortgage did not mention the loan or another mortgage on a property in Hartlepool. The Commissioner upheld the complaints against him. The Committee demurred. Mr Mandelson returned for a while to the back benches.

*Peter Mandelson (2).* He returned a year later as Secretary of State for Northern Ireland. He was forced to resign a second time, in January 2001, after it emerged that in 1998 he had made inquiries to the Home Office about a passport for Srichand Hinduja, an Indian businessman facing trial at home on corruption charges. Hinduja and his brothers had given £1 million to the Millennium Dome, for which Mr Mandelson had responsibility at the time. One of the issues was about the veracity of successive public statements made as events unfolded. On his second dismissal, the House of Commons bar ran out of champagne, mostly drunk by Labour MPs.

*John Prescott (1).* The Deputy Prime Minister was found to have failed to register an interest, a flat in south London that was provided by the RMT rail union and used by his son. The Standards and Privileges Committee urged him to register the flat. In what it took to be a gesture of defiance he never did so.

*John Prescott (2).* Further unwanted publicity came his way in April 2006, when it was revealed that he had a two-year affair with his diary secretary, Tracey Temple, who sometimes accompanied him on official engagements. Remarkable entries from her diary appeared in the press. Others were suppressed on the grounds of good taste but somehow got into the public domain. The personal and political embarrassment was acute. When in opposition, Mr Prescott had been a scourge of Tory sleaze. In 1996 he said: 'They are up to their necks in it!' He apologised for the affair.

*John Prescott (3).* His trials were still not over. It was reported in July 2006 that he had accepted the hospitality of Texas millionaire Philip Anschutz, who hoped to turn the Millennium Dome into Britain's first super-casino. Mr Prescott did not have responsibility for the Dome, but he did for the development of the Greenwich site on which it stood. His gifts included the Stetson, spurs, buckle and belt of a hand-stitched cowboy outfit. Eleven months later he declared them. The Commissioner noted that there was a real risk of conflict of interest. Mr Prescott was mildly rebuked.

*David Blunkett (1).* The Home Secretary in Labour's second term had an affair with Kimberley Fortier, the American publisher of *The Spectator* magazine. When the affair ended he went to court to establish the paternity of her as-yet-unborn child. This was a private matter, until it was alleged that an attempt was made to expedite a visa for her Filipino nanny. An independent investigator, Sir Alan Budd, concluded that there was a chain of events linking the Home Secretary to the visa application. Mr Blunkett resigned.

*David Blunkett (2).* In 2005 he returned to the Cabinet as Secretary of State for Work and Pensions. During his time out of office he became a director of a bioscience company and bought £15,000-worth of its shares. There was a potential conflict of interest between his position and his business connections. He should have consulted the Advisory Committee on Business Appointments, but did not, despite three reminders from the Committee to do so. When this was known, he resigned for a second time. The Prime Minister's spokesman said that his position had become untenable.

*Tessa Jowell.* The Culture Secretary co-signed a mortgage application form with her husband David Mills for £408,000. Her husband was being investigated by Italian prosecutors over claims that he was paid £344,000 for giving helpful testimony in a corruption investigation of the Italian Prime Minister Silvio Berlusconi. The mortgage was quickly paid off. Ms Jowell denied any wrongdoing and said she did not know of a £344,000 'gift' he had received. They later separated. The Prime Minister said he had full confidence in her.

*Stephen Byers.* In 2001 the Transport Secretary assured the Transport Select Committee that he had no plans to pull the plug on Railtrack. He later admitted that this answer was untruthful, although he could not remember why. He was ordered to apologise by the Standards and Privileges Committee, and did so.

*John Reid.* In 2000 the Secretary of State for Scotland (later Party Chairman, Health Secretary, Defence Secretary and Home Secretary) came before the Commissioner and the Committee in the most complex and difficult case of the 1997 parliament. It was also the case with the most far-reaching consequences. He was accused of having misused his parliamentary allowances for work by his son Kevin on the first election campaign for the Scottish Parliament. The Commissioner upheld the complaints against Dr Reid and described his conduct as an attempt to frustrate her investigation. The Committee did not uphold the complaints and found only that Dr Reid's contact with another witness gave rise to 'misunderstandings'.

## Standards and Privileges

The policing of the conduct of MPs, other than as ministers, remained a matter for the Commons itself; but the House was always wary of self-regulation; adopted it only reluctantly in 1996; and continued to give itself a bad name, quite unnecessarily, in the New Labour years that followed. The damage was entirely self-inflicted. It was another case, as if any more were needed, of an opportunity lost and a promise broken. Something of value could really have been achieved. Instead it was lost in the daily din of adversarial politics.

The old House of Commons operated as a gentleman's club. The theory was that no disciplinary system was needed because a gentleman's word was as good as his bond; and the automatic right of MPs to be trusted was bequeathed to them naturally on their election to the House. But that depends on how you define a gentleman. It was G.K. Chesterton who observed that the class of English gentleman has historically been as corrupt as any on the face of the earth. Certainly the House has accommodated more than its share of rogues and scoundrels over the years. It still does. And it has consistently resisted a system that might expose and exclude them. Enoch Powell, who was a peculiar character but neither a rogue nor a scoundrel, refused on principle to declare his private interests in the Members' Register when it was first introduced in 1975. He believed in statutes but not in voluntary codes. He was threatened with sanctions, but they were never applied.

The easy-going code of conduct, in so far as it existed at all, was more appropriate to a London club or an officers' mess; codes of dress and address were strict, with the rules of procedure running to thousands of pages; it was important to know who was a right honourable member (a privy councillor), an honourable and learned member (a QC) or an honourable and gallant member (an officer of the rank of major or above – having been only a corporal, I could never be gallant). But that was as far as it went. The outside interests of MPs, their schemes for self-enrichment and whether these might possibly conflict with their duties, were matters left to the honourable and right honourable learned and gallant members themselves.

That changed decisively in the 1980s and 90s. There was a shift in the political culture. The gentlemen retreated and the spivs advanced. A series of scandals arose, including the notorious cash-for-questions affair in which two Tories, Tim Smith and Neil Hamilton, were accused of receiving £20,000 each in brown envelopes from Mohammed al Fayed, the owner of Harrods, for advancing his interests in government; Smith admitted to taking the money and resigned, Hamilton denied it and fought on. They were not the only ones. Twenty other MPs were accused of having bent or broken the members' code of conduct. They either disappeared from view or were thrown out by the voters.

Such was the impact of these scandals, and the cloud of wrong-doing that hung over the House, that the Prime Minister, John Major, set up the Committee on Standards in Public Life, initially under the chairmanship of Lord Nolan; and a new system of regulation was rather reluctantly adopted. It had to be done but did not go far enough. MPs would continue to have the final say in whether to acquit, censure, or even suspend a member of the club charged with a breach of the rules. But they would have before them the report of a newcomer, the Parliamentary Commissioner for Standards, who would examine the allegations and either dismiss them or send a report to another new body, the Select Committee on Standards and Privileges. In theory the Commissioner was independent, but in practice still an officer of the House and thus only semi-detached. This was a fudge – and, as fudges tend to, it failed. The theory and practice were to collide with damaging consequences.

In a number of cases, most of them high-profile and high-voltage, the Commissioner and Committee failed to agree. This applied even to the most contentious case considered by the first Commissioner, Sir Gordon Downey, which was that of Neil Hamilton. Sir Gordon found 'compelling evidence' that the MP for Tatton (who was by then the former MP for Tatton, since someone else had taken his place) had received cash for questions. The MPs were not so sure. They agreed to another fudge, that they could neither 'add to nor subtract from' the Commissioner's findings. One of the Conservatives on the Committee, Ann Widdecombe, resigned, and in due course I took her place at the table. The chairman, Robert Sheldon, was especially welcoming; as were two other members of the Committee, Peter Bottomley (Conservative) and Alan Williams (Labour).

So I was left with a ring-side view of the inter-party battle over sleaze, and a privileged position from which to judge the performance of MPs when dealing with members of their own party who had, in some cases, quite clearly broken the rules. It would be a snapshot of the state of politics in the post-Tory era, and a practical test of Labour's intentions on the issue that brought it to power. The Committee was supposed to be non-partisan. Some of its MPs properly parked their party allegiances at the door.

But it was soon clear that others did not. In particular there was a group who were consistently sympathetic to Labour MPs, especially those of ministerial rank, when they came before us. These party loyalists pleaded extenuating circumstances. They were concerned about the impact of an adverse finding on a member's career – and especially a minister's, because a minister had more to lose. They argued for raising the standard of proof to a height where no charge, however well-founded, could possibly clear it. They seemed less interested in the detail of the discussion than in its outcome. Nor did they care, when the Committee's final report was published, what the public would think when the 'fix' was so obviously in. The most assiduous of them was an eyes-down character who read from documents that may or may not have been prepared by someone else. There was even an occasion when one of the group, being out of town for some reason, submitted a paper, like a lawyer's brief, for the rest of us to consider. Whether they were doing the whips' bidding I had no way of knowing. But their words and actions would not have been so different if they had been. Maybe it was just serendipity, telepathy or the on-message mind-set of the time. MPs wore their pagers like badges in those days. I was new to Parliament, over-impressed but still quite shocked, and minded to add new words to a familiar verse:

> No need to whip the poor back-bencher
> With threats of punishment or censure;
> For, seeing what the man will do
> Un-whipped, there is no reason to.

Because sleaze had been the defining issue in the 1997 election, the two main parties used the disciplinary procedures to throw mud at each other. Sadly, they succeeded and a lot of it stuck. As a result of their efforts, Parliament as a whole fell further into disrepute. The party leaders or whips could have called a ceasefire; but they didn't. They finally agreed to one only after the damage was done.

Labour and the Tories complained relentlessly about the conduct of each other's MPs. The principal complainants were Chris Leslie MP for Labour and David Heathcoat-Amory for the Tories. Apart from one case, which did not even involve a sitting MP, the Liberal Democrats were left out of it. The motivations in making these complaints were clearly partisan. I protested that no party had ever shown the slightest concern on the Committee about the conduct of one of its own. I was pulled up short on that: there had in fact been a single case of a complaint brought by one Labour MP against another: but that was about the Balkan business interests of Bob Wareing, the Member for Liverpool West Derby, who belonged to the party's awkward squad and was deeply out of favour with the leadership. Whether this was at the whips' instigation I had again no way of knowing; but if it was it didn't work. Bob Wareing remains an MP to this day and a gremlin in the New Labour machine.

In February 1998 Sir Gordon Downey retired. He was succeeded by Elizabeth Filkin, formerly Adjudicator of the Inland Revenue. She was no stranger to independent investigation, but she was a stranger to the Westminster wonderland, and that was a bond between us. The way she went about her business, firmly and fearlessly, soon had the natives whispering against her. The whispering reached gale force during her inquiry into the related cases of John Reid and John Maxton. Maxton was in his last term as an

MP, but Reid was one of Labour's rising stars with much to lose if the Commissioner and the Committee found that he had misused his parliamentary allowances. This was the case in which the Committee satisfied its Labour diehards by raising the standard of proof from the balance of probabilities to the allegations being '*significantly* more likely to be true than not'. It noted that: 'A case like this has serious implications for the holders of public office.'[1] It is my greatest regret in four years as an MP that I should have resigned from the Committee at this point, but did not.

It was not that the emperor had no clothes, but that his courtiers refused to see how shabbily he was dressed.

Sir Gordon Downey, the first Commissioner, noted that the new procedure ran into the most difficulty in cases involving senior MPs. He was bruised by the Neil Hamilton case, but his problems were slight compared to Elizabeth Filkin's. These were compounded by the presence on the Committee of three new members. These were MPs who at the start of their parliamentary careers were required to sit in judgement on senior figures in their own party. (I was also a new MP but without a party.) Robert Sheldon, the veteran Labour MP who was the Committee's chairman, had no say in who was appointed to it. He said later: 'I was surprised, astonished in fact, when I was informed of the membership of the Committee back in 1997 … they asked for volunteers … I was just astonished.'[2] Kenneth Clarke MP added: 'It is extraordinary how party political people can be in their first two or three years in the House until they discover that the other side are human.'[3]

In due course the three new MPs received promotions to the modest rank of parliamentary private secretary. I am not for a moment making the suggestion that they acted improperly; or that their advancement was connected in any way to their service on Standards and Privileges. But there could have been at least a perceived conflict of interest. This was recognised by the Committee on Standards in Public Life, which reviewed the system two years later. It advised that no parliamentary private secretaries should sit on the Committee, and this advice was followed.

What was fascinating to watch, in the most contentious cases, was the extent to which the Labour ultras round the table found themselves impaled on the code of conduct that we all inherited; they then tried to wriggle out of it. On taking office, MPs are bound to sign on to the seven principles of public life, laid out unambiguously by Lord Nolan in 1995: selflessness, integrity, objectivity, accountability, openness, honesty and leadership. On accountability, for instance, the code states: 'Holders of public office are accountable for their decisions and actions to the public and must submit themselves to whatever scrutiny is appropriate for their office.' This raised awkward questions in cases like Peter Mandelson's mortgage application. Did the code apply, as his defenders maintained, only to his actions as an MP, *or to everything he did?* There was nothing in the code suggesting any such reservation: because the seventh principle was leadership, MPs were supposed to set an example both inside and outside Parliament. Mr Mandelson's defenders even went on a bizarre treasure hunt for a restrictive interpretation of the rules that they were sure had been written down somewhere when the code was drafted, but had mysteriously been mislaid. It was like the search for the Holy Grail. The rules meant what they said. But it was an issue that divided the Committee, usually but not always along party lines, between realists and idealists. Too often the realists dug in their heels as if their careers depended on it, and complaints were dismissed that should have been upheld. The result was the scandalisation of politics and the further erosion of public trust in public life. The press and the public rightly detected the baleful influence of party politics in those sensitive cases where the Commissioner's conclusions went one way and the Committee's the other.

There was one point on which criticisms of the new procedures, made by senior Tories like John Major and Kenneth Clarke, were entirely justified: an MP's reputation could be tarnished by the mere fact of an allegation being made, even if there was no merit to it and the Commissioner dismissed it out of hand. This was a licence for mischief-makers inside and outside Parliament. The complainant would alert the press, the Commissioner would confirm that the complaint had been received and was being investigated, and that was enough to let loose the dogs of defamation. The charge of misconduct would be front-page news. The dismissal of the charge would go unreported, except perhaps in the MP's local paper, but even there the damage was already done. But this was a defect not of the system but of the frenzied nature of the media and of party politics itself. Any regime for the regulation of MPs is open to be abused in such a way. The alternative is to have no regulation at all. It was tried for many years, and it did not work. 'Trust me, I'm a politician' is not exactly a confidence-building gambit.

On one occasion an MP on the Committee saw the draft of the Commissioner's report on a senior MP of his own party whom she had investigated. 'You have him bang to rights', he said. And then, under political pressure, he voted not to uphold the Commissioner's findings. This happened over and over again. Although the Committee met behind closed doors, the aroma of party politics seeped out into the corridors and lobbies and from there into the press until it reached the public. It was the politicians, who reproached the Commissioner for not sufficiently understanding the difficulties of their calling, who dug their own hole and fell into it.

It is possible – or more likely, downright certain – that I am technically in breach of privilege in recounting some of the internal debates of the Committee during Labour's first term. But those were the pivotal years of self-regulation. And there is a strong public interest defence in bearing witness to the mistakes that were made during those years so that they will not be repeated. It cannot be right to operate a system in which there is one law for the powerful and another for everyone else. To have more to lose is not a reason to be treated differently under the rules; it is a reason to observe them more carefully. And if I am summoned to the High Court of Parliament and consigned to the Tower of London as a punishment (for the Commons still has the power of arrest), I look forward to the hospitality of the Yeomen of the Guard, senior NCOs who were platoon sergeants to today's generals; and it is they (the senior NCOs, not the generals) who are the engine room of the army. So I know I shall be well looked after. I have been there before. Fieldcraft is about the calculation of risks.

Elizabeth Filkin was in effect removed from her post for doing her job too well. Towards the end of her three years she wrote to the Speaker, Michael Martin: 'The degree of pressure applied has been quite remarkable. In some cases this has been applied directly by Members. In other cases it has been applied by unchecked whispering campaigns and hostile briefings.' Of more than 600 MPs, only 48 rallied to her defence. Peter Bottomley, who was one of them, resigned from the Committee. Alex Salmond, who was another, spoke of her departure as a 'political assassination'. It was a disgraceful episode which did untold damage to the reputation of Parliament, such as it was. The press was unanimously on the Commissioner's side. The flood of supportive letters she received showed what the people thought of those who were supposed to represent them.

## A NEW BEGINNING?

I was among those approached by Whitehall's head-hunters when they started their search for Elizabeth Filkin's successor. I replied that I had no intention of applying for the post, since the House of Commons Commission, in its treatment of her, had shown that it had no use or time for a truly independent Commissioner. It wished to be regulated only by itself. The chosen candidate was Philip Mawer, Secretary-General of the Synod of the Church of England. In short order he became Sir Philip. So two of the three Parliamentary Commissioners for Standards received high honours and one did not. Was I surprised by this? Knowing the House as I did, not at all. The word in the smoking room was that it had been hinted to Elizabeth Filkin that a damehood awaited if she would be so kind as to conduct her inquiries with a little more discretion.

Sir Philip certainly kept a lower profile, but the cases he dealt with were fewer and, on the whole, less contentious than those that faced his predecessor. Initially he worked only a three-day week. The atmosphere was calmer. The parties had ceased to use the complaints procedure as a weapon of war. They were aware of the damage they had done to themselves as well as to each other, and to the institution of Parliament itself. The House had accepted the idea that the Committee should be chaired by a senior opposition MP, and the respected Tory Sir George Young was appointed. He asked for a fresh start: 'We cannot control what use other people may make of our complaints system, but we in this House should not use it to do down political opponents by making trivial or politically motivated complaints.'[4]

The Commons complied. Sir Philip had to contend with no furious ministers, whispering back-benchers or MPs who defied his authority; he operated independently – and, in the opinion of most, effectively. He was well within the rules when he dismissed a complaint that I made against a very senior MP because, although it was well-founded, the principal witness wished to remain anonymous. In his report on the 'cowboy' allegations against John Prescott, he concluded that the gifts received 'might reasonably be thought to influence his actions as both a member and a minister'. Ministerial conduct was for the Prime Minister to deal with. But the Commissioner thought it right to border that territory. It was a bold and necessary departure.

Sir Philip said: 'What erodes public confidence is the number of allegations that are around and the absence of clear machinery for resolving them.' He called, as many have, for an independent figure to investigate these allegations and report to the Prime Minister. Without such a figure there is one set of rules, clear and specific, for MPs, and another, much vaguer and looser, for ministers. This leaves an ethical vacuum at the heart of government.

The old way of dealing with charges of ministerial misconduct, which had a record of consistent and serial failure, was to have them investigated inside Downing

Street by the Cabinet Secretary. This reached the level of tragicomedy in 1994, when the First Secretary of the Treasury, Jonathan Aitken, reached for his 'sword of truth and trusty shield of British fair play' when accused by *The Guardian* of lying to clear his name. The paper's editor, Peter Preston, took his allegations to the Cabinet Secretary, Sir Robin Butler: 'A very busy man. He didn't even read the paperwork; he didn't quiz Mr Aitken. He gave the minister a clean bill of health and allowed Jonathan himself to draft the push-off letter to me.'[5] Sir Robin was a distinguished public servant, but this was not his finest hour. Mr Aitken told him a pack of lies and was jailed for perjury five years later.

For most of his three terms, Tony Blair also used this tried and untrusted route. It was rough justice, and it could be unfair to the ministers themselves. The second time Peter Mandelson was summarily dismissed, in January 2001, he might well have been vindicated by a more thorough investigation. He never had the chance. In March 2006, when the Culture Secretary Tessa Jowell was accused of breaking the code of conduct over links to her husband's business affairs, the case was again investigated by the Cabinet Secretary, Sir Gus O'Donnell. He did not actually clear her. He said that the Prime Minister was 'the right and proper person to take a view on matters arising from the ministerial code'. It was the Prime Minister who took the decision. Sir Alistair Graham, chairman of the Committee on Standards in Public Life, described the system of policing ministerial conduct through the Cabinet Secretary as 'pretty bankrupt'.[6]

But then Mr Blair changed his mind, or at least his practice. In the next case, that of Mr Prescott's cowboy gifts from a Texas millionaire, he brought in an outside adjudicator, Sir John Bourn, the Comptroller and Auditor General. But Sir John did not have the permanency of the Parliamentary Commissioner for Standards. It was still for the Prime Minister to decide when or whether he should be called in. As the Downing Street spokesman put it: 'There had to be a common sense acceptance of when an investigation was needed.'[7] After nine years of scandals, whenever his ministers were accused, Mr Blair remained the judge and jury and court of appeal. In July 2000 he had declared 'no one will be better governed by fine-tuning the ministerial code'.[8] He was not only above the law. He *was* the law. It is hardly a 21st-century way of proceeding when the king has the power to decide which of his barons should stay and which should go, whatever the evidence of misconduct against them.

Things don't have to go from bad to worse. There are encouraging signs that they are changing for the better. Whether the Prime Minister saw the half-light or half-saw the light, there is a dawning awareness that things cannot continue as they were. The next step is to move from an occasional outside adjudicator to a fully-fledged Ministerial Commissioner for Standards. Would it be too expensive? No more so than one of those costly government task-forces that roam the country compiling reports which are quickly cast into oblivion. The mere fact of its existence would galvanise ministers' private offices and have a restorative effect on public trust.

It is said of a fish that it rots from the head down. A government doesn't have to.

## CHAPTER THREE

# WHAT KIND OF DEMOCRACY?

*In the city set upon slime and loam*
*They cry in their Parliament 'Who goes home?'*
*And there comes no answer in arch or dome,*
*For none in that city of graves goes home.*
*Yet these shall perish and understand*
*That God has pity on this great land.*

G.K. Chesterton, 'Who Goes Home?'

## WHO GOES HOME?

How frail a thing is this democracy, which we recommend to others, even seeking to impose it by force of arms in Iraq and Afghanistan; or setting up imitation Westminsters in Africa and the Caribbean, complete with Speakers and wigs and robes and maces, as we did in the past in the process of decolonisation. Some have survived and others have not. The Canadian House of Commons is the only one with a claim to be an improvement on the original; which is not hard to achieve, with the original in so sad a state of disrepair. Most have ended up as rubber stamps for some all-powerful executive – which is exactly what has happened to our own. The democracy we practise is so imperfect that there should be another name for it – elected autocracy, perhaps, or democratic Bonapartism. Our upper chamber does not have a single elected member in it. As for the Commons, in 2005 the Labour Party was returned for its third term in government despite being the choice of less than a quarter of those entitled to vote, an unimpressive 22 per cent. After two terms in office it somehow managed to mislay 4 million voters. Only the weakness of the opposition kept it afloat. Its total vote, 9.54 million, was its second lowest since 1945. It had lost in the past with millions more votes than that. Three voters in ten stayed away. The rest split their votes between other parties, with more than usual going to those outside the political mainstream. Two-party politics was dead and buried. Labour's minority status made no difference. It still retained a comfortable majority, and had no incentive to change the system that delivered it.

But when first elected, in 1997, it was on a commitment to electoral reform that would have to be bent, if not broken, if the winning formula of first-past-the-post were to stay in place. The manifesto promised a referendum and half-promised a switch to proportional representation:

> We are committed to a referendum on the voting system for the House of Commons. An independent commission on voting systems will be appointed early to recommend a proportional alternative to the first-past-the-post system.[1]

The commission was duly set up, under the chairmanship of Lord Jenkins. And in September 1998 it suggested a compromise known as AV+, which would combine a system of proportional voting with some elements of first-past-the-post. That was the end of it. The promised referendum was never held. The Liberal Democrats, who thought they had a deal with Labour on electoral reform, were led up the aisle and abandoned at the altar.

Under the electoral system we have (we can hardly be said to *enjoy* it), unless there is a political earthquake the next election will be won and lost in just 48 marginal constituencies. People who live in other constituencies, more than 90 per cent of the population, might just as well not have a vote for all the difference they can make to the result. And we dare to call this democracy.

The existing system, which is a distortion of democracy, stayed in place because it delivered solid majorities for the Labour Party in three successive general elections. This was party politics at its bleakest. Especially after the death of Robin Cook, a genuine reformist, there was no one in power who dared to change or challenge a winning formula. Electoral reform was kicked into the long grass, which took the form of a Cabinet committee on constitutional affairs chaired by John Prescott, the very incarnation of Old Labour and an enthusiast for first-past-the-post. The then leader of the Liberal Democrats, Charles Kennedy, said that this was 'like putting Herod in charge of the maternity ward'.[2]

The first-past-the-post, winner-takes-all formula that we have for the Westminster parliament, and always have had, would be an adequate if sometimes flawed reflection of the popular will in the two-party system which used to operate but is now a thing of the past. We have a three-party system in England, a four-party system in Scotland and Wales, and even a five-party system in Northern Ireland: and that is even without factoring in the Greens, UKIP and the BNP, who are no longer as marginal as they used to be. While not winning seats for themselves in general elections, they draw off more and more votes from the mainstream parties and can affect the results substantially – as can Independents in special circumstances. 'None of the above' is an option with growing appeal. Political allegiances are now so frail and fragmented that, with every election, first-past-the-post distorts the results so much that they become a parody of the national will. It may deliver decisive majorities. But it is not in any real sense democratic. Elections are in some respects as much a game of chance as the national lottery.

Could there be a worse system? It is hard to believe, but actually there is. It is the one we use for elections to the European Parliament, and is even suggested for elections to the House of Lords if the dream of a democratic upper house ever becomes a reality. This is the list system, a sort of Soviet affair, although actually Belgian, having been devised by a Monsieur D'Honte, who in his day enjoyed fame of a sort as one the world's most famous Belgians. (The others include Tintin, Georges Simenon, the Singing Nun, the genocidal King Leopold II and the saintly Audrey Hepburn who was born in Brussels.) Under D'Honte's scheme, the parties set out their candidates for election on a list in order of preference – their preference, not the voters' – in a multi-member constituency. I had personal experience of this, since I stood as an Independent in 2004 in the Eastern Region, where 2 million voters were invited to elect seven MEPs to the parliament in Brussels. The main parties listed seven candidates (six for the Tories), with little chance of getting any but the first two or three (or in the Lib Dems' case, one) elected. By and large, the voters had never heard of any of them. I, of course, as a one-man minority, was the first and last on a list of one. And winning 93,000 votes – about 30,000 short of what I needed – was a creditable showing under the circumstances. I had a point to make about democracy; and failing to become a member of the European Parliament was not the worst thing that ever happened to me. We all learn from our mistakes; and I now realise that spending less than £650 of my own money from start to finish of the campaign was not the smartest way to get elected. I had two brilliant people to help me, the agent Paddy Seligman and the chairman Nick Lyons, but no posters or leaflets except on the internet. This was fortunately not quite enough. And when it was over, a lady from Hertfordshire told me that she hadn't known I was standing until polling day, when she saw my name on the ballot paper; and then, supposing that I was an impostor, she voted for someone else.

One thing we were able to do in that campaign was to expose the iniquities of the list system. The Conservatives went into it with four MEPs and hoped to have all of them returned to Brussels. One of them was Bashir Khanbai, who, because he was placed third on their list, seemed assured of re-election. He lived in Sevenoaks but gave a Norfolk address on his website: No. 57 Peninsula Cottages, Staitheway Road, Wroxham. The *Eastern Daily Press*, which initiated and supported my campaign, sent one of its reporters to the road, who discovered that No. 57 did not exist. It was a postal address. The Conservative Party then dropped Mr Khanbai from its list of candidates, over allegations of falsely-claimed travel expenses. (He believed that he was the victim of a racist campaign by elements of the party; for all I know he was an excellent MEP, but the ambiguous address was his undoing.) If the matter had come to light after nominations closed, the party would have had to stand by him and I would probably have attracted enough disaffected Tories to win a seat. The deeply undemocratic nature of the system was out in the open for all to see. Voters could choose between parties but not between candidates of the same party. People wishing to make an intelligent choice had not the slightest chance of doing so.

The entire system was gerrymandered by the political parties to protect their electoral monopoly, and to lessen the ferocity of competition within them. This is what they do on all issues of electoral reform: they start with the desired end state and work back to the system that will deliver it. The end state is a cosy duopoly in which one party will be in government and the other awaiting its turn in opposition. If the system that will deliver it is as grotesquely undemocratic as the party list, they will nonetheless adopt it without hesitation. Even the Liberal Democrats go along with it, who ought to know better: it rewards them with seats which would otherwise be beyond their reach.

I have travelled the world and seen how others do it. Most of them do it better. A case can be made that the will of the people is better expressed in an Arab *diwaniah* or an Afghan *loya jirga* than in the organised fiasco of a Euro-election. Even in the unreformed Gulf States they improve on the party list system. A process of consultation goes on. The Crown Prince or heir presumptive is not necessarily the eldest son.

So is there an answer? Actually, there is. The most democratic solution would be the variant of the alternative vote in which voters list candidates in their order of preference in a single-member constituency. This retains the constituency link and results in the election of the candidate who, if not actually the most popular, is the least unacceptable to the greatest number of people. That's real democracy, in which the people, not the parties, decide who represents them; and the MPs' primary loyalty is to the people, not the parties. The parties complain that it would result in the election of too many mavericks, oddballs and football mascots. This is a self-serving objection. The oddballs and football mascots are as entitled to seek election as anyone else. And the House of Commons is stuffed to the rafters with far too many machine politicians and not nearly enough mavericks. It needs more. Since the retirement of the Honourable Member for Linlithgow in 2005, it still has a Tam Dalyell-sized hole in it.

## THE AUTOCONFORMISTS

I am often asked, because I take an interest in these things, how politicians can become, if not more trusted, at least *less untrusted.* The politicians ask this themselves, if only on a point of self-esteem, for who would wish to be held in such low regard not just for who they are but for what they are? Members of the House of Lords are especially vexed about it, and eager to point out that their peerages were earned or inherited rather than paid for. This leaves the few remaining hereditaries, for once, in an enviable position. They owe their places in the Lords, in the first place, not to party membership but to an accident of birth. One of their ancestors may have paid for it through the patronage of an earlier time, but they did not. They also pay less attention to the whips and speak more freely than in the Commons. You can attend a Commons debate, as I used to out of curiosity, and wonder: 'How ever did such-and-such an honourable member ever get selected, still less elected?' Go into the Lords on any day and you will almost always, if you stay long enough, find someone worth listening to.

Politicians will commonly blame the press for their predicament, and their allies in the press will dutifully join in the media-bashing. In 2000 I served with Peter Riddell of *The Times*, whose columns were so lapidary they could have been set in stone, on a commission on the selection of parliamentary candidates, set up by the Electoral Reform Society. The commission happened. Electoral reform did not. In the final report, which he wrote himself because the party representatives could not agree, he observed:

> The television image of jeering or scoring points off each other in the Commons, or dodging questions in broadcasting studios does not encourage involvement and reduces trust. Media coverage of politics (itself much reduced in scale and trivialised) often portrays a game played at Westminster over the heads of the electorate, who seem powerless to affect what happens.[3]

Of course it is true that the press are relentless axe-grinders. Whatever course the Labour government had followed since its election in 1997, it would have encountered the implacable hostility of Associated Newspapers. If St Francis of Assisi had been one of its ministers, he would have been shredded in no time by the *Daily Mail*: 'Strictly for the birds', it might have said, and its sister paper would have launched an inquiry into his domestic arrangements and the conditions in his aviary. But the partisanship worked both ways. Whatever the government decided on, up to and including an illegal war, it would enjoy the support of the Murdoch press across the board from *The Sun* to the *Sunday Times*. Mr Riddell himself would duly weigh in with judicious columns which were in general sensitive to the government's wavelength. He once described the war in Iraq as a 'niche issue'.[4] Some niche, some issue!

The broadcasters, by contrast, tended to go with the flow. The cause of the war in Iraq was surely lost when, rather late in the day, the BBC's John Simpson turned against it: a gifted reporter, he is also a political operator who knows better than most the strength and direction of the gusts that blow through Whitehall.

And the political classes, desperate to find someone else to blame, have found an additional culprit – the new media and the mushrooming blogosphere. Matthew Taylor, Downing Street's outgoing adviser on political strategy, attacked the bloggers' 'shrill discourse of demands' which he said was responsible for a crisis in relations between politicians and voters. He asked: 'What is the big break-through, in terms of politics, on the web in the last few years? It's basically blogs which are, generally speaking, hostile and, generally speaking, basically see their job as every day exposing how venal, stupid and mendacious politicians are.' And he came up with a striking conclusion: 'We have a citizenry which can be caricatured as being increasingly unwilling to be governed but not yet capable of self-government.'[5]

Oh dear, oh dear – the ungrateful people, who should know better, are not worthy of the government which serves them so devotedly! It would be hard to find a sadder or more eloquent betrayal of the new politics promised in 1997. Instead we have the old politics, not just autocratic but Bonapartist. And we cannot say that we were not warned. We were. The constitutional scholar, Peter Hennessy, recalled a breakfast meeting he chaired in March 1997, two months before the Labour landslide, at which top businessmen and civil servants were addressed by a senior figure from the Blair camp. On the verge of taking office, this outrider of the project told them: 'You may see a change from a feudal system of barons to a more Napoleonic system.'[6] So indeed it came to pass. Our Bonaparte bestrode the stage. And Iraq was his Waterloo.

Matthew Taylor had a point. The bloggers are unrepresentative of the electorate at large – which is just as well, or we would be a nation of unbalanced people. There is a furious, foaming, swivel-eyed quality to much of what they write, as if their fingers work faster than their brains. Many of them seem to resemble those constituents who attend MPs' surgeries year after year nursing the same ancient grievances in documents carried in a scuffed old plastic bag; or who write letters in green ink with much underlining. A full moon shines permanently on them. Some of them even came to my surgeries pretending to be constituents when they were not. They are victimised twice, first by their grievance and then by their obsession with it. But the most widely read of the anti-government blogs, by Iain Dale and Guido Fawkes, are not like this at all. They are literate, well argued and good-humoured. The same applies to the broadly pro-government views of Oliver Kamm, who is just about the last man outside the barricades of Downing Street who still believes the war in Iraq was justified (and in whom I have to declare an interest, since I happen to be his uncle). The bloggers are not a big battalion but a mass of little platoons, often firing furiously upon each other. Politicians will not rise or fall by the pounding of their artillery.

But politicians *can* rise and fall by what they do to themselves. The majority who behave honestly are tainted, time after time, by their association in the House of Commons with the minority who do not. Good behaviour stands alone and is seldom even noticed. Corruption spreads and draws massive press attention. Neither the old nor the new media are to blame. The damage is self-inflicted by those whom we elect to represent us.

Here is an example of how it happens. An MP on an important committee moves an amendment to the annual Finance Bill which, if passed, will save an oil company £70 million a year in taxes. There is nothing wrong with that. The industry has lobbied him, which it has every right to do, and persuaded him that the tax break is in the public interest. The committee, under Treasury pressure, rejects the amendment. Still so far so good. But after the business is over, the MP invoices the oil company for a fee of £10,000 for his parliamentary services. The company's executives are rather surprised, since they have expected him to help them with no thought or question of payment. Years later, it all comes out in a libel trial, the now-retired oilmen give evidence and the MP is found to be corrupt – 'on the take and on the make', as the avenging angel of an accusing barrister describes him. His reputation is permanently shredded.

Here is a second example, no more fictional than the first. An MP with a cash-flow problem asks a wealthy friend for a £5,000 loan to tide him over the local difficulty. The friend obliges. Again, so far so good. There is nothing in the code of conduct that prevents an MP, like anyone else, from borrowing money from time to time, so long as no conflict of interest arises from it. But a few days later the MP writes to Downing Street recommending his friend for an honour. In due course this linkage is made public. A complaint against the MP is upheld by the Standards and Privileges Committee and he has to apologise to the House of Commons.

Both men broke the rules by acting corruptly and using their public positions for private gain. Their misconduct rubbed off on others as well as themselves. But what interested me, as someone outside party politics, was the strength of party loyalties in both cases: their constituency associations stood by them. Both were subsequently re-adopted to fight the next election. One lost and the other won. But the loss was unusual, the result of an unprecedented popular rebellion, and nothing quite like it has happened since. When Members of Parliament are well entrenched in safe seats, almost nothing that they do is thought to disqualify them from enjoying the sinecure of a lifetime. A sense of comfort and entitlement settles around them. Even bone idleness will not debar them from office. An MP can win an election, take the oath on the floor of the House and disappear to the beach or the golf course for the next four or five years – and there is nothing the disciplinary system can do about it. If there were, the parties would use it to score points off each other.

The demands on an MP's time and attention are neither more nor less than the MP wants them to be. There is the legend from a long time ago of a Member for a south coast constituency who visited it on his yacht occasionally – and in an election year he actually disembarked! Something like it still happens from time to time. I was contacted by some voters in Lincolnshire seeking advice on the mystery of their missing MP. They wanted him to help them on a local issue, and he had simply disappeared. No one had seen him for months. I regretted that I had to tell them there was nothing they could do to unseat the invisible MP until the next election, when they would have a chance to remove him democratically. (He wisely retired.) De-selection by an MP's party, which is the obvious remedy, is also extremely rare. In his report on candidate selection, Peter Riddell observes: 'Having navigated the selection procedure, the candidate in a safe seat should not automatically feel assured of a job for life regardless of subsequent performance.'[7] But it almost always happens. And it is an observable fact that the most bone-headed MPs tend to occupy the safest seats, with nothing but the division bell to disturb their slumbers, in the library or the smoking room, before they sleepwalk through the lobbies. I knew a man who drank himself to death in Annie's Bar. It did not bother the whips, so long as he could drag himself upstairs in time to vote.

In TV production there is a device known as an auto-conformist, which stores and organises images in a computer. It is the perfect term for so many of the Labour intake of 1997, who missed a once-in-a-generation chance to revive democracy and practise a new sort of politics: kinder, gentler and closer to the people. They could have done so much and they did so little. They put their consciences into cold storage and voted for a war that few of them believed in. To watch them in action was the stuff of nightmares. They followed their leader with the shining faith and blind obedience of the disciples of a cult. And when he was on song at Prime Minister's Questions, as he was more often than not, he carried them with him and conducted them as if they were a tabernacle choir. They came close to chanting 'Hallelujah!' back at him. They were his autoconformists.

## BRITAIN'S *VOLKSKAMMER*

In the Parliament of 1997, the permanently hard-pressed Liberal Democrats lent me one of their seats on the standing committee on the Armed Forces (Discipline) Bill, bringing military law into line with the requirements of the European Convention on Human Rights. Standing committees matter. They scrutinise and amend the detail of legislation before it returns to the floor of the House for a vote. And they don't stand, of course, but sit. The Bill was also a measure of practical importance. It gave more powers to military lawyers and reduced those of commanding officers on active service to administer summary justice in the field – a practice as old as the British Army itself. As a result, the Army Legal Service is closer than ever to being a front-line force.

Serving on this committee was, against stiff competition, one of the most shocking experiences of my life. I was surprised to see that, on the government side, only the junior minister advancing the legislation was apparently entitled to speak. The other six Labour MPs sat there paying little attention to anything except their constituency correspondence and their fingernails. And a whip was present, as always, to ensure their compliance. Their eyes were down, their minds were not engaged; and if a division was called on a disputed clause, their votes were cast without a moment's thought on the whip's instructions. If the minister had proposed the return of the cat-o'-nine-tails on Royal Navy ships, or the revival of the press gang to improve recruitment, they would surely have nodded these measures through as part of the New Labour project. On the opposition side, some important points were raised by two Tory MPs, Andrew Robathan and Crispin Blunt, both former army officers. My own interventions, from the lesser vantage point of a former corporal, were dismissed as the ramblings of an eccentric. I was so exasperated that I challenged the dumb majority to say something – *anything* to break the silence – on pain of being named and shamed in a book that I was writing. They smiled at me patronisingly and went back to writing their letters. There was no real debate, and the government carried the day on every point. So the Bill was not scrutinised. It was rubber-stamped. The autoconformists prevailed. It was a matter of parliamentary oversight in the most literal sense. Over the next five years, there would be men and women serving in the armed forces charged with some breach of the regulations, who would feel the effects of such an arbitrary abuse of power. *This also undermined trust in public life.*

The better MPs are well aware of the extent to which they are failing their Parliament, and it is failing them. They need no lectures (as they are fond of saying) from the party opposite: they can deliver these lectures themselves. I have a friend who is a senior figure in one of the main political parties. He holds a safe seat and has served a fair number of terms. He occupies a grand office in the Palace of Westminster. He has an important position on an important select committee. He is a Right Honourable Member. But he is in a state of despair. Because of the subordination of the legislature to the executive, and the Napoleonic tendencies of the Prime Minister's office, he reckons that almost all of his parliamentary work, except for what he does for his constituents, is a whisker away from being a total waste of time. If he wished to make a difference in the debate, he now believes, he should have chosen a career in the media rather than politics twenty years ago. It may be that he exaggerates the importance of the media. He does not exaggerate the decline of the House of Commons, relative to what it used to be and could be.

This is not – or at least not yet – an argument for a Parliament of Independents, although a few more would be a healthy corrective to the present state of affairs. Peter Riddell writes that 'Political parties must not be allowed to wither' – to which I am inclined to ask: 'Why not?' If they no longer serve a useful purpose, have lost the trust of the people and are unable to fund themselves honestly, perhaps they *should* be allowed to wither; and the time may come when it will be only humane to turn off their life-support systems. Endangered species normally attract our sympathy, because they are endangered by other species (mostly human) and by their inability to adjust to a changing world. Political parties, by contrast, have no one to thank but themselves for their threatened extinction.

They have so far been necessary to government, which seems to have a hard time doing without them, except in the Isle of Man. They bind like-minded people to a common purpose. But after all that has happened they should see themselves as being on probation. They need a measure of discipline to function, but surely not so much as to prevent independent-minded people from joining them, invigorating them, adding value to them and correcting their lemming-like tendencies. The over-whelming power of the whips makes such incomers feel unwelcome. It has increased, is increasing and ought to be diminished.

When I first took my seat in the House of Commons I sat and listened for a while as new Members should, to get the measure and feel of the place and to work out what kind of a parliament it was. After a couple of months the uneasy feeling dawned on me that it resembled nothing so much as the old East German *Volkskammer*, to which I had been accredited just before it voted itself out of existence in 1990. It was an assembly where the system counted for everything and the people for nothing, and some of the parties themselves, like the old German *Bauernpartei* (the farmers' party), were mere shells of what they used to be or pretended to be. Were we on the same road to the same destination? Was there anything to admire except the history and the architecture? Why did we allow this arthritic grip on the windpipe of democracy? And was this really the best that we could do, remembering what happened when the East Germans lost faith in the whole corrupted system of state power?

The columnist Simon Jenkins has described the British Parliament as 'God's gift to dictatorship'. 'If I were an absolute monarch,' he wrote, 'I would get one immediately.'[8] His dismay is widely shared inside the House of Commons as well as outside it, although some of its inmates remain deaf to reason and blinded by their privileges.

It should be the free parliament of a free people. That is a long way from what we have now. Only half of it is even voted for. Far from being a beacon of democracy and an example to others, it serves rather and in many respects as a model of malpractice. We have to reclaim it from the minority of unrepresentative politicians – mediocre, self-serving and self-satisfied – who have far too much power inside it.

## A Modest Proposal

How do we do that? So much of what is wrong and remediable revolves around the power of the whips. Their role as the pillars of the parties in Parliament has enabled them to survive with the system crippled but their power intact. That power must now be trimmed back in the public interest. Like all enforcement agencies they are averse to change; so reform will come, as it usually does, from pressure outside abetted by atrophy inside. This is how empires decline and fall; and it works. What follows is a modest proposal for democratic reform by whip reduction.

First, there should be fewer lines for MPs to toe. Every week the whips send out a circular to their troops in Parliament, with lists of the expected divisions and voting instructions heavily underscored. A single line means that the issue is not important and absence or even abstention will be forgiven. A double line means that MPs are expected to vote as the party directs. A triple line means that a vote is mandatory, rebellion could have awkward consequences and only a serious illness can excuse an abstention. My proposal is simple: subtract a line in each of the three categories. A one-line whip becomes a free vote. The former two-line whip becomes a one-liner. And a two-line whip replaces the old three-liner, with MPs encouraged within a much looser party discipline to think and speak for themselves. The three-line whip disappears altogether. Persuasion replaces coercion. Sometimes MPs need reminding that they were chosen by parties but elected by people. And they represent those who didn't vote for them just as much as those who did.

Second, the whips should lose the power to choose members of select committees. All too often these enviable assignments – envied, at least, by other MPs – are handed out as the reward for obedience. As a result, the committees are stuffed with stooges. Committee members should be chosen instead by the MPs themselves through their parliamentary parties. And the whips should stay away from standing committees, so that bills can be scrutinised as fairly and freely as possible. If we are ever to resemble a real democracy, MPs must learn to work with rather than against each other. In the better-led committees, they already do so.

Third, the handful of Independents should have the same rights as other MPs, not be treated as stateless citizens. They are at present excluded from both select and standing committees because they don't belong to any recognised group. But that's the whole point of them. It is true that the Kidderminster MP, Dr Richard Taylor, has a seat on the Health Select Committee – but only because first the Tories, and then the Liberal Democrats, lent him one of theirs. As Parliament's leading authority on the NHS, he should be there by right.

Fourth, it is time for the parliamentary private secretaries to leave the stage. There are some 50 of these autoconformist MPs, serving as message-passers and bag-carriers to government ministers. Although unpaid, they are part of the so-called 'payroll' vote and bound to loyalty on all occasions. Thus, on an important vote, like the one on Iraq, their constituents are in effect disenfranchised since these legislative ciphers are forbidden to think for themselves. (An honourable handful did resign rather than vote for the war – and I should put in a special word here for Michael J. Foster, MP for Hastings, with whom I have tangled in the past.) One of the roles of PPSs is to persuade their friends on the back benches to table helpful questions to their ministers. The planted question is one of the curses of Westminster, since it denies time to real questions requiring real answers. There are more plants to be found in these ministerial sessions than in *Gardeners'*

*Question Time.* An end to this practice would make the House of Commons a better place than it is.

Fifth, the parties have to ease back on their efforts to impose their will on their memberships in general and their MPs in particular. They should listen more and discipline less. A case in point was the Conservatives' attempted de-selection of Sir Patrick Cormack, their long-serving MP for South Staffordshire, in February 2007. There are dozens of members whose de-selection would be in the public interest, but Sir Patrick is not one of them. He was the only Tory MP to have offered serious opposition to his own government's non-policy on the Bosnian war. His offence this time, allegedly, was a lack of partisanship: he had not sufficiently featured the word 'Conservative' in his campaign literature in the general election of 2005. He had every reason not to; and he was not the only one. The party at the time was a contaminated brand, and its candidates were wise to shy away from it in the spirit of *sauve qui peut.* He achieved a swing to the Conservatives that was three times the national average. He survived the attempted coup because of an irregularity in the conduct of the meeting in which he was voted out. *More votes were cast than there were people actually present.* Let's hear it for the wonders of British democracy!

Sixth – and this is the hardest of all – there has to be a climate change in parliamentary behaviour. The Conservative leader, David Cameron, is on to something when he objects to the puerile, schoolyard quality of so much of what passes for debate: 'People despair at the predictable and juvenile partisanship of Westminster politics, and yearn for a more political debate.'[9] It alienates the people to an extent that the politicians are only just beginning to understand. My own experience was that serving in the

House of Commons was like being enrolled in an old and particularly unruly boarding school – a sort of ill-tempered Hogwarts. It is time for the parties to join the real world, in which people do not normally behave like that, or they will find that the real world passes them by because it sees them as a freak show.

There is surely a case for a House of Commons whose members are chosen for their character and record, not for their service to faction; who vote for or against a measure on its merits and not on the instructions of a whip; whose only allegiance is to the people they represent; and in which the parties, having served and outlived their purposes, become interesting relics of the past like Beefeaters and Yeomen of the Guard. I have even started work on a *Requiem for Political Parties*. All it needs is a versatile (and non-party) composer to come up with a suitable score – something for bugles, muffled drums and at the close a fanfare of rejoicing.

> *Indifferent to the people's warning,*
> *The parties headed for a fall,*
> *Labour, Tories and Lib Dem;*
> *At the going down of the sun and in the morning*
> *We will of course remember them,*
> *But miss them not at all.*

## Chapter Four

# HOW MUCH FOR A PEERAGE?

*When rogues like these (a sparrow cries)*
*To honours and employments rise,*
*I court no favour, ask no place,*
*For such preferment is disgrace.*

John Gay, *Fables*

In 2005 Angus MacNeil was elected as the new Scottish National Party MP for Nah-Eileanan, also known as the Western Isles. It is the country's remotest constituency, measuring 200 miles and taking five hours, including two ferry crossings, to travel from north to south: it includes the rocky outpost of St Kilda, which is home to a handful of voters and millions of seabirds, and which even its MP has not yet visited. His victory surprised a lot of people but not himself; it came at the expense of the Labour veteran Calum MacDonald, whom he described in his maiden speech as a highland gentleman and very nice man. It says a lot for the Hebrides that the ritual unpleasantness of Westminster does not reach to their remote and windswept islands.

Angus MacNeil's maiden speech was notable for something else. With the permission of the Speaker, he began it in Gaelic. According to his own account, the English-speaking MPs hardly noticed for the first minute, concluding that here was another Scottish MP, like the Speaker himself, with a rather impenetrable accent.

So the new MP took his place, and looked, as is the way with all MPs, for the issues that went with the territory. Besides following tradition in promoting his constituency – including the beach on Eriskay 'where Bonnie Prince Charlie started his epic and, sadly, failed adventure' – he demanded a change in the graphics of the BBC's new tilting weather map, in which Scotland, containing 40 per cent of the UK's land mass, was reduced to 10 per cent of its screen size. The BBC backed down and corrected the tilt.

Then in March 2006 an event occurred which put him under the media spotlight to an extent very rare for a first-term MP (except one embroiled in a scandal, which he was not). It was reported that four of the Prime Minister's recommendations for peerages had been turned down by the House of Lords Appointments Commission. These were men who had given donations or loans to the Labour Party, of between £250,000 and £2.3 million, to fund the election campaign of 2005. In 2000, under the new electoral law, the Commission had replaced the old Political Honours Scrutiny Committee as the body which, so far as possible, should try to apply some standards to the award of peerages. When the change occurred, Tony Blair hailed it as removing 'an important source of patronage from the hands of the Prime Minister of the day' – although as things turned out, that was not what it actually did. The new Commission had an easy act to follow. The Scrutiny Committee was donor-friendly and had been the softest of touches for the cash-strapped parties. Its chairman, the former Conservative Cabinet minister Lord Pym, gave the game away when he said that it considered a contribution to a political party a point in a candidate's favour, in that the would-be peer had 'put his money where his mouth is'. In other words, all else being equal, a rich man could acquire a peerage that a poor man could not. He might as well have advertised a rate card.

Now the cat was out of the bag for a second time. The House of Lords Appointments Commission believed that a line had been crossed in the Prime Minister's proposal to reward so many of those who had paid for his party's most recent campaign. It was a line laid down in the Honours (Prevention of Abuses) Act 1925, following Lloyd George's fire-sale of honours to his fundraisers and favourites. The only man ever charged and convicted under it was his bagman, Maundy Gregory. The traffic in peerages may also have been in breach of the government's own Political Parties, Elections and Referendums Act of 2000, if the loans were given at non-commercial rates. For if the rates were commercial, why go to an individual rather than to a bank in the first place?

Large sums of money had flowed from wealthy individuals to political parties. The leaders of those parties had nominated a number of those people for high honours, knighthoods and peerages. On the face of it, it was an open-and-shut case of commercial and institutional corruption.

Angus MacNeil succeeded where I had failed. In New Labour's first term, the promise to clean up politics still resonated. So I got to my feet in the House one day and asked: 'Does the Prime Minister accept that the task of restoring public confidence in public life is as important in this Parliament as it was in the last? In view of the widespread perception that political honours are being sold to party contributors on a scale not known since Lloyd George's time, will the right honourable gentleman fulfil his promise to clean up politics?' The Prime Minister replied: 'We accept the duty to ensure that our political life is clean, but I do not accept the honourable gentleman's statement about political honours.'[1] My only reward was a little note slipped to me by Charles Kennedy, then the leader of the Liberal Democrats, gently reproaching me for my reference to his predecessor. It told me that my application for membership of the Lib Dems was cancelled!

The MP for the Western Isles did better. He moved the issue onto the national stage, where it should have been from the start. He wrote to the Commissioner of the Metropolitan Police complaining that the law, or laws, may well have been broken, and asking for a criminal investigation. The SNP had an interest in the matter because, like all the small platoons of politics, it had to do battle with the big battalions at election time. The big battalions were well-funded. And if the funding was illegal, there was every reason why the small platoons should challenge it. The MP for the Western Isles had made some powerful enemies, and it was no surprise that he became the target of an attempted character assassination. Initially, Angus MacNeil's intervention was dismissed by the major parties as a stunt, in line with their general view that politics properly belongs to the big players, and the minor parties are interested only in making headlines and mischief. The general expectation at Westminster was that the police would go through the motions, and in due course would dismiss the complaint for lack of evidence.

Instead they took it seriously and launched a wide-ranging investigation that shook the political establishment and reached all the way to Downing Street. As they did so, the atmosphere grew murkier. It emerged that a number of wealthy individuals who wished to remain anonymous had agreed to supply funds to the parties not as gifts, which would have to be declared, but as loans, which would not – so long as the loans were at the prevailing market rate (if they were not, and they were in a sense gift-wrapped, that too might be against the law). On the advice of the Prime Minister's principal fundraiser Lord Levy, who played a pivotal part in this episode, Chai Patel, Director of the Priory Healthcare Group, loaned £1.5 million to the Labour Party, with a view to converting it to a gift at some later time. He was also nominated for a peerage, but asked that his name be withdrawn. 'I gave money to the party,' he said, 'because I happen to believe in what it stands for.' Among Labour's benefactors, as the affair unfolded, there was a very real sense of grievance that their motives were misunderstood and misrepresented. The scandal had the perverse effect of tainting the reputations of public-spirited people who wished to give money to causes they believed in. The parties were left with empty coffers and disaffected donors.

The bulk of the £17.94 million that the Labour Party raised for its campaign in 2005 came from loans of this kind, anonymous and undeclared. The party's treasurer, Jack Dromey, knew nothing of them. A picture was emerging of a party-within-a-party, run by the Prime Minister's inner circle and funded discreetly outside the usual channels. The Labour Chairman, Ian McCartney, tried to justify it: 'Bear in mind too that we fought the 2005 election in the face of a very heavily funded Conservative campaign – a large part of which was reportedly funded by loans, and targeted at individual Labour MPs.'[2] This was indeed true. Some of the money had flooded into Labour-held marginals long before the campaign itself began. And the Tories' lenders included foreign nationals who were forbidden by the Act of 2000 from giving money directly. The law was being bent in every way imaginable. But the Tories' acrobatic accounting was nothing new in a party that preferred the secrecy of the smoke-filled room. Most of the attention remained on the Labour Party, not only because they were the party of government which had set the new rules, but also because they had promised to do things differently. Their 1997 manifesto was entitled 'New Labour because Britain deserves better'. And they had described the Tories as 'knee-deep in dishonour'.

The investigation went wide and deep. In a little over six months the police questioned 35 members of the Labour Party, 29 Conservatives, four Liberal Democrats and 22 people, including Downing Street staff, without known political affiliations. Witnesses were not just interviewed, but in a few cases they were arrested and questioned under caution. The first was the little-known but influential Des Smith, a head teacher involved in the promotion of city academies, a favoured Downing Street scheme to involve the private sector in state education, especially in under-privileged areas – and an admirable initiative, so long as the deal did not include the exchange of honours for sponsorship. Mr Smith later gave a graphic account of being arrested at his home in Wanstead, warned not to try to escape and consigned to a cell in Stoke Newington police station, 'a very unpleasant Bastille-type place'.[3] He demanded equal treatment for the Prime Minister, when it was Downing Street's turn, and said he would never, ever, vote Labour again.

And the police were closing in on Downing Street. The

most prominent witness, arrested not once but twice, was the Prime Minister's friend, tennis partner, fundraiser and Middle East envoy Lord Levy. By all accounts he found it an upsetting experience. He accused the police of using their powers of search and arrest 'quite unnecessarily'. Downing Street's director of government relations, Ruth Turner, was also arrested at her home and questioned under caution. The range of alleged offences under scrutiny had widened to perverting the course of justice. Assistant Commissioner John Yates, who led the investigation, told MPs: 'You go where the evidence takes you.' And he said that his team had uncovered 'significant and valuable evidence'. The investigation was the most politically sensitive in the history of Scotland Yard, and a real test of its independence.

There were repercussions abroad as well as at home. President Putin of Russia, no novice in dealing with the power of oligarchs, picked up on the British democratic deficit with relish, after the questioning of the Prime Minister's chief fundraiser: 'There are other questions,' he told Tony Blair slyly in St Petersburg, 'let us say questions about the fight against corruption; we'd be interested in hearing your experiences, including how it applies to Lord Levy.'[4]

As the complainant, Angus MacNeil remained in touch with the investigating detectives and was satisfied by their commitment and thoroughness. He called a news conference with his party leader Alex Salmond MP, Elffyn Llwyd MP of Plaid Cymru and myself to demand that no further appointments be made to the House of Lords until the police inquiry was complete. In the climate of the time it was an easy case to make. If the Angel Gabriel had been nominated for an honour the press would be looking for under-the-counter payments. The cash-for-peerages scandal had knocked the stuffing out of the old system of patronage.

It also abounded in the potential for conflicts of interest; and whether these were perceived or real made little difference, since the one so easily blurred into the other and had the identical impact on public confidence. Sir Ian Blair, Commissioner of the Metropolitan Police, stood aside from the case because he had worked so closely with the Prime Minister on issues of national security. The Director of Public Prosecutions, Ken MacDonald, also excused himself because he came from the same legal chambers as the Prime Minister's wife. The Attorney General, Lord Goldsmith, was in an especially difficult position. He owed both his post and his peerage to his friend the Prime Minister, yet he had the power to halt a public prosecution that he felt was not in the public interest: to do so in this case would lead to a legitimate public outcry. He had taken the Prime Minister's side before, on the legality of the war in Iraq, and his reputation had been damaged by it. He bowed to pressure and promised to abide by the ruling of a senior and independent QC on whether or not certain suspects should be prosecuted. But he would not relinquish his right to be involved. And he intervened to suppress a BBC report about the police investigation which, although accurate, would have embarrassed the government. Was he defending the law, or just the beleaguered denizens of Downing Street? The issue resolved itself when Lord Goldsmith left office at the same time as his patron Tony Blair.

The Prime Minister himself was questioned twice on either side of a deeply troubled new year. He was not arrested or cautioned. He was a witness, it was said, rather than a suspect; and he described it as 'perfectly natural' that he should 'have a chat' with the police, since he had been named in the original complaint. Here was an eloquent commentary on Labour's trajectory over nearly a decade in office: it was perfectly natural that its leader should be sought by the police as a principal witness in the criminal investigation into a political matter. It would not have been perfectly natural ever before.

After thirteen months the investigation was closed and the police sent to the Crown Prosecution Service a 216-page report distilled from more than 6,000 pages of evidence. The sheer scale of the inquiry gave credence to reports that they had uncovered evidence of serious wrong-doing. It was up to the CPS to decide whether charges should be brought. Whatever it decided would be a reputation-shredder and inflict further harm on a government staggering through its final months in office. If there were charges, those who would have to defend themselves would inevitably be close to the Prime Minister. If there were not, the CPS would be accused of submitting to intense political pressure. It was in this respect that the Attorney General's refusal to separate himself entirely from the matter was unfortunate – especially so, because he did not have a reputation for resisting pressure from Downing Street. Lord Goldsmith was in the position of a man who stands on a railway track with an express train thundering towards him, loudly protesting his claim to a right of way. History may be kinder to him, but as an early obituarist of the New Labour project I would judge that, no doubt unwittingly, he did its reputation more damage than any other member of the Cabinet than the Prime Minister himself.

It was ominous news for the Labour Party that the Crown Prosecution Service, having studied the evidence, asked for more police work on the case. On the credit side, its financial woes were slightly eased, early in 2007, by a gift of £2 million from the Indian steel magnate Lakshmi Mittal, reputed to be the fifth richest man in the world. He was a controversial contributor because, after an earlier donation in 2002, Mr Blair had written to the Romanian government, backing his bid for the country's formerly state-owned steel industry.[5] That is the problem with gifts of this kind: the motives of both givers and takers, pure as the driven snow though they may be, are too easily misunderstood.

It is not to criticise Mr Mittal, or any of the other millionaires who gave to the party out of the goodness of their hearts, to note that they are hardly representative of its rank-and-file supporters. These are the people whose confidence Labour has to retrieve to give it a fighting chance of winning future elections. If it fails, it will be as unelectable as it was in the 1980s – only, this time, because of a different sort of bankruptcy. That was Tony Blair's real political legacy: to threaten with ruin the party he led but never really cared for.

Everything connects. It was the government's disastrous war in Iraq that drove its natural supporters away and forced it even more into the embrace of millionaires. When it pursued that course to the edge of legality, its voters stayed away from it and its tycoon-dependency became more acute.

Like a monsoon cloud, the cash-for-peerages scandal hung over the final phase of the Blair years to his very last day in office. It will not be dispelled until the successor regime reconnects with the voters, which it cannot do until, sooner or later, the Great Mistake is admitted. On taking over, Gordon Brown called the war in Iraq 'divisive'. But it was more than that – it was dreadfully and demonstrably *wrong,* at every level of idea and execution. To remain in denial was no longer a plausible option. In the real world, human error is acknowledged and learned from – but not, it seems, in the shadowland of politics. If we want a politics funded by millionaires and practised by stooges, we are going the right way about it.

## So Who Pays the Bill?

With peerages no longer available at knock-down prices, most of Labour's big spenders turned their backs on the party or gave on a much smaller scale. So where was the money to come from? The obvious answer was the taxpayer. From within the Labour Party, and its champions in the commentariat, the argument was made that the existence of the parties themselves was in the public interest – they were national institutions like the Old Vic and the Tower of London – and the shortfall should be made up from public funds. But the scandal itself had made the case much harder to argue. Sir Alistair Graham's Committee on Standards in Public Life conducted a poll, after the cash-for-peerages affair became public, which showed that less than a quarter of the people trusted ministers to tell the truth, seven out of ten believed that MPs habitually lied, and that politicians were thought to be less trustworthy than estate agents. Sir Alistair laid some of the blame on the media, whose reporting of politics could be 'cynical and sensationalist', but most on the politicians themselves. They had brought this on themselves. Cash-for-peerages had caught them with their hands in the money-box. It was not a good time to be asking for public money.

Most people had little idea how much the parties cost them already, and there might well have been a public outcry if they *had* known. By 2006 the so-called 'Short money' (introduced in the 1970s by the Labour minister Ted Short) supported the opposition parties, to be used in the running of their offices, to the tune of £5.6 million. The main beneficiaries were the Conservatives with £3.6 million and the Liberal Democrats with £1.5 million. These were not trivial sums. Even Sinn Fein, which did not take its seats in the Commons, drew £86,424 under a parallel scheme for the discharge of its 'representative duties'. Independents of course received nothing. Nor did Labour, because it was in office – which worsened its plight but left the voters unmoved. As it alienated its supporters, members and subscriptions continued to drain away from it into the sump of public disaffection.

It makes sense that people should give to parties as they do to charities, because they believe in the cause and feel they can do something worthwhile to assist it. This certainly applies to some of their wealthy backers, whether or not an honour is part of the *quid* for the *quo*. But among the population at large, the relief of distressed political parties is hardly a cause to tug at the purse- and the heart-strings. Most people believe the parties should be left to fend for themselves, and if they fall into poverty they should, like everyone else, adjust their lifestyles accordingly. It is a simple lesson in home economics: if we get into debt, we have no right to go running to the taxpayer to get us out of it. Sir Alistair observed dryly: 'I do not think there is much goodwill from the public for substantially increased state funding of political parties. Indeed, I have been struck by the widespread recognition from MPs that the public are not in a mood to bale out the parties.'[6]

The government was aware of this when, to try to take the curse off the issue, it commissioned Sir Hayden Phillips, one of the most rarefied of Whitehall mandarins, to conduct a year-long inquiry into the reform of party funding. To no one's surprise, the one thing that the parties agreed on was their need for more taxpayers' money. Sir Hayden suggested an extra £23 million, which in due course is almost certain to become the law of the land. If these were private corporations siphoning off money surreptitiously from shareholders or customers, they would properly be taken to court for racketeering, larceny or fraud. But because they are political parties, they can get away with it. If the parties wish to do something shifty, shady and deeply dishonest, all they have to do is to use their powers in Parliament to vote it into law. And at that point it neatly ceases to be illegal. This is the give and take of politics: if we don't give, they take. So the public end up bailing out the parties, whether or not they are in the mood to do so. Under this formula, so many parties will qualify for the hand-out that people will necessarily end up giving more money to the parties they oppose than those they support. And if they don't support any of them it will make no difference at all. There is no contracting in or out, and no escape from this poll tax. A citizen who is, say, of the Round Earth persuasion and deeply hostile to the policies of the Flat Earth Party will find himself enriching the Flat Earthers against his wishes.

This is hardly democracy. Rather, it is the politics of the pig trough. *And it further undermines trust in public life.*

## CHAPTER FIVE

# DEFENDING THE INDEFENSIBLE

*Can any one on earth believe that if the seeing and telling of the whole truth were really one of the ideas of the English governing class, there could conceivably exist such a thing as the English party system?*

G.K. Chesterton, *All Things Considered*

## BRAVE NEW WORLD

At least the government tried; and in so far as it had a defence on the malpractices of party funding, including cash-for-peerages, the fact that it tried was the best defence that it had. It had promised in its 1997 manifesto, as part of the brave new world on offer, to deal with the sleaze and scandals of party funding. It did not renege on its promise, but came up with the Political Parties, Elections and Referendums Act which passed onto the statute book in 2000. On the face of it, the reforms were necessary and unexceptionable. An independent Electoral Commission would be set up to police the political parties' campaigns and ensure that elections and referendums were fairly and openly conducted. It proposed to restrict the amount spent by political parties on general elections to a limit, depending on the number of seats they contested, of about

£17 million each. It required the parties to name their donors of £5,000 or more, so (it was claimed) turning off the flow of cash from secretive millionaires. Even if a number of folk who valued their anonymity felt able to sign cheques for only £4,999, the proclaimed outcome was that the scandals of the past would remain in the past, and a new age of transparency and openness was dawning.

Except that it wasn't. As an MP at the time, I protested that the interests of Independents had been completely ignored;[1] and I tried to obtain a seat on the standing committee that scrutinised the Bill, supposedly going through it clause by clause and looking for the loopholes that needed closing. Party politics brings out the worst in people; and there never was a piece of legislation likely to have more loopholes crafted into it. So I felt that there was a case for having someone on that committee, as on Standards and Privileges, with no party axe to grind. I failed. Membership of standing committees is in the gift of political parties and their whips. The parties themselves had too much at stake: they were setting the rules of engagement for their future campaigns. They were fearful of any concession that might disadvantage them. They were not in a giving mood. The result was an Act of the dodgiest draughtsmanship since the Control of Dogs Act of 1986: it was so shot through with loopholes that the parties could drive their gilded coaches and horses, or uncontrolled dogs, through them as they wished. Whether or not that was the intention, it was certainly the effect. If the parties knew it, they were guilty of dishonesty; and if they didn't, they were guilty of negligence.

The most conspicuous loophole was that, while gifts to a party had to be declared, loans did not. The result was that the financial needs of the two main parties had so far outrun their resources that at election time they were funded mainly by anonymous lenders rather than identified donors. Not only were the loans not declared – some of them on the Tory side were provided by foreign benefactors – but a number of the Labour lenders were nominated for peerages in short order. And let it be remembered that this was a party that had been voted into power in 1997 amid what its leader called 'a sense of hope beyond ordinary imagining'.

Molière said: 'It is the public scandal that offends: to sin in secret is no sin at all.'

A further defect of the Act was that it set the parties' spending limits roughly at existing levels, which were far too high for the practice of honest politics, as they have now begun to recognise. An election war chest of some £17 million could not be raised from their rank-and-file supporters. The usual subscriptions, raffles, coffee mornings, and wine and cheese parties could contribute only a fraction of what was needed. The rest would come from big donors – or, as it turned out, big lenders who might or might not want something in return. Cash-for-access is not as flagrant a breach of trust as cash-for-peerages; but if a government changes a policy in a way which, quite by chance, benefits one of its donors, a whiff of perceived corruption will hang over it; and that was the essence of the Bernie Ecclestone affair.

It would have been better to have set the spending limit at £10 million or even less. That would have been a more realistic target, given that there are some wealthy people who genuinely give to political parties as they would to charities, because they like doing it, and expect nothing in return except perhaps a feeling of having acted in the national interest. The parties would also have helped themselves, and can still do so, by agreeing to a ban on billboard advertising, which costs them millions and is unremittingly negative. They have already adopted the Liberal Democrats' technique of the virtual advertisement. The Lib Dems, unable to afford much in the way of regular advertising, devise a poster for mobile display, invite the TV cameras to its launch, hold a news conference and then tow it away, never to be seen again.

Or you can buy your way in. It is actually possible, in our supposedly settled and mature democracy, to purchase a seat in Parliament. Limits are properly applied to the amount that a party or candidate can spend in a constituency campaign; but there are no limits to what can be spent before it starts. And MPs always run scared: they tend to begin campaigning for the next election on the morning after the last one. Their careers depend on it. In the general election of 2005 the Labour Party were not the beneficiaries but the victims of this mile-wide loophole in the law. Twenty-three of the 31 marginal seats that the Tories won were targeted by millionaires who bypassed the central party and lavished their money on constituency associations, where it revived the grass roots for months and even years before the election was called. The swing to the Conservatives in those seats was 4.5 per cent, against a national average of 3.1 per cent. One of the unseated and outspent MPs, Peter Bradley in The Wrekin, complained to the Electoral Commission: 'It cannot be right that elections are decided not by who wins the argument but by a handful of millionaires in a handful of marginal seats.'

What has this got to do with cash-for-peerages? There is no way of knowing, unless the titles speak for themselves. Michael Ashcroft, whose company Bearwood Corporate Services gave £844,000 to the constituency campaigns, is a member of the House of Lords. Leonard Steinberg, who gave £101,000, is also a peer of the realm. And Robert Edmiston, who gave £370,000, would have joined them if his nomination had not been blocked by the House of Lords Appointments Commission.[2] Like Lord Ashcroft, he was questioned as a witness on cash-for-peerages.

If you are a wealthy man seeking to help your party – and this is a general point, not necessarily applying to any of the recent givers and lenders – it is devilishly hard to know how much of your money to spend to make the difference. You can throw away millions, in pounds or dollars, to no effect at all. But just a few thousand targeting the right campaign at the right time can turn defeat into victory. Irish Americans were famously good at those judgement calls. Joseph P. Kennedy (father of JFK) was reputed to have said: 'Don't buy a single vote more than necessary. I'm damned if I'm going to pay for a landslide!'

## A VERY BRITISH CORRUPTION

When the scandal broke, the Prime Minister's first line of defence on cash-for-peerages was that rich people were as entitled to honours as poor people – a political version of the old advice not to marry for money but to marry where money is. 'Nobody in the Labour Party to my knowledge has sold honours or sold peerages', he said in July 2006. 'The fact that is sometimes excluded from the public's mind in relation to this debate is that there are places in the House of Lords reserved for party nominees for their party supporters.'[3]

The weakness of this argument was that the would-be noble lords were not party supporters like any others. They didn't knock on doors. They didn't stuff envelopes, attend branch meetings or get out the vote on polling day. They didn't spend achingly tedious hours in steering committees and policy forums. Some of them weren't even party members. *But they did sign cheques.* The rich were different from the rest of us: they had more money and, in due course, the honours to go with it, acquired for public services in the party political bazaar.

Another fall-back was the Dagenham defence, which took its name from the old days at the Ford Motor plant when an employee's car would be searched at the security gate and found to have something in it that belonged, strictly speaking, to the company. The excuse was that the practice was widespread: he did it only because everyone else did. The same argument was regularly employed by MPs under investigation by Elizabeth Filkin in her exemplary term as Parliamentary Commissioner for Standards, and she gave it the very short shrift that it deserved. Now the parties themselves were trying it in the arms race of election spending. If party A ennobled its millionaire benefactors, party B would follow suit, perhaps throwing in an extra 'K' (knighthood) or 'big P' (peerage) along the way for good measure. This was peer pressure in its most literal sense. But the Dagenham defence should have no conceivable place in politics. If law-makers are law-breakers, either nationally or internationally, that is the end of the rule of law. The great American jurist, Louis Brandeis, observed: 'If the government becomes a law-breaker, it breeds contempt for the law; it invites every man to become a law unto himself; it invites anarchy.'[4]

An alternative argument, also deployed against Elizabeth Filkin, was that politics was such a special calling that no policeman or parliamentary commissioner could begin to understand its mysteries, and the politicians should therefore be left to themselves to practise it as they wished. But it was precisely because they *had* been left to themselves, and had practised it only too much as they wished, that it had been necessary for the regulator, and ultimately the police, to investigate their behaviour. Yates and Filkin served the public interest and enjoyed strong popular support in doing so.

When the government fell into its greatest difficulties, usually self-inflicted, there were two members of the commentariat who could always be relied on to rally round and try to pull it out of the ditch. David Aaronovitch of *The Times* and John Lloyd of the *Financial Times* remained generally so loyal through thick and thin that they probably did more to deserve an honour than some of those who actually received one. The game they played was a sort of political 'X Factor': in the cause of the government of the day, there was nothing they couldn't explain and no one they couldn't excuse, exonerate or exculpate. On cash-for-peerages they were on especially fine form. David Aaronovitch called it much ado about nothing:

> In the end, I think it is unlikely that much – if any – influence was bought, or much policy bent, by donors to political parties. And, by and large, I would guess that the sort of people who act as benefactors to the Labour, Lib Dem and Conservative Parties are the same kind of people who go around benefacting everywhere else as well. Rich people who spend their cash on things other than their own pleasures tend to find some reward in advance of Heaven.[5]

John Lloyd believed that Labour's mishaps were largely the fault of the press; and he wrote a strange, mad book on the subject, whose villain was depicted on the cover as a white-suited toad with a press pass. He too had words of comfort for those who wished to pay for a place in Westminster's sunshine:

> The House of Lords is a handy place for such people, since it rewards them for supporting the democratic system (which they do) by giving them an agreeable place in central London to mingle and meet with interesting, important and influential people. That seems to be the deal, and as deals go in a fallen world it isn't too bad a one. That is, it's not very corrupt.[6]

This would have been an attractive defence if the wealthy had been paying for membership of the Worshipful Society of Apothecaries or the Royal Antediluvian Order of Buffaloes, although the Apothecaries and Buffaloes might have had something to say about it. But they were not. They were buying their way into the high court of Parliament and the national assembly which makes the laws of the land. That was quite a difference.

A parallel line of defence adopted by the government's apologists was that London wasn't Kinshasa, Nairobi or, for that matter, Washington. Relative to so many other countries, corruption in Britain was moderate, restrained, discreet and so thoroughly British that we should almost be proud of it as part of a great tradition. And those who were up to their gentlemanly necks in it had, in most cases, sought to benefit their parties, not themselves; so if they had brought themselves accidentally into disrepute, that was the price they had paid for acting in the public interest. It takes the British to make a national virtue and an art form out of hypocrisy.

The answer to this sort of nonsense is threefold: first, that we have set ourselves up as a model of democracy, even presuming to impose it by force on countries denied its blessings; second, that any corruption anywhere is too much corruption, and you can't be a little bit corrupt any more than you can be a little bit pregnant; and third, that the peculiar institution of the House of Lords is not only itself anti-democratic, but it offers distortions of democracy neither practised nor even understood by democrats elsewhere. Try explaining the seductions of the upper house, as I have, to Ukrainian television or a Slovakian parliamentary delegation, and you will be met by a blank stare of incomprehension:

'You mean, the Prime Minister can personally appoint his own hand-picked men and women as members of the national assembly?'

'Not only he can, but so can the members of the other parties.'

'Do they all do it?'

'All except the Scottish and (usually) the Welsh National Parties.'

'But surely that can't happen in a modern democracy?'

'It not only can, but it does.'

'But why can they get away with it?'

'The classic British answer: because they always have done.'

The Slovaks and Ukrainians never got it. But the British understood it all too well; and a few of them stood to benefit in ways that money, and money alone, could buy. So arise, Lord Megabucks. Step this way, Lady Cashpoint. The ermine awaits, Lord Lucre and Lady Lavender of the List. The rules of admission have been drafted to secure you a seat at the grander end of the Palace of Westminster. And a soft landing for life, unless the rules are changed.

It can of course be subtler than that. Cash-for-peerages is against the law. Column-inches-for-knighthoods are not. Governments of both parties have routinely handed out honours to the editors of newspapers who back them in good times and bad. A Conservative prime minister will usually reward the editor of the *Daily Telegraph*, and a Labour prime minister will usually, although not invariably, reward the editor of *The Times*. The present incumbent still awaits recognition for the considerable services he has rendered in sidelining news unfavourable to the government, or banishing it to the least-read corners of his paper. There is no need for the 'spike', the butcher's hook on which Fleet Street used to skewer unwanted news, when it can be so discreetly buried at the foot of column six on page 44.

Forty years ago the Canadian Roy Thomson, with his eye on the ownership of the *Sunday Times*, noted that all proprietors of British newspapers seemed to become members of the House of Lords. He liked the idea, and in due course it happened to him too – as it did to Conrad Black of the *Telegraph*, whose ennoblement was opposed by the Canadian Prime Minister Jean Chrétien, but not by his British counterpart. Lord Black of Crossharbour duly took the ermine, and a fulsome account of his induction appeared in his newspaper. What happened next is news, if not yet history. In March 2007 he faced racketeering charges in a Chicago court; and no one would want to have his life story written by Tom Bower, certainly not the noble lord and his lady, Barbara Amiel. Bower's book *Conrad and Lady Black: Dancing on the Edge* told the whole amazing story of rise and fall.[7] Bower is the rudest man in England. To be fair, he says the same of me. The difference is that I mean it and he doesn't.

'When I want a peerage,' Lord Northcliffe is reputed to have said, 'I shall buy one like an honest man!' But there are other ways of acquiring a title than crudely paying for it. Such are the dignities that go with being an ordinary MP that most incumbents in safe seats will be reluctant to step down, and will serve one term too many, or maybe more. But there comes a time in their careers when they will hope to be asked, shortly before a general election, to make way for a candidate favoured by the leadership; and if they are not actually at death's door, they will be rewarded with a seat in the House of Lords. The Labour Party's rules are actually drawn to put such a 'parachuting' mechanism in place, allowing it if necessary to override the objections of a constituency association to the candidate pressed upon them.

Or an MP out of favour with his own party may cross the floor of the House in the hope, or even on the promise, of a place in the Lords when he has served out the full term. The whips have an interest in promoting such defections *pour encourager les autres.* Peter Temple-Morris was elected to Parliament in 1997 as the Conservative MP for Leominster. Now he sits in the Lords as a Labour peer.

More seriously, I sat and watched one day, in utter amazement, as an MP actually traded his vote for a peerage. I was not the only witness to it and am in no doubt that it happened. He was a serious politician with a reputation for integrity; and he knew that his decision, on an issue on which he carried some weight, was under scrutiny by the party. It was not a 'grey area' vote. He understood the rights and wrongs of it very well; and he voted for his promotion and against his principles. The speech that accompanied the sell-out was eloquent and high-sounding, but I am convinced that he did not believe a word of it. He justified it later as an issue of party loyalty. And now he has his seat in the House of Lords. *This also undermined trust in public life.*

## MANNING THE RAMPARTS

As the cash-for-peerages scandal deepened, the last-ditch defenders of the status quo took refuge in ever more ingenious and far-fetched arguments. One of their cheer-leaders was Steve Richards of *The Independent*, who dared to play the BNP card in denouncing an anti-politics movement that served no public interest:

> The bigger parties struggle for cash while smaller extreme parties flourish in local elections. Mean-while, senior politicians are accused with casual complacency of being corrupt. No wonder that the fanatics of the BNP and elsewhere rub their hands with glee.[8]

The logic of this argument was that the greater the misconduct, the less attention should be paid to it, for fear of throwing fuel on the fires of extremism: as if all small parties are extremist and large parties are not, which is actually not the case. It was arrant and self-serving nonsense. The Kidderminster Hospital and Health Concern Party is about as extremist as Rotary International. Its MP, Dr Richard Taylor, looks every inch the ultra-respectable 70-something retired physician that he is. The ranks of the Scottish and Welsh National Parties include some of the most dedicated parliamentarians in Westminster. The Labour Party, by contrast, really is extremist in its deference to Downing Street and its orchestrated and systematic attacks on civil liberties. The mainstream parties have been driven to desperate – I would even say extreme – measures to defend their threatened lifestyles.

The same Steve Richards described the police investigation into cash-for-peerages as 'deranged'. There is surely something amiss, or even deranged, in the state of a nation if its police, acting independently, cannot follow a trail of evidence in a criminal investigation without attracting this kind of incoming fire. The Prime Minister's biographers were especially zealous in his defence. They were manning the ramparts as if their careers and intellectual property were under threat, as in a sense they were. John Rentoul's headline, 'Kindly leave the stage, Mr Plod', over a column about 'the amateur theatricals of Yates of the Yard', gives some idea of the quality of the argument.[9] The last resort of the Prime Minister's diehards was to hint that the police inquiry was politically motivated – the likes of Yates of the Yard would never have called on Margaret Thatcher or John Major – and that when it was over they (the diehards) would 'get' the Metropolitan Police just as they had 'got' the BBC over the reporting by Andrew Gilligan. They even suggested, as a last throw of the dice, that if the Prime Minister was not trusted then there must be something untrustworthy about the very nature of politics itself – 'a low trust business', as Mr Rentoul rather morosely described it.

Whenever the former Prime Minister's biographers get to meet their Maker – an experience that Mr Blair himself apparently looks forward to – they can expect to be taken aside by some seraph or other outside the pearly gates and quizzed about their attitude to the central issue of trust in public life. If they really thought it did not matter, they did their leader no service at all by saying so.

A mention in despatches for courage and common sense in these media wars was earned by Martin Bright, political editor of the *New Statesman,* one of the few left-leaning columnists who was not in denial about the affair: he understood from the start its significance not only for itself but for its wider effect on democratic politics:

> The humiliation is not the Prime Minister's alone. No politician acts in isolation from those that elect him. Tony Blair came to office bearing the hopes of the nation like no other post-war prime minister since Clement Attlee. He brought with him an idea of Britain as forward-thinking, enlightened and idealistic. When he finally leaves Downing Street, we will not only have lost a prime minister but an idea of ourselves. We share in his shame.[10]

The ennoblement of nonentities was by no means Labour's worst mistake. No lives were lost because of it. No weapons of shock and awe were launched to promote it. There was nothing against it in the UN Charter. It even had the democratic merit of enabling the party to fight the Conservatives on more or less equal terms in the 2005 election (without it, they might actually have lost, as they did in most of the marginal seats where they were so heavily outspent). It helped a number of wealthy individuals to keep the score in the great game of life and then, being clad in ermine and grandly titled, to feel that they had achieved something. No harm in that. According to this philosophy, who dies with the most gongs wins. But it was not a sufficient excuse for bending the law of the land to breaking point. *This also undermined trust in public life.*

That the government was hung out to dry on this issue was like Al Capone being done for tax evasion.

If anyone should have blown an early whistle on the scandal it was the Electoral Commission, which was established in 2000, one of New Labour's first-born, to ensure fairness and transparency in the conduct of elections. It chided me for forgetting VAT in my minuscule Euro campaign expenses, but on the serious scandal of cash-for-peerages it failed to sound the alarm. In a report in January 2007 the Committee on Standards in Public Life noted that: 'It does not appear to have taken any further action on this issue until it became a major controversy in 2006.'[11] The Commission's chairman, Sam Younger, admitted that it did not intervene in the matter because he feared 'we might well be criticised'. That's worth repeating. Play it again, Sam: '*We might well be criticised.*' In the bear-pit of politics there is no regulation without criticism. Ask Elizabeth Filkin. Ask Yates of the Yard. Ask Sir Alistair Graham of the Committee on Standards, whose reward for pointing this out was to be let go at the earliest opportunity, while plots were hatched for the disbandment of his Committee. That is the price that you pay for telling the truth. Criticism is also, as Sir Alistair observed, a key performance indicator of effective regulation: if it works, it hurts. The watchdogs are dealing with ruthless people who will stop at nothing to get elected and believe in regulation for others but not themselves. It is the only life they have. A reluctance to face criticism is not a sufficient excuse. Soldiers set a better example. It is a court martial offence for a sentry to fall asleep at his post.

More than any other issue, the abuse of patronage contributed to the air of moral dishevelment that settled over the government in its third term of office. The Conservatives of course were equally culpable though less conspicuous in their own honorific transactions. The Electoral Commission must also take its share of the blame for failing in its basic task of scrutiny. So must Labour's cheerleaders in the media for aiding and abetting the traffic in peerages by turning a blind eye to it.

The ingenious Danny Finkelstein, a professional contrarian, wrote a column in *The Times* under the amazing headline: 'What British politics needs is more corruption.'[12] It was no wonder that the people despaired.

## CHAPTER SIX

# IRAQ – A WAR TOO FAR

*The people of England have been led in Mesopotamia into a trap from which it will be hard to escape with dignity and honour … Things have been far worse than we have been told.*

T.E. Lawrence, 1920[1]

## MOMENTS OF UNTRUTH

Governments receive information from the security services that the rest of us do not. They have a duty, when the national interest is threatened, to explain the nature of the threat and deploy the armed forces if necessary, and in the last resort, to deal with it. But equally, when the national interest is not threatened, they have a duty to examine the intelligence diligently, such as it is, and to act on it with caution and good judgement, whatever the pressure from powerful allies. What is remarkable about the rush to war from March 2002 to March 2003 is the extent to which the threat from Iraq (formerly Mesopotamia) was not just exaggerated, but *manufactured*, in a series of dossiers and statements which were shot through with falsehoods. In his statement in the House of Commons on 24 September 2002, the Prime Minister introduced a 50-page dossier setting out the threat allegedly posed by Iraq's imagined weapons of mass destruction. We now know that the reservations and doubts of the security services were wiped from the record. The voices of sceptical experts were silenced. Speculation was presented as hard fact:

> The weapons of mass destruction programme is not shut down. It is up and running now. ... The intelligence picture that they [the security services] paint is one accumulated over the past four years. It is extensive, detailed and authoritative. It concludes that Iraq has chemical and biological weapons, that Saddam has continued to produce them, that he has existing and active military plans for the use of chemical and biological weapons, which could be activated within 45 minutes, including against his own Shia population, and that he is actively trying to acquire nuclear weapons capability.[2]

In his preface to the dossier, the Prime Minister wrote:

> What I believe the assessed intelligence has established beyond doubt is that Saddam Hussein has continued to produce chemical and biological weapons. ... I am in no doubt that the threat is serious and current, that he has made progress on WMD, and that he has to be stopped.

None of this was true. The chemical and biological agents did not exist. Nor did the means to deliver them. The 45-minute claim applied only to tactical battlefield shells which did not exist either. And the press was encouraged to make alarming claims that the British sovereign base areas in Cyprus were within range of these phantom weapons. The 'assessed intelligence' was not only false but falsified, both on its way to Downing Street and inside Downing Street, where the Director of Communications, Alastair Campbell, assumed the chairmanship of a group that went through the intelligence from a presentational point of view, suggesting a hardening of its language on WMD. Some of these changes were incorporated in the final dossier. Dissenting voices were filtered out. Question marks were turned into exclamation marks, and conditional judgements into absolute certainties. The 45-minute claim was allowed to stand, unqualified, to make a good headline. The intelligence services were rolled over. The senior and respected Conservative, Kenneth Clarke MP, described the outcome as 'the worst military decision taken by this country since the Suez invasion'.[3] Lord Hurd, a former Foreign Secretary, said: 'Something went dangerously wrong at the heart of the decision-taking processes of our country.'[4] So it was that the armed forces were mobilised and sent to war on the basis of a falsehood about weapons of mass destruction and a whim about regime change – although the regime change argument was a later addition: on 18 March 2003 the Prime Minister told the House of Commons: 'I have never put the justification for action as regime change.'[5]

The door was slammed shut by David Kay, who led the Americans' search for WMD. On 28 January 2004 he told the Senate Armed Services Committee: 'We were almost all wrong, and I certainly include myself. ... It is important to acknowledge failure.'

The decision to take the country to war on such

insubstantial and shifting grounds was more than a breach of trust. It was a form of corruption – of thought, of language and of the political process.

## THE SOLDIERS' STORY

The armed forces sent to fight the war initially believed in the existence of weapons of mass destruction as the *casus belli*. They had no reason not to. Then, when it turned out that the prospectus was false, a deep disillusionment set in. This was the untold story of the war – untold, because the men and women in uniform were silenced temperamentally by their loyalty and institutionally by their terms of service. 'Theirs not to make reply, theirs not to reason why, theirs but to do and die.' I tried to tell it for them in a TV documentary, *Iraq: the Futility of War*, broadcast by Channel 4 in January 2006. It mostly reflected the views of the army rather than the other services, because the soldiers were closer to the ground and suffered the greatest casualties; but it was widespread across all three services. Their views have hardened since that time, and remain a standing reproach to the men who so nonchalantly put them in harm's way.

I was a soldier once, and not a very good one, as the regimental sergeant major never tired of reminding me. I served in the ranks, because I failed the War Office Selection Board's intelligence test; and when the brigadier, who doubted that I could be quite so stupid, ordered me to take it again, I failed it again – which didn't trouble me so much until I saw the cadets who had passed. So then the battalion posted me to its intelligence section, where I moved pins on maps and wrote subversively for the regimental magazine. The army of today is better than the army I served

in, not least because it no longer has Corporal 23398941
Bell M serving in it. (The last thing a soldier ever forgets is
his army number.) Those two years were the best education
I ever had – and from them I retained a deep respect for
the army. I came across it again as a reporter, from
Northern Ireland to Bosnia to the Gulf; some of the
captains I knew became its generals; we have a shared
history together; I occasionally lecture at its academies,
attend its mess nights and so on.

Because of these contacts I was aware, within weeks of
the start of the war in Iraq, of a groundswell of disquiet
within the military. This was not the campaign they had
signed on for and been led to expect. The disquiet started
with the medics, the doctors and nurses, who were not only
mostly reservists and closer to civil society than the rest, but
had to deal with the casualties which were the immediate
human cost. It spread to the infantry, the cavalry (tanks
and armoured reconnaissance), the engineers, gunners,
logisticians and other supporting arms. It affected the
army's nerve endings of recruitment, retention and
discipline. Serving soldiers were occasionally bold enough
to express it. The Chief of the Defence Staff, General Sir
Mike Walker, whose non-resignation at the time of the Iraq
war remains a mystery to this day, attributed a falling-off in
recruitment to what he called the forces' 'guilt by
association' with the war. He would not have said that if he
felt, after the event, that the war was justified. And further
down the chain of command, the army's Director of
Recruiting, Brigadier Andrew Jackson, dared to venture
further into this political no man's land: 'We cannot
pretend Iraq isn't a factor. It is reasonable to assume that
the officer community might have thought more deeply
about the army's role in Iraq.'[6]

Former soldiers could express their views more freely, and did so in the television documentary. General Sir Michael Rose, a respected commander and until recently the Adjutant General, laid the blame squarely where he felt it belonged: 'I think the politicians should be held to account, and my own view is that Blair should be impeached. And that would prevent the politicians taking a country quite so carelessly to war.' He also raised the question of why there had been no resignations by any of the chiefs of staff in the early months of 2003.

'Would you have resigned?' I asked him.

'I most certainly would have done. I would not have gone to war on such flimsy grounds.'

Another witness was General Sir Rupert Smith, described by the military historian Sir John Keegan, who knew them all, as 'Britain's outstanding soldier of modern times'. He was also the one with the greatest operational experience: commander of the British 1st Armoured Division in the Gulf in 1991, commander of the UN force in Bosnia in 1995, commander of British troops in Northern Ireland, and deputy commander of NATO at the time of the interventions in Kosovo and Serbia in 1999. He is a modest man who, retired from soldiering, uses neither his title nor his rank. But he does use his experience. His influential book *The Utility of Force*, published two years after the war in Iraq, is a distillation of that experience and an eloquent account of how industrialised warfare, with its high-tech weapons of shock and awe, regularly fails to deliver the outcomes that the politicians expect of it: 'You can have the biggest infantry in the world and the most super kit. Go in amongst the people, and every time we use our strength we fail to achieve our objective. We often reinforce our opponent's ability to achieve his objective, because his strategy is always to get us to over-react.'[7]

So it proved with the British and Americans in Iraq in 2003, and with the Israelis in Lebanon in 2006. It was to the disadvantage of the armed forces, but perhaps the relief of the politicians, that Rupert Smith never rose to be Chief of the Defence Staff, a position for which he was well qualified and which, if he had been promoted, he might have held at the time of the war in Iraq. It could then have taken a rather different course. The campaign was conducted in violation of every one of the principles he sets out.

It was left to another thoughtful soldier, General Sir Richard Dannatt, to pick up the post-war pieces. After only two months as Chief of the General Staff, the army's senior soldier, he gave an interview in which he told people what their government did not want them to hear about the war in Iraq: 'We should get ourselves out sometime soon, because our presence exacerbates the security problems.' And he added: 'I think history will show that the planning for what happened after the initial and successful war-fighting phase was poor, probably based more on optimism than sound planning.'[8]

The Army Rumour Service, the soldiers' unofficial website, resounded with approval. Comments included: 'Respect to the man, he's saying what everyone thinks'; 'After years and years *at last* someone at the top has had the balls to stand up and be counted'; and 'In other news, the Prime Minister is reported to be taking a new and unexpected interest in the appointment of a new defence attaché to Greenland.' But the general was safe in his job: to have shown him the door for telling the truth would have provoked too much of an outcry. He was criticised for crossing the line between the political and the military, but in truth he did not so much cross the line as move it; and it *had* to be moved, because the covenant between the armed forces and the nation was breaking down.

These were the gap years of British politics. Not only was there a widening gap between the government and the people, but also between the government and the armed services. The witnesses to that included General Dannatt's predecessor as CGS, General Sir Mike Jackson:

> Throughout my career I have been taught, and I have striven to instil, that soldiering requires the Army's leaders always to have in the forefront of their minds that it is the soldiers themselves who will make the endeavour succeed. … Sadly, I did not find this fundamental proposition shared by the Ministry of Defence.[9]

General Jackson waited for his retirement before speaking out. But General Dannatt was still serving, and for that reason became a hero to his troops – which, as any soldier will tell you, is a rare occurrence.

In 1515 Erasmus wrote: *Bellum dulce inexperti* – war is sweet to those with no experience of it.

So it happened that, on New Labour's watch, troops were sent to fight unwinnable wars in distant places by politicians who had, themselves, not a day's experience of soldiering between them. In my Commons days I would look across the floor of the House at the government front bench and note that there was no one on it – not a minister or junior minister – who had worn the Queen's uniform or known anything of the reality of warfare. Not a single one. The best the government could come up with in its third term was a parliamentary private secretary and former major in the Adjutant General's Corps, Eric Joyce MP, who as a soldier had been described by his brigadier as 'uncommandable' and then became the most compliant of Labour back-benchers. And to think that once, when he was still in uniform, I initiated a debate in the House of Commons on his behalf!

The Prime Minister, when he was weighing the options about any of his wars, had no one around him who could tell him what the real thing was like or could bring a whiff of cordite to the discussion. This was an entirely new phenomenon in British politics. The Duke of Wellington, the ultimate soldier politician, once said of his old adversary Napoleon that no one ever lost more armies than he did: 'I could not risk so much: I knew that if I ever lost 500 men without the clearest necessity, I should be brought upon my knees to the bar of the House of Commons.'[10]

More recently, Churchill's post-war Cabinet included no fewer than three veterans of the Battle of the Somme: Harold Macmillan, Harold Alexander and Oliver Lyttleton: Macmillan was badly wounded and saved by his sergeant major who, being a Guardsman, asked permission to carry him away.[11] Macmillan himself was the last prime minister to have had the benefit of seeing the world from the bottom of a shell hole. When Ted Heath was Prime Minister, most of his Cabinet had wartime experience. Margaret Thatcher could rely on the advice of Willie Whitelaw and Lord Carrington, both of whom had served with distinction in Normandy. Harold Wilson was well supported by his Defence Secretary Denis Healey, who had been a beach-master during the Allied landings at Anzio in 1944. Tony Blair had no one of that calibre beside him; and on Iraq he refused to take the advice of those who offered it, including

Lord Healey, by then a sprightly octogenarian. Healey observed: 'I don't think that people who had war experience would ever have got us involved with the Americans in the way that Tony Blair did.'[12]

## FAMILIES AGAINST THE WAR

It took this government, and its war in Iraq, to break with centuries of military tradition and provoke an uprising of the families of the fallen. Not all of them took part in it: but enough of them did to suggest that the covenant between the nation and the armed forces had been broken. In its place arose the phenomenon of Military Families against the War.

In June 2003, an army staff car headed south from Bala in Wales, and turned right on a narrow lane in the village of Llanuwchllyn. In it was a major of the Royal Military Police, in his role as a casualty notification officer. When a soldier is killed on active service, the Ministry of Defence no longer informs the next of kin by telegram, but does it, properly and directly, with a personal visit by an officer of the same regiment or corps. It is the least coveted assignment in the armed services, and anyone would wish it to fall to someone else. The officer cannot bring back a lost life, but he can help to catch a falling family.

Reg Keys was working in the garden of the home on the hillside that he and his wife Sally had bought when they moved from Solihull in retirement – he from a career as a paramedic and she from the NHS. Both of their sons were in the army, Richard in the Royal Engineers and Tom in the Royal Military Police, having transferred from the Parachute Regiment at his father's suggestion: a steadier job, Reg Keys supposed, and less in the line of fire. (Tom had taken part in a storming rescue operation by the Paras in Sierra Leone three years earlier.) The last time Reg had seen him was at Birmingham International Station in February 2003, marching proudly down the platform and off to war. As soon as he saw the staff car he knew what had happened. It was like a cold hand on his heart.

Tom Keys was one of six military policemen assigned to visit a police station in Al Majar Al-Kabir. Shortly before that, their equipment had been downscaled. They carried less ammunition than in wartime. They had no satellite phones. And their radio antenna would take longer to assemble than they would have time for in an emergency. Close by, and unknown to them, men of 1 Para had run into opposition from a hostile crowd, angered by weapons searches, and had withdrawn. The crowd, some 400 strong, then stormed the police station. The six RMPs barricaded themselves in a single room; they were out of touch with their headquarters; and when they ran out of ammunition they were killed. Tom Keys' body was riddled with more than twenty bullets, the last two to the head.

The army's board of inquiry, which reported in November 2004, concluded that the incident was a surprise attack which could not reasonably have been predicted. Although it called many witnesses, including the battle-group commander and others in the chain of command, it found no one at fault. Its remit was tightly drawn. It was directed not to attribute blame or recommend disciplinary action, but to ensure that such a tragedy did not occur again. To the families, it was an evasion and a whitewash. The criminal investigation also ran into the ground. Reg Keys believed that his son had been betrayed in life and was now betrayed in death.

Herodotus said: 'In peace sons bury their fathers; in war fathers bury their sons.'

Bereavement affects different people in different ways. Reg's response was to start asking questions. Why was the men's equipment downscaled just at the time when the supposed liberation of Iraq was (in the soldiers' phrase) going pear-shaped? Why did they not have the communications equipment that could have saved their lives? Why did the rest of the battle-group not know of their plight? And what warnings had the Paras received of the likely effects of their weapons searches in communities where it was normal and even necessary to be armed?

Then there were the wider political questions. At the time of the invasion, most soldiers believed what they had been told: that the reason they were risking their lives was not regime change, but to rid the region of Saddam Hussein's weapons of mass destruction. By the time the six redcaps were killed, it was obvious that he didn't have any. Subsequent surface-skimming inquiries shed little light on the matter. In no forum, including the high court of Parliament, had the government been fully and independently held to account.

So Reg Keys decided to do it for himself. In the general election of May 2005, he first considered standing as an Independent against the Defence Secretary, Geoff Hoon, in Ashfield. (Hoon is passionately disliked within the military.) Then he reasoned, in his own words, 'Why go for the monkey when you can go for the organ-grinder?' He stood against the Prime Minister in Sedgefield. The difficulties were considerable. The field was already crowded with no-hope peace and protest candidates. He had no experience of electioneering and no idea of what he was getting into.

I called up and offered to help, and spent the next month by his side. He was a marvellous candidate, convincing on the doorstep and with a compelling reason for entering the fray. He wasn't doing it for himself, but doing it for Tom. His inexperience was actually an asset, for he was a man of transparent honesty and without a shred of political ambition. He became a familiar figure on market days in Newton Aycliffe and Ferryhill, where other candidates including the mainstream opposition, Tories and Liberal Democrats, were seldom to be seen.

He attracted a wider variety of support than any other candidate in the entire election. He did particularly well with old soldiers, in one of the army's main recruiting grounds. His coalition ranged from the peace activist Bruce Kent on the left to the novelist Freddie Forsyth on the right, which is about as wide as the spectrum goes. Other high-profile supporters included Brian Eno, Richard Dawkins and Rory Bremner. Freddie Forsyth delivered a grand patriotic speech on his behalf, resonant with Shakespearean references, in the rain opposite the Sedgefield war memorial. Of great local value was Derek Cattell, formerly on the executive of the Sedgefield Labour Party. He defected to Reg's campaign after some heart-searching; it cost him a few fair-weather friends, but the candidate had no more loyal supporter from start to finish.

Sometimes the campaign's leftists fell out with each other, as leftists tend to, leaving us alone on the doorstep. I felt that Reg needed cheering up.

'You do know that if this goes right,' I said, 'and whether or not you win, you will have the chance to stand up and say your piece on election night?'

'I had never thought of it,' he said, 'but will the Prime Minister have to be there?'

'He will, and Cherie will be with him. The eyes of the nation will be on Sedgefield. So it's worth considering what you want to say.'

It is part of the romance of standing for Parliament that, notwithstanding the canvass returns, you have really no idea how you are doing. My attempts, through friendly MPs, to persuade the main opposition parties to withdraw their candidates had come to nothing. The Tory candidate, Group Captain Al Lockwood, a former coalition spokesman on the war, had the nerve to suggest that Reg should stand down in his favour: as a former officer, he seemed to imply, he would be better placed than a mere other rank (Reg) to call for a full inquiry into the war. As a former other rank myself, I found such notions beyond belief.

On polling day, Sally bravely came over from Wales. Their surviving son Richard was there, on leave from the army. I was touched that he asked to borrow one of my Suffolk Regiment ties. Having done all I could, I stayed away and watched from home.

I know better than most how hard it is for an Independent to challenge the political parties: every vote has to be won the hard way. In Sedgefield Reg Keys, a bereaved father and good man, had taken on the might of the Labour machine and the party system. He came fourth with 4,000 votes, 10 per cent of the total. It was the second highest non-party vote of the night except for those of the two elected Independents in Wyre Forest and Blaenau Gwent. And it earned him his place on the podium. His speech at the count was the most effective and highly charged of the whole campaign. Its dignity and grief visibly discomforted Tony and Cherie Blair. It was restrained and eloquent, delivered from the heart and to the point:

'I dedicate this campaign to my son Tom, who was killed in Iraq four days short of his 21st birthday. He was sent to war under very controversial circumstances. If the war was justified, then I would not be here today. If the war had been just I would have been grieving but not campaigning. If weapons of mass destruction had been found, then I would not have come to Sedgefield, the Prime Minister's stronghold, to challenge him on its legality. ... I hope in my heart that one day the Prime Minister will be able to say sorry to the families bereaved in this war, and that one day he will be able to visit in hospital the soldiers that have been wounded in it.'

He ended his words with the names of the six dead military policemen. His speech had an enduring impact. In any record of the Blair premierships – perhaps presidencies would be a better word – it will remain as a standing reproach to Labour's leader on his greatest mistake. It certainly reads better, in the after-light of events, than most of the Prime Minister's own dazzling performances, including the speech that launched the war on 18 March 2003 and was said by those who heard it to be one of his best.

## MISSION TO BASRA

The lights in the RAF Hercules were blacked out as it flew over the Kuwaiti border into Iraq – which after three invasions in thirteen years, once by the Iraqis and twice by American-led coalitions, was one of the most breached in the world. The plane was on its nightly milk run taking British soldiers into and out of Basra. For the buzz of active service, the loadmasters preferred sliding supplies out of the back of the aircraft to the men of the Queen's Royal Lancers on permanent armoured patrols in the desert near the Iranian frontier. Air drops were used because whatever moved on the roads was likely to be ambushed. The Americans' nightmare around Baghdad was not being replicated in the south, but the war was not going well anywhere. The British comforted themselves with 'at least we're not struggling'.

I was not on a regular reporting mission, but completing a radio programme about the work of army chaplains. That couldn't be done without visiting the sharp end, and the chosen sharp end was Iraq. The padres were men of peace among men and women of war. Most if not all were against the war, as indeed were their Churches and many of the soldiers still escorting convoys, conducting raids and guarding bases. For soldiers are not automatons, but can and do think for themselves. And they had reasonable concerns about a war that never ended. On the ninth rotation of British troops, it was still taking the lives of too many for no clear purpose. 58 Battery of 12 Field Regiment Royal Artillery had lost four men out of 110 on the previous tour of duty. Those were not negligible casualties.

Marooned in the desert and living hard lives under canvas, 7,200 British soldiers were facing six months of concentrated reality in which their survival skills would be tested to the limit. Every road movement was conducted as a meticulous military operation, often led by a corporal whatever the rank of the soldiers in the convoy. The RAF Regiment, who seldom receive the credit they deserve, were specialists. At least one of the bases would come under attack each day, usually by mortar and rocket fire: a weapon of choice was the Chinese 63-1, a version of the Soviet

Katyusha rocket. Three of these were fired at the Shaibah base during our stay there – just daily routine. The chaplains were in more demand than they would have been in peacetime. They dealt with the doubts and dangers individually. The Reverend Andrew Martlew, padre to 40 Field Regiment Royal Artillery, said: 'This is quite a difficult thing to say and an even more difficult thing to think, but almost by taking the Queen's shilling we're putting elements of our conscience into cold storage, and in order to help the guys we might not be economical with the truth, but we might want to give them encouragement and help rather than pull them down.'

The churches, Portakabins behind 10-foot-high blast walls, were the safest places on the base. They were furnished with crosses and makeshift altars; one of them even had two small stained glass windows; and when Shaibah was closed they were towed away. Army chaplains had one advantage over village vicars: they could name their churches after whichever saint took their fancy, and often did so. Andrew Martlew inherited the Church of St Paul in the Desert, and turned it overnight into St Jude's. Padres are unarmed, and the only weapon that they carry is a saving sense of humour. Beside his biblical distinction as a man of peace, St Jude is also the patron saint of lost causes.

There could be few more desolate places on earth than the old RAF field at Shaibah. The red-brick open-air cinema was crumbling to dust. Wooden gables were collapsing at drunken angles. The roofs of verandas were falling onto the floors. The abandoned control tower, built to the colonial standards of the 1930s, was deserted but for a Gurkha piper practising the Gaelic tune 'Mist Covered Mountains', to be played that evening at the lowering of the regimental flag. He was there only because it was the emptiest place on the base that he could find. The ghosts included long-forgotten aircraft. In its heyday Shaibah was the busiest airfield in the region, buzzing with the old Vickers Valentia and Hawker Audax, bought on the cheap and reconfigured as bombers against the Luftwaffe, the pro-German 'Golden Square' of Iraqi officers, and tribesmen who resisted British rule in 1941. The British then marched on Baghdad. And the RAF, like the Germans at Guernica, learned the uses of bombing against unde-fended targets. In those days they called it 'air control'. *Plus ça change* ... Flares from the encircling oil fields were a burning reminder of why we were there in the first place. The rise and fall of an empire were embalmed in this emptiness. Ozymandias, king of kings, must have had a monument around here. The Prime Minister who knew no history could have learned so much from Shaibah.

He got close. I was waiting for my flight out of the Basra Air Station as he arrived for his fourth and last pre-Christmas visit to the troops. So of course I asked to see it for myself. The answer that came back from the Downing Street advance staff was 'Absolutely not'.

Thirty minutes later an accompanying officer's phone rang again. It was the functionary from Downing Street.

'Martin Bell won't be there, will he?' she demanded.

'Of course not,' said the soldier. 'It's as you wish.'

Some time later, there was yet another call:

'*He won't even be in the same building as the Prime Minister, will he?*'

And so it went on. My army friends were amused that I was such a pariah in Downing Street. I explained that it may have been because I was once a politician myself; or because as a journalist I had never been a member of the

Lobby, the magic circle of political correspondents who sign on to certain agreements in these matters. But there were no hard feelings at all, at least for my part. Worse fates have befallen me than not getting to see the Prime Minister.

What was fascinating was to observe, from the outside, how the visit was managed. Of the thirteen officials accompanying him, more than half were press handlers of one sort or another, from the Official Spokesman to the Special Adviser (Press) to the Director of Events and Visits, the Press Logistics Officer and no fewer than four other press officers. They were outnumbered by the travelling journalists by less than three to one – an extraordinarily high ratio of sheepdogs to sheep. The aircraft hangar was rigged like a stage, with two Challenger tanks outside, two Warrior battle taxis, a Lynx helicopter and 300 troops inside – truly a theatre of war in the most literal sense. The camera angles were calculated to perfection, but the soldiers were unimpressed.

'Tell the pilot to keep the engines running,' said one. 'He'll be off again in a moment.'

'Hardly time for a fag break,' said another.

'Remember that he's your boss,' countered the first soldier.

'No, mate', said the second, 'my boss is the Queen.'

Even in warfare, spin was king of the hill. It did not matter so much that the army of occupation was failing, so long as it wasn't *seen* to be failing, as the general debacle unfolded. The burdens that soldiers have to bear, especially in distant and inexplicable wars, include not only their weapons and body armour but the 'lines to take' dictated to them by their civilian masters and advisers. These lines tend to diverge from reality to the point where, in this case, they were sticking out at jagged angles to it. This was especially so on the term to be employed for describing the forces attacking British troops. 'Terrorists' wouldn't do, because although soldiers can be frightened they cannot be terrorised: terrorism is the use or threat of violence against civilians to achieve a political purpose. They experimented with 'criminal gangs', and indeed there were such gangs in Basra, but when they were not threatening each other they were united in trying to expel the foreign invaders. The spin doctors then tried 'anti-Iraqi forces', but that wouldn't work either, since an Iraqi firing a rocket at a British base was by definition anti-British, but hardly anti-Iraqi; he wasn't aiming the rocket at fellow Iraqis. The obvious term was 'insurgent', but they wouldn't use it because it was politically neutral. As George Orwell noted, the corruption of thought and language infect each other.

In the course of a visit rather longer than the Prime Minister's, I met not only the chaplains but fighting soldiers of many ranks and regiments. They were old friends from Gulf War One and Bosnia. Some were on their second, third or even fourth tours of duty in Iraq. They had seen for themselves the shift from liberation to occupation. Their only contact with Iraqis was contact in the military sense of being under fire. They were shot at, shelled and ambushed, not because they were liberators but because they were occupiers.

Out in the desert an experienced officer dared to speak his mind. He had been in Iraq through the euphoria of liberation, to the early tensions between the liberators and the liberated, and now to the hard grind of occupation. He had the medals to show for it. 'I'll tell you what this feels like,' he said. '*It feels like being a German in the Wehrmacht in*

*France in the Second World War. We too are an occupation force.
And that's how it seems to me.'*

## ENDGAME

One by one, except for the British Prime Minister and
the American President, the architects of the invasion
recanted, were removed from office or peeled away from
the cause. By the time that Donald Rumsfeld, a whirling
Dervish of a Defense Secretary, was dismissed after the mid-
term elections in November 2006, even he was having
second thoughts: 'In my view, what US forces are doing in
Iraq is not working well enough.' In October, President
Bush was still assuring the American people: 'We are
winning in Iraq.' Rumsfeld's replacement, Robert Gates,
thought otherwise. An exchange at his confirmation
hearing, before the Senate Armed Services Committee,
went as follows:

> Senator McCain: 'We are not winning the war in Iraq.
> Is that correct?'
>
> Mr Gates: 'That is my view, yes sir.'
>
> Senator McCain: 'And therefore the status quo is not
> acceptable?'
>
> Mr Gates: 'That is correct, sir.'[13]

So the next day President Bush was in the White House
Cabinet room receiving a document which told him in
effect that the invasion had been a mistake, the war was lost
and that 'staying the course' was no longer an option. This
was the report of the Iraq Study Group, a committee of
Washington veterans including James Baker and Edwin

Meese, who had served the President's father with distinction. The group also included Lee Hamilton, a respected Democrat from the same era. In those days partisanship stopped at the water's edge. Essentially it was a group of elder statesmen drafted in to read the riot act to their successors, who were advised that they could accept all of the report or none of it. The time for fighting until victory had passed. American combat troops should start withdrawing from Iraq in about a year. It was the end of a costly and tragic delusion. The 'we shall prevail come what may' brigade had lost, and the realists thought they had won.

But they had not. Against all reason, the President rejected the advice of the wise men. He ignored the will of the people expressed emphatically in the mid-term elections. Instead of American forces being reduced, he announced in January 2007 that they would be increased. It was as if nothing was learned, and nothing remembered, from the lessons of the past. Senator Chuck Hagel, a Republican with presidential ambitions, called it the most dangerous foreign policy blunder since Vietnam.

At this point the rhetoric and the reality finally parted company, as did the British strategy, quietly and discreetly, from the American. The Prime Minister's line, still an echo of the American President's, was: 'Don't be in any doubt at all. The troops will stay until the job is done.' But even as he made that pledge, in his pre-Christmas address to the troops in Basra, the engineers were starting to dismantle the logistics base at Shaibah.

Here is a sound war-zone rule: pay no attention to what they say – pay attention to what they do. Even the Pizza Hut on wheels was being driven to somewhere safer. By the early summer of 2007, what remained of the camps inside eight miles of perimeter wire were handed over to the

Iraqis. British bases in the city of Basra were closed. Three of the departing battle-groups were not replaced. Most of the remaining troops were concentrated around the airport, the obvious launching pad for an exit strategy. British tanks and armoured personnel carriers, the thunderous symbols of the occupation, were pulled back behind the wire. The British were redefining success, on a downward scale, in line with what was achievable, which was less and less with every month that passed. The senior British commander in Iraq, Major General Richard Shirreff, said: 'When I came here and initiated the operations we have been conducting, I was looking for a 100 per cent solution. But this is Iraq, this is Arabia and this is reality. A 60 per cent solution is good enough for me.'[14]

In 1920, T.E. Lawrence wrote: 'Mesopotamia will be the master of the Middle East and the powers controlling its destinies will dominate its neighbours.'[15] It was Mesopotamia's misfortune that the powers controlling its destinies were the Americans and British.

In four terrible years the so-called coalition had lurched through all the phases and phrases of military intervention, from shock and awe to hearts and minds and finally – this was the curtain call – to a qualified cut and run. It would be presented as a victory. It was in fact a retreat. There was even a certain symmetry to it. The war would end, as it had begun, on the basis of a falsehood.

## CHAPTER SEVEN

# SHADING
# THE TRUTH

*I could not dig: I dared not rob:*
*Therefore I lied to please the mob.*
*Now all my lies are proved untrue*
*And I must face the men I slew.*
*What tale shall serve me here among*
*Mine angry and defrauded young?*

Rudyard Kipling, 'Epitaphs of the War'

## THE CREDIBILITY GAP

It was an everyday scene in 'liberated' Baghdad: flames swept through a building in the city centre. Smoke filled the air and debris littered the street outside the Interior Ministry. Rescuers worked to carry away the wounded. Fourteen people had been killed and 40 wounded in a suicide car bombing at the outer checkpoint. Seven American soldiers also died that day, the victims of IEDs, improvised explosive devices, which were the insurgents' own weapons of shock and awe. On the same day, 59 Iraqis lost their lives in sectarian clashes, Shia against Sunni, further south near Diwaniyah, bringing the total to about 10,000 in three months, and unknown hundreds of thousands in three years. It was at that point that the new British Defence Secretary Des Browne, on a visit to Baghdad, looked the camera straight in the eye and declared: 'Things are improving and the challenge is to maintain that improvement.'[1]

*Why did he ever say that?* It ran contrary to all the known facts. Things were not improving: they were unravelling. Just about everyone outside the political class could see that: the politicians obstinately refused to. Back in my parliamentary days, when most of my early votes were cast for the government, I was aware of many disappointments but no single big mistake in Labour's first term, unless perhaps the Bernie Ecclestone affair, foreshadowing future scandals. The big mistake of its second term without question was the war in Iraq. The big mistake of its third term was the sequel to that war – the bone-headed pretence that a new Iraq was being built and the consequences of the conflict were so positive as, retrospectively, somehow to justify it, however mistaken the original *casus belli*. It was as if those who held power were progressively blinded by it – and the longer they held it, the less they could see. The fatal error of ministers, especially the Defence Secretary and the Prime Minister himself, was to maintain that things were so when they were manifestly not. The words pointed one way and the evidence pointed another. The words were clearly nonsense. The people understood, even from the filtered and fragmentary reports on the nightly news, that they were nonsense. So how could they trust a government that was telling untruths to the extent that it lived in a parallel universe all of its own and had, apparently, taken leave of its senses? Not only its competence but its balance of mind were called into question by the multi-plication of its mis-statements, day after day, month after month and year after year. As the free-spirited Labour MP Paul Flynn observed: 'For New Labour only the future is certain: the past is always changing.'

The government's way of proceeding was not only intellectually dishonest and even criminal, for the denial of evident truth is a crime of the mind, but self-defeating. Few would believe it any more. The people's trust deserted it and never fully returned. For these – again – were not trivial issues but matters of life and death. Kipling was prescient:

*If any question why we died,*
*Tell them, because our fathers lied.*
'Epitaphs of the War', 1919

Martha Gellhorn, one of the greatest of war correspondents, used to call it 'official drivel'.

If the people's faith in government is shaken, it can sometimes be restored by admitting error, but not by denying it. There was surely never a time in our country's history when the government's statements about a crisis were so out of kilter with the people's understanding of it; and in this case, the people knew better. *This also undermined trust in public life.*

A Labour government, of all governments, should be aware of what happens when such a separation occurs, and the popular misunderstanding of an emergency is at odds with the official version of it. This has happened before. It was precisely because of this kind of contradiction that the party was cast into outer darkness – or, more precisely, eighteen years of opposition – in 1979. Jim Callaghan, the last Labour prime minister before Tony Blair, was locked at the time into a struggle with the public sector workers who should have been his allies. The unions were strong. The pound was weak. Inflation was running at 10 per cent. The Callaghan government tried to restrict public sector pay rises to 5 per cent. It was challenged by transport workers, engineers, NHS staff, council workers and others. Even the grave-diggers went on strike. No one was working to capacity except the cartoonists. The press described it as the winter of discontent. And in that winter, as uncollected rubbish piled up in the streets and squares, the Prime Minister was unfortunately scheduled to attend a summit meeting with American president Jimmy Carter and French president Valéry Giscard d'Estaing on the Caribbean island of Guadeloupe. It fell to me, as Washington correspondent, to head south and report the event for BBC television. The winter of discontent was a world away geographically, but not politically. We were well aware of the context. I patrolled the beaches with my tireless cameraman Bob Grevemberg, formerly of the New Orleans police. We tried – oh, how we tried! – to secure an image of the Prime Minister swimming in warm waters. In the climate of the times, that was the scoop to be had and we never got near it. It was in an age of innocence before there were spin doctors, but we were quite properly thwarted by Callaghan's press secretary Tom McCaffrey and his political adviser Tom McNally (now Lord McNally, the Liberal Democrat Leader in the House of Lords). The Prime Minister had actually been working hard to agree an alliance position on nuclear disarmament negotiations and was genuinely upset by the criticism from home. But the summit did for his government all the same.

On his return to London, and on McNally's advice, the Prime Minister held a news conference at Heathrow airport, to head off the clamour in the press that he had been taking his ease in the sun while the country suffered. (Even Tony Blair would face this kind of criticism a generation later, when he was merely on holiday and New Labour had left Old Labour far behind: although, after Iraq, there were some who felt he should take more and longer holidays to reduce the chance of further foreign adventures.) This is what Jim Callaghan said: 'I promise that if you look at it from outside, and perhaps you are taking a rather parochial view at the moment, I don't think other people in the world would share your view that there is mounting chaos.' An increasingly anxious Tom McNally hovered over his shoulder. The message was supposed to have been 'I'm back, and I'm in charge'. A creative sub-editor on *The Sun* distilled this into the headline 'Crisis: what crisis?', and the rest was history, including the history of Labour's hopes for re-election. In the opinion of many, it was this more than anything else – an off-the-cuff remark distorted by a headline – that brought Jim Callaghan down, and opened 10 Downing Street's door to Margaret Thatcher. Words can have consequences, which in this case were long-term. She stayed there for twelve years, and her successor John Major for a further six-and-a-half.

It may be that the Labour Party made the mistake of forgetting its own folklore. We were a poorer country then, which is not to say an unhappier one. The issues and symbols were important: strike-bound factories, un-dug graves and uncollected refuse. Just imagine the impact they would have today in the age of instant commentary, rolling news and weblogs by the yard. Even at the time, they affected ordinary voters in a way that distant and ill-reported conflicts did not. But (except for the graves) they were hardly matters of life and death. Twenty-seven years on, with another Labour government in office, the fall-out from the war in Iraq was of a different order. Lives were lost and families bereaved on a pretext that was demonstrably false. The weapons of mass destruction did not exist. Tony Blair was fortunate in that, throughout this affair and in spite of it, he still commanded a solid majority in the House of Commons. (His Labour predecessor was brought down by a single vote, 310 to 311, on a motion of no confidence moved by the Scottish National Party, which was itself pulverised as a result.) To remain in denial on an issue of such magnitude was to risk the same outcome, but for two differences. The first was that Labour was protected by the size of its majority, its leadership-friendly constitution and the support of its friendly press barons. The second was that the Conservative Party, having unwisely supported the war, was in no position to propose a motion of no confidence about the conduct of it. It was one of the mysteries of his ten years in office, and which said a lot about the demoralised state of the opposition, that Tony Blair never had to face a single vote of confidence, or even a debate on Iraq, initiated by the Conservatives. Rank and file Tories – even some senior Tories – had reason to believe that their party let them down.

They also let themselves down. An interesting example of their misplaced faith in the government was Nicholas Winterton, the usually independent-minded Cheshire Conservative whom I greatly respected as my parliamentary neighbour and would have proposed for the Speakership had I not been committed elsewhere. In the fateful debate on the war on 18 March 2003 he said:

I have sent a petition to the Prime Minister carrying about 700 signatures from my Macclesfield constitu-ents expressing their concern and their opposition to the war. I say to them: 'On this issue, put your trust in the Prime Minister. I fervently believe, as your member of Parliament, that he is right.'[2]

By contrast, only a handful of Tories understood that he was wrong. One of them was Richard Bacon, the new MP for South Norfolk:

He has not persuaded world opinion. He has not persuaded the British people. He has not persuaded my constituents in South Norfolk. And he has not persuaded me.[3]

The war in Iraq, among the multitude of its other failures, was a failure of party politics.

## A QUESTION OF HONESTY

Politics is not straightforward and too often brings out the worst in otherwise decent people. Nor do I believe that those who practise it should always and in all circumstances tell everything they know regardless of the consequences. On questions of national security there are times even in a democracy – perhaps especially in a democracy – when discretion is a necessary virtue. Any government has a right and duty to make its case to the people, especially when, given the ill-intentioned nature of politics, the opposition is bound to misrepresent its record. Such is the way that the political game is played. But for reasons of self-interest as well as principle, those who conduct our affairs should not tell egregious falsehoods either, or they will fall deeper into the hole that they have dug for themselves. There is a reasonable balance to be struck between discretion and disclosure. And always has been. In his first speech as Prime Minister in 1894, Lord Rosebery, Gladstone's successor, described England in relation to Ireland as 'the pre-dominant partner', and by so doing provoked a storm that he never understood. His colleague Sir Henry Campbell-Bannerman, a more professional politician and indeed a prime minister in waiting, tried without success to enlighten him. Sir Henry wrote later: 'It showed how little political and parliamentary education Rosebery had that he thought it a sufficient defence of a public utterance that it was true.'[4]

Our sympathies here should surely lie with Lord Rosebery. It *should* be a sufficient defence of a public utterance that it is true; but in the winner-takes-all world of party politics this is not always possible. It puts a weapon into an opponent's hands, and, more damagingly, into those of the attendant posse of spin doctors and word-twisters, who can turn honour into dishonour at the drop of a press release. In the 2004 presidential election in the United States, the Democrats fielded a candidate with an impeccable war record in Vietnam. While most of his privileged contemporaries evaded the draft, or used family influence to remain on safer home postings, Lt John Kerry of the US Navy was commanding a patrol boat in the dangerous waters of the Mekong Delta. By the time the pack of scavengers had done with him, this was portrayed in the campaign as in some way discreditable; the message-merchants around President Bush, who had done barely the minimum in the Texas National Guard, were able to blend his service record, such as it was, with his folksy 'bring 'em on' defiance of terrorism, to turn a questionable episode into an electoral asset. The truth had nothing to do with it.

When I entered Parliament in 1997, I was in a position to set myself a test – a one-man experiment in honest politics: how long would it be before I too ceased to tell the truth, when a half-truth would cause me less difficulty? I passed the test with flying colours for just about a month. Then in June 1997 one of the local weekly papers, the *Knutsford Guardian*, asked me whether I was enjoying the experience of being the new MP. A truthful answer would have been that I was exhausted, less relaxed and more anxious than at any time in my life, more apprehensive even than in the war zones, and that I regretted every moment of the decision to stand for election. But I did not wish to give such easy satisfaction to the vengeful Neil Hamilton, who had brought his defeat upon himself, still less to his wife Christine. Goodness knows what they would have made of it in their later career as a comedy double act. I had nothing personal against them, but found them difficult people to admire. So I prevaricated. Call me in a couple of months, I told the newspaper. By that time I had found my feet, learned the basics of parliamentary procedure and taught myself how to survive in such mixed company. So I did not lie, but admit to having shaded the truth to make life a little more bearable.

From this I developed the *Knutsford Guardian* principle, a bomb-dodger's guide for rank-and-file MPs. It can do for politicians what fieldcraft does for soldiers, which is to help them stay alive in dangerous places. Most of it is common sense. It is being careful how you fill in your mortgage application form. It is not employing your relatives at public expense (although some do). It is scrupulously listing gifts and benefits in the Register of Members' Interests. It is listening to the advice of those you respect. It is not taking loans from millionaires whose affairs (if you are a minister) your department may happen to be investigating. It is not proposing friends or creditors for knighthoods and peerages. It is not going looking for wildlife in motorway service areas or taking late-night walks, with attendant moments of madness, on Clapham Common. Whatever you do, whatever you say in Parliament or out of it, on whichever side you vote or don't vote, whether you decide to abstain on a big issue, even where you take your holidays, whatever interviews you give to the unholy trinity of press, radio and television – on all these things, just ask yourself how they will look in the headlines of the *Knutsford Guardian*, or its equivalents in 600 other constituencies. If they look OK, you have passed the test and have nothing left to worry about. If not, then think again. Your first mistake can so easily be your last. However creditable your previous record, you will be remembered for that error and nothing else, and for your subsequent apology to the House.

Part two of the *Knutsford Guardian* principle is that if you do make a mistake, then it is vital to admit it rather than to cover it up and let the truth seep out a little at a time. If you acknowledge a mistake, the public and even the press will usually forgive you; and may even credit you, deservedly or not, with showing an unusual degree of honesty – 'I was wrong!' is a disarming political battle-cry. It wrong-foots the ill-intentioned and leaves them at a loss about how to get back at you. If you cover the mistake up, you will deservedly die the death of a thousand cuts. The difficulty here is that, being human and therefore fallible, you may not admit even to yourself that you have made the mistake in the first place. Something of the kind happened to me when as a still-serving MP I wrote a book about Parliament. I maintained that the members of the Standards and

Privileges Committee, on which I served, left their party allegiances at the door in considering the various cases that came before us. I wished it to be true, and even for a while I must have believed it to be true. But it was not true in most of the disputed cases involving senior Labour Party figures. These brought out the partisanship in four of the eleven members, although some of them let it show more subtly than others. There was no excuse for what I wrote, although looking back on it I can only conclude that hope got the better of experience. Or maybe I was over-impressed by the architecture. I should have known better.

For ministers, of course, the stakes are higher – and for the Prime Minister, highest of all. The consequences of his government's most extreme error, the war in Iraq, were so catastrophic as to be beyond cover-up. That left the choice of admitting the mistake or denying it. He chose denial. What was worrying was that this was no masquerade. He even *believed* in it, with all the fervour of a member of the Flat Earth Society, and was just about the last man in the country still to do so. A rueful hush descended on his co-believers. Some defected, others just fell silent. The argument was comprehensively lost, more than any that I can ever remember in public life. In all New Labour's first decade there was nothing that did it more damage than the opening up of this gap between truth and fiction. Its epitaph should be a dodgy dossier engraved upon a tombstone.

## STATES OF DENIAL

Tony Blair's post-war pronouncements on the action that he ordered in Iraq, his most controversial and consequential decision, should properly be allowed to speak for themselves. They show him on a journey through various sorts of denial, from obstinacy through injured innocence to mystical self-belief.

On 28 April 2003, with the 'hot war' barely over and the Iraq Survey Group still searching for Saddam Hussein's elusive WMD, he said: 'Before people crow about the missing weapons of mass destruction, I suggest they wait a little.'

They waited and they waited; and no such weapons were found, because none existed. So, at his party's conference five months later, the Prime Minister was obliged to acknowledge the reality while evading responsibility for it. He could have expressed contrition. He chose not to. It was not in his vocabulary, any more than it had been in Margaret Thatcher's, whom he not-so-secretly admired and who was in fact much better than he was at executing a discreet U-turn when a policy was failing. The hardest act in politics is to stand on the deck when the ship has been holed below the water-line and pretend that it is all plain sailing. In the most difficult and carefully crafted speech of his premiership, this is what he said: 'I ask just one thing: attack my decision but at least understand why I took it and why I would take the same decision again … Imagine you are Prime Minister. And you receive this intelligence. And not just about Iraq. But about the whole murky trade in WMD. So what do I do? Say "I've got this intelligence but I have a hunch it's wrong?" Leave Saddam in place with the democracies humiliated and him emboldened?' What was conveniently omitted, because it was not yet in the public domain, was the extent to which the evidence on WMD had been made more definitive than it actually was by the Downing Street spin machine; so it was not (as it should have been) the intelligence that drove the policy, but the policy that drove the intelligence.

By the time of the Labour Party conference a year later, in 2004, the rhetoric had left the real world in its slipstream and soared into the thinner air of a faith-based foreign policy: 'Do I know I'm right? Judgements aren't the same as facts. Instinct is not science. I'm like any other human being, as fallible and as capable of being wrong. I only know what I believe.'

*I only know what I believe* is the strangest of watchwords for a head of government in such dangerous times. It can only be damaging in the making of foreign policy. To act in good faith is not enough, when what the country cries out for is good judgement.

What was lacking was a sense of history. In his self-belief, Tony Blair resembled none of his predecessors so much as Neville Chamberlain. After a particularly difficult debate in the Commons in June 1938, Chamberlain wrote: 'I think that what enables me to come through such an ordeal successfully is the fact that I am completely convinced that the course I am taking is right and therefore cannot be influenced by the attacks of my critics.'[5]

Tony Blair never lost his capacity to astonish. A classic example, late in his reign, came from a visit to Dubai during one of those swings through the Middle East that tended to produce little more, in the final analysis, than the square root of not very much. This is what he said: 'The art of leadership is learning to take decisions. Sometimes you are right, sometimes you are wrong. Some of the decisions are very difficult and someone also gets angry.'[6] A lot of people also get dead. It was the sheer insouciance of the decision-making that took the breath away.

It is precisely because a Prime Minister is as fallible as anyone else that he has a special obligation, in committing the armed forces to war, to take the advice of those who should give it, including the chiefs of staff of the armed forces – always remembering that they are not his to commit. When the band marches onto parade it does not play 'Soldiers of the Prime Minister': it plays 'Soldiers of the Queen'. Constitutionally we do not have a commander-in-chief – nor, after recent events, would we wish to have one. It was a sad reflection of the decline of accountability when the Prime Minister, having committed the armed forces to an ill-fated expeditionary war, refused to allow an inquiry into his actions on the grounds that to do so would have endangered the troops he committed. The logic of this argument was that the more he put them in the line of fire the less he should be answerable for doing so. *This also undermined trust in public life.*

I believe that future historians, when they come to assess this episode in our national life, will find it strange, if not incredible, that Tony Blair initially survived his misjudgements on Iraq to win a substantial, if reduced, majority in the election of 2005. It had to do in part with the tribal nature of politics. Such is the rallying of the party faithful in times of crisis, especially of war, that a prime minister may be able to gather the clan around him and survive a single catastrophic mistake. (The exception was Anthony Eden in 1956.) But a pattern of misjudgements, one following fatally after another, will bring the show to a close. The war in Iraq lit a bonfire of Labour Party membership cards. But it was Tony Blair's unconditional support for George Bush, and indirectly for Israel, in the 34-day conflict between Israel and Hizbullah in Lebanon in July and August 2006, and his refusal to call for an immediate ceasefire, that finally turned his Cabinet and MPs against him. His 'complete inner self-confidence' in his judgement on this crisis repeated his dangerous certitude on Iraq. The MPs had had enough of it. They were away from Westminster at the time, closer to their constituents, in many cases fearful for their seats and at the final limit of their loyalty. It wasn't the awkward squad that did for him, but hitherto supportive back-benchers. He was forced to outline a timetable for the long good-bye.

Even as he did so, his states of denial over the war in Iraq became more acute, and therefore untenable, as the security situation deteriorated. The violence there 'spiked' to the highest level in two years. An American offensive to pacify Baghdad during the month of Ramadan resulted only in a sharp increase in suicide bombings and sectarian warfare. The general responsible for the operation described the outcome as 'very disheartening'. 105 Americans died in October 2006, pushing the total to nearly 3,000. President Bush's officials started looking for a way out, although he himself vowed to stay the course until victory, even if Laura (his wife) and Barney (his dog) were the only ones beside himself left believing in it. And the comedians were saying that he couldn't be sure about Barney. There were even conflicting signals, as in Vietnam more than a generation earlier, about what victory might consist of – perhaps a tripartite state, a local ceasefire, a 'forcing mechanism' to hand over power and a phased American withdrawal. Whatever it was, it would be a long way short of the original objective of a new democracy in a remade Middle East. To those with an eye for historical parallels Iraq was Vietnam all over again, and the Ramadan attacks were its Tet offensive.

The parallel was not exact, but close enough to be shocking. There were ominous similarities, but certain differences too. One was that that the British had not been involved in Vietnam. It was the wisest decision of an earlier

Labour government under Harold Wilson to resist President Lyndon Johnson's pressure to join the coalition in support of MACV, the Military Assistance Command in Vietnam. Just as in Iraq, the troops committed were a coalition of the United States as the main force with other countries in a lesser supporting role – South Korea, Australia and New Zealand; and it came under strain south of Saigon in 1967, when the New Zealand gunners shelled the Australian infantry by mistake. All that the Americans wanted from the British was a token force to broaden the coalition. President Johnson's Secretary of State, Dean Rusk, suggested that a battalion of the Black Watch would have been enough (just as in Iraq, where it was committed in the most hazardous circumstances, the Scottish regiment had an important symbolic significance for the Americans). The Labour government was not to be moved. The national interest did not require it. Nor did the 'special relationship' with the United States. Years later, when another Labour government faced a similar decision, it was as if the lessons of Vietnam had never been learned. Downing Street forgot its history. On judging whether to support American military adventures, the old guard had a notably better record than the new one.

History does not repeat itself, Mark Twain said, but it rhymes. Some of the Americans themselves saw the rhyme and unreason of it, or at least the older and wiser of them, that for the second time in 30 years the Congress, the people and the press had been rolled over to support a disastrous foreign war. One of these veterans was the octogenarian Robert Byrd, a lone voice of dissent in the Senate. Another was the investigative reporter Seymour Hersh, who broke the story of abuse of prisoners at Abu

Ghraib. In the second year of the war, he asked in a speech at Berkeley, California:

> How can eight or nine neo-conservatives come and take charge of this government? They over-ran the bureaucracy, they over-ran the Congress, they over-ran the press, and they over-ran the military! So you say to yourself, how fragile is this democracy?[7]

## ENDANGERING THE PEOPLE

The bearing of false witness was nowhere more conspicuous, and more damaging, than in the government's denial of the effects of the war that it launched. As with the war itself, it promoted falsehoods as truths.

The common-sense advice to doctors, *first do no harm*, should equally well be applied to politicians. A government's obligation is to the people it serves. In times of war and emergency, its paramount duty is not just to protect them but to refrain from actions and policies which will further endanger them. The decision to go to war in Iraq was just such an action and policy. Obviously it endangered the armed forces committed to it, as all wars do. More than 100 British servicemen were killed in the first three years, for the war did not stop with the unwise 'mission accomplished' statement on the USS *Missouri* in May 2003. It also divided communities at home and radicalised, or even criminalised, a small but growing group of young Muslim men. The bombings on the London Underground in July 2005 were carried out not by foreign fighters but by five such men, mostly from Yorkshire's Muslim communities. The government took these atrocities as evidence of the extremism that it was determined to root out. The greater the danger, the more it claimed to be vindicated. It confused cause and effect. It operated entirely within the cocoon of its own convictions. It denied the link between the bombings and its policy of waging war in Islamic countries.

But the link was obvious to just about everyone else. The retiring law lord, Lord Steyn, said: 'After the dreadful bombings in London, we were asked to believe that the war did not make London and the world a more dangerous place. Surely, on top of everything else, we do not need to listen to a fairy tale.' Lt Col Tim Collins, a good soldier who commanded his battalion of the Royal Irish Regiment in the war, observed: 'History might notice the invasion [of Iraq] has arguably acted as the best recruiting sergeant for al-Qaeda ever.'[8] The Americans' Joint Intelligence Estimate, the shared analysis of sixteen agencies, concluded against the grain of White House policy that the war in Iraq was fuelling the global spread of Islamic militancy. And two weeks before the bombings, the British government's own Joint Terrorism Analysis Centre noted that the Iraq issue provided a 'motivation and focus' for UK-based terrorist activity.[9] This was confirmed by someone better placed than any analyst to know what was in the bombers' minds – Shehzad Tanweer, who was one of them and blew up himself and others near Aldgate Underground station. In a 'martyrdom video' aired a year later on al-Jazeera television, he said: 'What you have witnessed is only the beginning of a string of attacks that will continue and become stronger … until you pull your forces out of Afghanistan and Iraq.'

There was certainly a string of reported plots and conspiracies. These included a plan by a group of British

Muslims of Pakistani origin allegedly to blow up as many as a dozen aircraft bound for the United States, three at a time, with liquid explosives and detonators smuggled separately on board by the conspirators and then assembled in flight. The suspects arrested were again not foreign fighters but British citizens with British accents and British addresses, mostly in Walthamstow and High Wycombe. The evidence seized by the police included computer records, explosive materials and 'martyrdom videos'. The head of MI5, Dame Eliza Manningham-Buller, rang alarm bells when she revealed that up to 30 terrorist plots were being investigated and more than 1,000 suspects were under surveillance.

The war in Iraq left one group of British Muslims in an especially exposed and vulnerable position: the 325 men serving with the armed forces, mostly in the army but some in the other two services. In January 2007 the police made a number of arrests in Birmingham in connection with another alleged plot, to kidnap and behead a British Muslim soldier. One man was charged. Muslim families faced strong pressure from within their own communities to persuade their sons to resign from the armed forces and even the civil service. No such pressures had been applied before the ill-fated war.

The government's view of its critics was 'Those who are not with us are against us', or alternatively 'They just don't get it'. The critics could counter in identical terms: it was Westminster and Whitehall that just didn't get it. The government's policy was not mistaken *because* it incubated terrorism. It was mistaken *and* it incubated terrorism. It was wrong to go to war on a falsehood even if it had not endangered the people; but it had endangered them, and most of them knew it. The war came first and this particular plague of terrorism after. Before the war there had been no suicide bombings or related conspiracies in the United Kingdom; after the war, there was an ever-increasing number of them, representing a growing threat. To suggest that this was a coincidence was an affront to common sense. 71 per cent of people believed that their government's foreign policy had made them less safe, against 1 per cent – which is as near to zero as opinion polls go – who believed it had made them more secure.[10] Sir Rupert Smith, the general who should have been heeded but wasn't, wrote of the so-called 'war on terror' (which he called 'a term without useful meaning') that in the way it was being conducted it provided the terrorist with the high-octane strategic fuel that he needed.[11] Almost everyone understood the link, except those in power who persisted in denying it.

Among the British people, dismay at the government's policy was not confined to Muslims, but it was Muslims who felt its impact most acutely, especially when advised by ministers of the crown to spy on their children and root out the 'extremists' in their midst. So a group of the most influential – MPs, peers and the Muslim Council of Great Britain – wrote an open letter to the Prime Minister, at the time of the war in Lebanon, stating the obvious: 'Current British policy risks putting civilians at risk both in the UK and abroad. The debacle in Iraq and the failure to do more to secure an immediate end to attacks on civilians in the Middle East not only increases the risk to ordinary people in the region, it is also ammunition for those who threaten us all. Attacking civilians is never justified.' To this the government reacted furiously, accusing the Muslims of suggesting that policy should be framed in response to terrorist threats. This was the reverse of the truth. It was the government's own decisions, flawed and inflammatory, that were fuelling terrorism at home and abroad. They sidelined our diplomacy, turned our voice into an echo of the Americans' and singled out the United Kingdom, among all the countries of the world, as the second most favoured target of al-Qaeda – perhaps even the first, because more easily penetrated, and with more potential sympathisers, than the United States.

## SO WHY DID THEY DO IT?

Why did they repeatedly state that things were so which were manifestly not so? Why did they deceive the public? Why indeed did they also deceive themselves? Why could they never admit that a policy had failed, but only that circumstances had changed and it was therefore 'evolving'? I find these the hardest of questions to answer, because reasonable people outside politics don't act in this way at all. When they find themselves in a hole, they stop digging. Most politicians tighten their grip on the shovel. That is in the very nature of their trade. Party politics is adversarial. It for ever looks ahead to the next election. It allows consensus in committee, but resists it on the floor of the House. Those who practise it will choose a course of action, however speculative, to prevent their opposition from occupying the same ground or accusing them of indecisiveness for not having occupied it; and then when the course of action fails they will persist in it, shovelling all the more furiously the while, lest the same opposition will exploit an admission of error for electoral advantage. This is especially so in the case of an unpopular and contentious war. Macbeth can help us here:

*I am in blood*
*Stepp'd in so far that, should I wade no more,*
*Returning were as tedious as go o'er.*

*Macbeth,* Act III, scene 4

The novelist Martin Amis accompanied Tony Blair on his 'farewell tour' from Washington to Iraq. He wrote a shattering account of a meeting that the Prime Minister had at the Basra airbase with a group of officers, a padre and 25 young soldiers. The senior men talked to him about the 'hard and dark' side of soldiering, the lives and limbs that were lost. Amis noted: 'All the oxygen went out of him. It wasn't just that he seemed acutely underbriefed (on munitions, projects, tactics). He was quite unable to find weight of voice, to find decorum, the appropriate words for the appropriate mood. "So we are killing more of them than they kill us ... You're getting back out there after them. It's brilliant, actually."'[12] Instead of an answer there was an emptiness.

In matters of war, the blood sacrifice is decisive. Whoever embarks on it has to be able to assure the bereaved families that the cause in which their loved ones died was a good one, that those deaths served some larger purpose and that the country or the world is a safer place because of them. To do otherwise is to admit that the casualties were in vain. This does not excuse the falsehoods of war, but it does begin to explain them.

CHAPTER EIGHT

# DIPLOMATIC BAGGAGE

*To me, Goldsmith's March 2003 opinion on the legality of the Iraq war remains the fault line of the Blair governments. Like the permanent stain of Suez on Eden's reputation, it will not be eradicated from the memory of the Blair prime ministerships for generations to come.*

Peter Hennessy, constitutional scholar[1]

## REBELLION IN THE RANKS

The careers of those at the centre of government policy over Iraq prospered in spite of – perhaps even because of – its failure. They promoted it and were in turn promoted. In due course Ann Taylor MP, who reined in the Butler Inquiry and chaired the Parliamentary Intelligence Committee, became Baroness Taylor of Bolton. Donald Anderson, who squared away the House of Commons Foreign Affairs Committee, was ennobled as Baron Anderson of Swansea. John Scarlett, chairman of the Joint Intelligence Committee, was made head of MI6 and a Knight Commander of the Order of St Michael and St George. Sir David Manning, the Prime Minister's chief foreign policy adviser, was appointed ambassador to

Washington. Coveted honours were bestowed on lesser officials in the decision-making loop. CBEs, OBEs and Companions of the Order of the Bath abounded. Only Geoff Hoon was moved downwards, from Defence Secretary to Europe Minister. And Alastair Campbell found a use for his talents as a sports columnist for Murdoch's *Times*. (At least one of this group – not of course Mr Campbell – is now known to be regretful about the part that he or she played in the matter.) No one was dismissed. No one resigned. No one broke with the policy. *This also undermined trust in public life.*

The service chiefs belonged in a different category. They showed a proper deference to the civil power. They were also by nature 'can do' people, keen that the armed services should do what they were trained for, and knowing that if they were not used they would (on past experience) be cut. The top brass were not themselves hell-bent on the war, but they did accept the flawed (and revised) assurances that it was legal. The Chief of the Defence Staff at the time, Admiral Sir Michael Boyce, duly became Lord Boyce of Pimlico. The Chief of the General Staff, General Sir Mike Walker, became Lord Walker of Aldringham. I asked Lord Boyce, for a documentary I was making, if he would be willing to explain his reasoning. His answer was a gruff and naval 'I don't do that sort of thing' (though whether the kind of thing he did not do was explaining himself or appearing on television was left unclear). There is a better chance that Lord Walker, who does have things to say, will use his platform in the House of Lords to say them. Both former chiefs, in my view, owe this to the men and women who served under them. Lord Walker disputes my account of this affair, which he calls a 'false tale'.

Among others honoured were officials within the

Ministry of Defence who had played a part in the identi-
fication of Dr David Kelly, a weapons specialist in the
Ministry, as the source of a BBC report that suggested that
the evidence on WMD had been adjusted – 'sexed up' was
the word used – to make the case for war. Dr Kelly, a
candidate for a knighthood if ever there was one, was
beyond the reach of the honours system. He was a supporter
of the war, but believed that Downing Street's dossier had
been overstated.[2] He died apparently by his own hand in a
field in Oxfordshire – some say it was murder – after being
put through the grinder by the House of Commons Foreign
Affairs Committee. The BBC report was flawed in detail
but truthful in its thrust. The case for war had been sexed
up, massaged, doctored or falsified – the terms varied but
the facts were indisputable. It had been presented as
something other than it was. The only people to lose their
jobs over the report were the BBC's chairman and director-
general and the journalist responsible for it. No Orders of
the British Empire or Knights Grand Cross or Companions
of the Order of the Bath for them. But in the media wars,
as in the real wars, the winners lost and the losers won. The
people understood very well what had happened. If it
looked like a fix and smelt like a fix, then it was a fix. Greg
Dyke was the only director general in the BBC's history
ever to have been cheered by his staff as he took his leave of
them. The BBC's reputation stood higher as a result, and
the government's much lower.

The diplomats also understood very well what had
happened. In embassies across the world, and especially
the Arab world, they saw for themselves the damage being
done by their government's war policy to British interests
and influence. The Foreign Office itself was reduced and
marginalised. The decision to march in lock-step with the

Americans undermined the influence of every British ambassador in every capital in the world except Washington. The Rolls-Royce of government departments was at risk of turning into the Trabant. The rank-and-file were in revolt, but bound to silence by their terms of service. As with the soldiers, it was the retired officers who spoke for them. In an unprecedented move, 52 former ambassadors and other senior diplomats signed a letter of protest to the Prime Minister in April 2004. It was drafted by Oliver Miles, former ambassador to Libya, in an internet café in Tripoli. Other signatories included Sir Alan Munro, who had been ambassador to Saudi Arabia, Sir Marrack Goulding, a former head of UN peace-keeping, and Francis Cornish, an ambassador to Israel. It was not only the Arabists – the so-called 'camel corps' – who joined in. They wrote that there was no case for supporting policies that were unprincipled and doomed to failure:

> The abandonment of principle comes at a time when rightly or wrongly we are portrayed throughout the Arab and Muslim world as partners in an illegal and brutal occupation of Iraq. ... All those with experience of the area predicted that the occupation of Iraq by the coalition forces would meet serious and stubborn resistance, as has proved to be the case. To describe the resistance as led by terrorists, fanatics and foreigners is neither convincing nor helpful.

A fiercer broadside against the Prime Minister was fired by Sir Rodric Braithwaite, a former British ambassador to Moscow and chairman of the Joint Intelligence Committee:

Stiff in opinions, but often in the wrong, he has manipulated public opinion, sent out soldiers into distant lands for ill-conceived purposes, misused the intelligence services to serve his ends and reduced the Foreign Office to a demoralised cipher because it keeps reminding him of inconvenient facts.[3]

The man who, more than any other, was caught in the diplomatic crossfire was Sir Michael Jay, Permanent Under-Secretary at the Foreign Office before, during and after the invasion of Iraq. It is possible, though unlikely, that he did not share the doubts about the legality of the war which were held by just about everyone around him, and were the cause of one high-profile resignation. What is known for certain is his view, contrary to Downing Street's protestations, that the war incited Muslim extremism at home. On 18 May 2004, more than a year before the bombings on the London Underground, he wrote to the Cabinet Secretary, Sir Andrew Turnbull:

The issue of British foreign policy and its negative effect on Muslims globally plays a significant role in creating a feeling of anger and impotence among especially the younger generation of British Muslims. … These seem to be a key driver behind recruitment by extremist organisations.[4]

He might as well have spared himself the effort. Downing Street remained in denial about the effect of its policies. The Foreign Office's senior official retired in 2006 and was duly ennobled as Lord Jay of Ewelme in the County of Oxford.

Maybe it is a matter of temperament rather than

conviction. Most public servants go with the flow. A few do not. No prizes for guessing which group has the better chance of ending up with a seat in the Lords.

Among serving diplomats, so far as is known, there was only one who resigned immediately over the war in Iraq: Elizabeth Wilmhurst, deputy legal adviser at the Foreign Office, who kept her silence throughout (for which her employers were duly grateful); but her resignation letter, which entered the public domain through the Freedom of Information Act, showed that the lack of an authorising resolution was crucial to her decision:

> I cannot in conscience go along with advice … which asserts the legitimacy of military action without such a resolution, particularly since an unlawful use of force on such a scale amounts to the crime of aggression.

She was joined more than a year later by Carne Ross, former first secretary in the British mission to the United Nations, who also wished to make his protest privately, but whose views became public after he gave evidence to the inquiry led by Lord Butler. His is a particularly interesting case, not only for itself, but for the light it casts on the politicisation, and I would even say the *corruption*, of the service for which he worked.

## THE CASE OF CARNE ROSS

Young people dream of their future occupations – as tinkers, tailors, soldiers, sailors, or even in extreme cases journalists, politicians or spies. As a boy, Carne Ross's dream was to be a diplomat. The otherness of abroad interested him more than anything else, and he resolved to make a career of it if he could. He remembers: 'I decided quite early on that I was going to become a diplomat, and was very discouraged by everybody saying it was incredibly difficult and that only very clever people became diplomats.'[5]

He was clever enough to pass the Foreign Office's entry tests and be fast-tracked for promotion. His first foreign posting was to the British embassy in Bonn. This coincided with the war in Bosnia and its effects on Germany, which had to absorb hundreds of thousands of Bosnian refugees as well as the spiralling costs of German reunification. One of the young diplomat's tasks was to explain the British government's policy – or rather lack of it – on the Bosnian war. It was an early blooding in the diplomatic exercise of defending the indefensible, but on his own admission he knew nothing of the Balkans and was slow to grasp what he later called 'the debacle of British inaction over genocide in Bosnia'.[6]

From 1995 to 1997 he worked in London on the Middle East peace process and as speechwriter to Malcolm Rifkind, the Foreign Secretary. These were the early stages in a career that, if all went well, would end in an ambassadorship, a knighthood and whatever other trappings of office come the way of a diplomat at the top of his trade. He was not marked out as a trouble-maker or dissident like, for instance, Craig Murray, who resigned as ambassador to Uzbekistan in protest against alleged British complicity in human rights violations by the host government (in the cause, of course, of the ubiquitous 'war on terror'). Ross and Murray worked together in the Foreign Office in the early 1990s on the analysis of sanctions-busting by Iraq, but in spite of that, Carne Ross's career still prospered.

In December 1997, he was appointed to one of the most sensitive and exacting posts in the diplomatic service. He was responsible for Iraq policy within the British Mission to the United Nations, including sanctions, weapons inspections and the drafting of Security Council resolutions. Every working day for four-and-a-half years he read the British and American intelligence on Iraq, which came in a thick folder and was more impressive in quantity than quality. He could have found his way blindfold through the undergrowth of successive resolutions on Iraq – what use of force they mandated and, just as important as things turned out, what use of force they did not. He worked closely with the Ministry of Defence. One of his contacts and friends there was the WMD expert and former weapons inspector, Dr David Kelly. He attended Dr Kelly's funeral. He testified to the Butler Inquiry:

> During my posting, at no time did HMG assess that Iraq's WMD (or any other capability) posed a threat to the UK or its interests. On the contrary, it was the commonly held view among officials dealing with Iraq that any threat had been effectively contained. I remember on several occasions the UK team stating this view … during our discussions with the US (who agreed). At the same time, we would frequently argue, when the US raised the subject, that 'regime change' was inadvisable, primarily on the grounds that Iraq would collapse into chaos.[7]

Which of course was what happened. The Americans talked of a grand coalition. A grand demolition would have been nearer the mark. Carne Ross also testified:

I quizzed my colleagues in the FCO and MOD working on Iraq on several occasions about the threat assessment in the run-up to war. None told me that any new threat had emerged to change our assessment; what had changed was the government's determination to present available evidence in a different light.[8]

Ross was diligent and well thought of. He attended his meetings, sent his reports and briefed his masters. He wrote later: 'I became proud (to my present shame) of my Rottweiler-like reputation at the Security Council as the most effective and aggressive defender of British and American Iraq policy, sanctions and all.'[9] He even coined the acronym UNMOVIC (the United Nations Monitoring, Verification and Inspection Commission), the inspections regime that followed UNSCOM (the United Nations Special Commission) with the task of investigating Iraq's alleged WMD. UNMOVIC, whose first chairman was Dr Hans Blix, was created by Security Council resolution 1284 that Carne Ross drafted. It is not every diplomat who enters a phrase into the international lexicon.

Then 9/11 happened. He was attending an EU meeting, hurriedly adjourned after the second plane struck the World Trade Center. He walked home against a flood of people coming the other way, covered in ashes and weeping. He remembers the compassion of those Americans, lighting candles, praying and singing in Union Square, rather than thirsting for revenge. 'Tragically, that compassion is something that the governments of both the US and Britain seemed to ignore since.'[10] After 9/11, everything changed politically and diplomatically. He switched to Afghanistan after the fall of the Taliban. He spent six weeks in Kabul negotiating with warlords and seeing for himself the power vacuum which developed with such fateful consequences, as the ground was already being prepared and the troops held back for the next war, in Iraq. He returned to New York and, increasingly sceptical of allied policy, took a year-long sabbatical studying foreign relations at a college in Greenwich Village.

He was there at the time of the dodgy dossiers and the headlong rush to war. He thought of resigning, but did not see the point of standing up in front of a runaway train. 'Here my knowledge was my undoing, since I was immediately aware that the case for war presented by London and Washington was a gross exaggeration of what we knew. ... Moreover, Britain's behaviour at the Security Council was at best manipulative and at worst dishonest.'[11]

By then Carne Ross had lost his faith in the Foreign Office. When his sabbatical was over he arranged a secondment to the United Nations in Kosovo. He believed in the cause and in the role that the British played there – 'a constructive force in the Balkans'. It was while he was in Kosovo, in the summer of 2004, that he sent his secret, written evidence to the Butler Inquiry into the uses of intelligence in the Iraq war. He told the inquiry what he knew about WMD, and about the alternatives to war which were never fully explored. Once he had written it down, he also knew that his career with the Foreign Office was over. 'I had to quit. I couldn't honestly work for this government with a smile on my face.'[12]

Because he requested anonymity, his name does not appear in the Butler Report; nor was the force of his evidence adequately reflected in it. (The report, damaging to the government as it was, would have been even more so

1. 'We are the people of England ...' Victory speech at the election count in Tatton, May 1997.

**TATTON CONSTITUENCY**

2. With daughter Melissa at the Knutsford Royal May Day, just after the general election in May 1997. Neil and Christine Hamilton were also present.

3. 'Before we preach democracy to others we could try to practise it ourselves.' In the House of Commons in October 2000, proposing Conservative MP Richard Shepherd for the Speakership.

4. The campaign against cluster bombs – 'aerially-sown anti-personnel mines'. With actor Richard Wilson and an exploded bomblet from Kosovo, at a news conference by the Diana Memorial Fund and Landmine Action in February 2003.

5. With landmine victim Stuart Hughes, Julie Felix and Vanessa Redgrave in Trafalgar Square in April 2004. The sculpture of shoes was arranged by the Mines Advisory Group to mark Landmine Awareness Day.

6 'A bereaved father and good man … a man of transparent honesty': campaigning with Reg Keys in Newton Aycliffe in the Prime Minister's constituency during the 2005 general election campaign.

7. 'I was a soldier once, and not a very good one …' On parade with the old comrades of the Suffolk Regiment at Minden Day in Gibraltar Barracks, Bury St Edmunds.

8. 'The issue is one of a national debt. It is time that we paid what we owe.' With John Moore of the Royal Green Jackets, paralysed by a sniper's bullet in Northern Ireland in 1981.

9. With Pensioners in the first and last of the military hospitals, the Royal Hospital Chelsea, in January 2007. 'We have gone from a system that serves the soldiers to one that fails them.'

10. At 10 Downing Street in August 2006, with the petition for a ceasefire in Lebanon, presented by Oxfam, Save the Children, CARE and the Muslim Council of Great Britain.

11. 'If you educate a man you educate a man; but if you educate a woman you educate a family': a women's literacy class in Mazar-i-Sharif in Afghanistan, one of UNICEF's life-changing projects.

12. With General Sir David Richards in Kabul, November 2006: 'He had not a shred of respect for the Taliban except as warriors. He described them as a rotten lot.'

13. 'Men of peace among men and women of war': British army chaplains at the Shaibah Logistics Base near Basra, December 2006.

14. 'Martin Bell won't be there, will he?' As close to the Prime Minister as his minders allowed during a visit to British military HQ in Basra in December 2006.

15. En route to the Shaibah Logistics base in a closely guarded convoy: 'The Prime Minister who knew no history could have learned so much from Shaibah.'

16. An early priority in the invasion of Iraq was the protection of the oil fields: 'A burning reminder of why we were there in the first place.'

if Lord Butler could have been persuaded to write it in plain English, rather than in the silken understatements of his kind.) But when Carne Ross's resignation was known, his anonymity ended. In December 2006 he appeared before the House of Commons Foreign Affairs Committee, because one of its members, the Liberal Democrat Paul Keetch, knew him and suggested that he should. Andrew Mackinlay MP, one of the Committee's few free spirits, challenged him to publish his evidence to Lord Butler under the protection of parliamentary privilege. The Committee chairman, Mike Gapes MP, a Labour loyalist, intervened on the government's behalf and told him that, as Parliament was proroguing, he should not feel pressured into doing so. Carne Ross replied with dignity: 'Mr Chairman, I have given it years of thought. This has been on my conscience for a very long time, and I was waiting for an opportunity under privilege to share my evidence to the Butler inquiry.'[13] It was made public a week later.

## OIL SLICK DIPLOMACY

So here was the greatest of the departments of state, two-and-a-quarter centuries old in its grandeur, banished to the fringes of policy-making, especially on issues of war and peace, where it should have been at the centre. Ambassadors and high commissioners around the world were sending their analyses not to where foreign policy was made and shaped, but to what was little more than an unfavoured annexe of Downing Street. How did the Foreign Office establishment itself react? What were its own views on its future – if it had any views, that is, or any future? Fortunately we were not left to speculate. It published them in March 2006, as *Active Diplomacy for a Changing*

*World*, a wide-ranging document in which it set out its world view and its strategic priorities for the next ten years.

The Foreign Secretary at the time was still Jack Straw. Launching the review, he said:

> The strongly activist foreign policy we have pursued since 1997 has been as much about values as about interests. ... That is the reason why we have taken a much more active approach to helping weak and fragile states become more effective and accountable – and why we are now in Iraq and Afghanistan supporting the fledgling democracies there.[14]

*Active Diplomacy for a Changing World*, by contrast, had nothing to say about Britain's military occupations of those countries, the differing grounds advanced for them or the damage done to British interests by the decision to invade Iraq. Its predictions about the future were little more than 'more of the same' – climate change, globalisation, the forced migrations of peoples, the threats of terrorism – but its ideas on addressing that future seldom shifted beyond platitude. Its prophecies were like those of newspaper astrologers, too vague to have useful meaning.

The wheels of parliamentary scrutiny grind slowly and not very small. The Foreign Office's view of its future had been in the public domain for eight months before it came before the House of Commons Foreign Affairs Committee. The government has more control over the proceedings of that committee, as of most committees, than it would have in a healthy democracy. The effect of this is to blunt the edge of scrutiny. So the former diplomats asked to appear were not from the representative 'awkward squad' of 52 ex-ambassadors who had signed the protest on Iraq. Nor was

Sir Rodric Braithwaite invited to repeat his challenge to those who had demoralised the service.

The chosen witnesses were both former British ambassadors to the United Nations, where the United Kingdom prides itself on punching beyond its weight. Lord Hannay described the diplomatic service as 'a pretty robust animal' capable of adjusting to difficult circumstances. Margaret Thatcher had been no friend of the Foreign Office either, but it had found a way of working with her. It made a big difference, he said, that two of the Prime Minister's inner circle were diplomats: 'If they were people completely from outside, or special advisers, I think you would get a much greater degree of demoralisation.' The fact of demoralisation was accepted: only the degree of it was debated.

The other principal witness was Sir Jeremy Greenstock, for whom Carne Ross had worked at the United Nations and whose book on the run-up to war had been blocked by Downing Street. He was also the executive director of the Ditchley Foundation, the diplomatic reflecting pool that operates in the margins of the foreign service. He therefore still belonged in a sense to the diplomatic establishment. He defended the white paper's lack of specifics as a necessary part of the exercise. He claimed that there had been unity among officials on Iraq.[15]

The ghost at this feast was Carne Ross himself, lurking at the back of the room. In written evidence, he attacked the Foreign Office white paper with gusto: 'Like an oil slick, the opaque words of this document help conceal the troubled if not disastrous reality of British foreign policy today.' There had been no unity on Iraq, he said. The sufferings of the Iraqi people were the absent truths at the negotiating table. His was the view from the ranks of the foreign service, which he described as having been marginalised and politicised by the failures since 2001:

> The FCO would vehemently rebut this, but promotion to senior positions has been in part based on the political sympathies of officials. Those closely associated with Number Ten, and who are seen to be sympathetic to the Prime Minister's prejudices, are swept up into senior positions. … [A]nother consequence is easy to predict: officials increasingly tell ministers what they wish to hear.

Questioned by MPs, he told them of the fate of those who try to debate policy more openly:

> People inside the Foreign Office are marked in that way with a little red sign. It means, for instance, that you will never be ambassador to Washington. You might be ambassador to Belarus, but never to Washington.[16]

## 'BUILDING DEMOCRACY WHILE FOSTERING CHAOS'

The Foreign Office has a remarkable record, over the years, of surviving its obituary notices. Diplomacy was supposed to have died with the invention of the telephone, but it did not. Then it was said to be done for by the internet, by the speed and ease of air travel and even by videoconferencing between heads of state and government; but it was not. It will also adjust – indeed it already has – to the shift in foreign policy-making, on all important issues, from its own grand buildings in King Charles Street to the cul-de-sac across the road in Downing Street. This shift can be traced back at least to Winston Churchill, an incorrigible summiteer who roamed the world tirelessly and at great risk to himself to build and maintain his special relationships. Margaret Thatcher took it to a new level: I was based in Washington at the time, and heard it said of her meetings with Ronald Reagan, regular as clockwork every year for eight years, that first she told him what *she* thought and then she told him what *he* thought. Tony Blair did no more than continue and accelerate the trend towards personal diplomacy. It suited his style. He was pre-eminently a red carpet politician; even in retirement he still is one.

In his memoir *DC Confidential*, the then British ambassador to Washington, Sir Christopher Meyer, tells a revealing story of how, in September 2001, the Downing Street retinue tried to exclude him from a working supper with President Bush at the White House *so that a place could be found at the table for Alastair Campbell*. Meyer, hand-picked to speak for the British government in Washington, responded furiously: 'If this happens, you will cut me off at the knees for the rest of my time in Washington' (to which he added a couple of undiplomatic expletives).[17] A place was set for him; but this was the way that things were done in the years of sofa diplomacy. It was not only the ambassadors who suffered: for his four years as Foreign Secretary, Robin Cook spent much of the time trying to find out what the unelected officials in the Prime Minister's den were up to on what was supposed to be his fiefdom of foreign policy. To return to the motoring analogy: it was as if the Rolls-Royce was left parked in the garage while the kids enjoyed themselves cruising the streets in their sofa-fitted sports car. They enjoyed it most in wartime. As Carne Ross observed: 'There is nothing like the excitement of war, especially one where you yourself are at no risk whatsoever.'[18]

But what really troubled the diplomats was not so much that they were bypassed by the Prime Minister's attachment to personal diplomacy, or by his personal envoys like Lord Levy and Nigel Sheinwald, but that they were professionally undermined by his disregard of international law. The decision to go to war in Iraq without an authorising resolution was, for a diplomat, all but impossible to defend – and those who defended it, as many had to, would end up not liking themselves very much. In the desperate weeks of early 2003, the British delegation to the United Nations under Sir Jeremy Greenstock sought a second Security Council resolution for a very good reason, because existing resolutions did not sufficiently authorise the use of force. And then, lacking one, the Attorney General changed his mind and the government went to war anyway. It separated itself from international law, enshrined in the Charter of the United Nations, and resorted instead to the law of the jungle, which was replicated on the ground in Iraq. As Carne Ross observed:

> International law was undermined by the invasion of Iraq. ... Thanks to our own behaviour, we have stepped back to an international culture of Hobbesian 'might is right'. ... We are so inured to the rhetoric of anti-terrorism and macho posturing about building democracy while fostering chaos, that it is hard to imagine an alternative direction for British foreign policy.[19]

There is of course an alternative. It lies in respect for international law, collective diplomacy through a reformed

United Nations, and a determination to help the world's oppressed, including lawful humanitarian intervention where necessary, as in Sierra Leone and (if it can still be done) in Afghanistan. The advocates of action in the Balkans were *almost without exception* opponents of the invasion of Iraq. But our authority as an arbiter was compromised by our lawlessness as an invader. As the results were brought home – quite literally in the case of the military casualties – more and more stories seeped out of the Foreign Office about dissenting diplomats taking early retirement or sudden leaves of absence. Those who remained could only do so at some cost to their integrity.

I was reminded of a question that I put to a British diplomat at the height of the policy debacle in Bosnia in the early 1990s.

'How can you bear to live with this?' I asked.

'It is a question of boarding school allowances', he answered.

But the diplomatic service is not in fact a profession teeming with careerists. I would guess that it has as high a proportion of idealists in it as, for instance, teaching or medicine – certainly a higher one than journalism or politics, to take two examples not entirely at random. Diplomacy's highest purpose is the avoidance of war. To achieve that, diplomats will deal with the devils they know, euphemised as 'non-state actors' to take the curse off them: warlords, terrorists, tribal leaders, drug barons and tyrants with an entire machinery of government at their disposal. (The Dayton agreement on Bosnia was negotiated, through intermediaries, with a trio of indicted war criminals.) They will also, on issues of arms control, take whatever opportunities their defence ministries offer them to ban certain killing machines (like cluster bombs) so that new and less indiscriminate ones can take their place. Everything is compromise. Everything is dealing with the world as you find it, not as you wish it to be. A senior British ambassador puts it this way: 'Therein lies the moral dilemma which causes some to jump ship but is fundamental to our ability to deliver the result.'

But the diplomats operate under political direction. And if the politicians take the war path without even considering the alternative or planning for the consequences, that leaves the peace-seekers in an untenable position. It gives them every reason to jump ship. The war in Iraq claimed countless victims. British diplomacy was one of them. A demoralised Foreign Office will take many years to recover, if it ever can.

## CHAPTER NINE

# THE ROAD FROM SARAJEVO

*This might well be the spark that sets Bosnia Herzegovina alight.*

Lord Carrington, Chairman of the Hague
Conference, December 1991

## CHAIN OF EVENTS

Never underestimate the reach and power of the law of unintended consequences. There is a convincing case to be made that the fate and reputation of Tony Blair's government, in its far-reaching interventions in Islamic countries, were determined by events over which he had no control and in which he had at the outset little interest. They occurred too long ago to be on his radar. In April 1992 a general election – only his third – coincided with a war. It was an election that Labour expected to win, with prospects of advancement for the MP for Sedgefield, while it seemed that no one cared about the war. The first shots were fired in Bosnia at the same time as the first votes were cast in Britain. The soapbox hostilities of John Major and Neil Kinnock were all that mattered to the political parties – and to the media, who were no less blinkered than the politicians whose fortunes they followed. The clash of sound-bites in one corner of Europe monopolised the news to the exclusion of the clash of arms in another. In the early crucial stages of the war, Bosnia was a far-away country of which we knew little and cared less. Like most civil wars it was slow to start but, once started, unstoppable. I had built up a little credit in the BBC news bank by then, but I had to draw on some hard-earned reserves even to get assigned to it. The lack of interest was short-lived. And Labour lost the election.

I did not know it at the time, but the drive from Belgrade across the bridge at Zvornik and through Olovo to Sarajevo (it was all Yugoslavia then) was as near as I hope ever to get to the primrose path to the everlasting bonfire. We skirted a little-known place called Srebrenica. There was no destruction yet, and only a few road blocks. The houses were undamaged. A single petrol station was still open. Tractors and timber trucks clogged the road. Primroses carpeted the roadside. A fragile peace still prevailed. I aspired to be a peace correspondent, but failed. It was in that time and place that the second war in Europe since 1945 began. The first had ended three months earlier in neighbouring Croatia.

So where did the law of unintended consequences come in? Right there, amid the primroses of Bosnia. It started with nationalist movements in Slovenia and Croatia demanding independence in 1991, and a shoddy compromise in what was then the European Community to accommodate them. It continued with the war in Bosnia, which in turn connected to the destruction of the World Trade Center in New York on 9/11 and the 'war on terror' that is still with us. What linked these things was a chain of causes and effects, actions and reactions, assaults and revenges, intended by no one in the chanceries of Europe, but which cast a dark shadow over the world we live in to this day. The trail of blame began, in terms of domestic British politics, with a single decision by a Conservative government and continued with multiple decisions by a Labour government. One sowed the wind and the other reaped the whirlwind. Neither remotely understood the forces that they were contending with. Both unwittingly fanned the flames of international terrorism.

The links in the chain were circumstantial but the outcomes were lethal. These were not events that happened directly *because of each other*, but events that would not have happened *without each other*. If the causes and effects had been more apparent then statecraft might have avoided them – as, for instance, it avoided a war in Macedonia through the pre-emptive deployment of a UN force. But in Bosnia it did not.

In November 1991 the war in Croatia was at its height. The river town of Vukovar was overrun and destroyed by the Serbs, leaving it looking like Stalingrad on the Danube. The jewel of the Adriatic, Dubrovnik, was under bombardment. The besieged Croats, who had sparked the war by declaring their independence, were pressing for recognition by the European Community. They had the strong support of Germany, which had as much to do with its domestic politics as with the justice of their cause. But the Community was committed to the Hague Conference, under the chairmanship of Lord Carrington, which sought a solution for all the republics of the disintegrating Yugoslavia and opposed the piecemeal recognition of any one of them. Lord Carrington warned that the recognition of Croatia 'might well be the spark that sets Bosnia Herzegovina alight'.[1] His warning went unheeded. The

British should have held out against the Germans in the Council of Ministers, but failed to do so. At almost exactly the same time, they were seeking concessions from the Germans over the opt-out clauses of the Maastricht Treaty. No memorandum of understanding was signed. No formal deal was ever done. Whatever was done was diplomatically deniable. But when the Croatian issue was on the table, the British were reminded of the favour that they owed; and the British and Germans won from each other the concessions that they sought, *both primarily for domestic political reasons.* John Major was able to stand at the despatch box and present the revisions of the Maastricht Treaty as a triumph for British interests. The Germans secured agreement to the recognition of Croatia. And this was indeed, as Lord Carrington predicted, the spark that ignited the war in Bosnia, leaving it to be fought for by its three constituent peoples.

The war started four months later. No one intended the one to lead to the other, but it was not unforeseen either. It is hard to escape the conclusion that for the sake of a dodgy deal in Brussels, and for the internal cohesion of the British and German governments, Bosnia was plunged into a war that lasted for three-and-a-half years, cost up to 97,000 lives and drove 2 million people from their homes. Such was the power of the law of unintended consequences.

The repercussions did not end there. In the war's early months the Bosnian Serbs took the initiative in those parts of the republic that they thought of as their own, a little over half of the total, on the basis that wherever Serbs have lived or died the land belongs to them. There was no monopoly of suffering or evil in the war, and the Serbs were victims – in Bratunac, Kupres and elsewhere – as well as aggressors. I testified to the war crimes tribunal in The Hague: 'The world got an impression that Sarajevo was under constant and unprovoked bombardment. However the war was being waged by both sides. I would even say that the Muslims had a political interest in provoking the Serbs to use their heavy artillery.'[2]

But the two-sided war was actually one-side-and-a-half: the attacks and atrocities in the early phase were predominantly the work of the Serbs; and it was the Muslims who suffered the most, being neither ready nor equipped to fight. They had few heavy weapons and were hindered from acquiring them by an arms embargo that froze the war in place for two-and-a-half years. The iconic images of the time were toppled mosques, torched houses, bombarded markets and columns of desperate Muslim refugees. Since the television cameras had front-line access, these were the pictures that flashed round the world, and especially the Islamic world, to devastating effect. The governments of Saudi Arabia, Iran and Turkey, among others, flew in aid; and fighters from Islamic countries rallied to the cause.

The timing was significant. In 1989 the Russians had been driven out of Afghanistan by various ad hoc coalitions of local and foreign fighters. Volunteers from Pakistan, Saudi Arabia, Yemen and other Islamic countries had their first taste of combat and of victory in a holy war against the infidel. In some cases they were recruited and financed by Osama bin Laden, in others they were armed by the United States. After that blooding, they were soldiers with a taste for war but without a battlefield. Bosnia provided the battlefield. In 1992 and 1993 they found their way there in up to brigade strength, mostly through Croatia under some sort of humanitarian cover until the Muslims and

Croats started fighting each other in the spring of 1993. The Islamic volunteers served mostly in central Bosnia alongside, and nominally under the command of, the Bosnian Army's 3rd Corps. The 'El Mujahed' unit, as they were known, were used as shock troops in the side-war between Muslims and Croats in 1993 and 1994. After a dawn assault on the town of Vitez under cover of fog in January 1994 the HVO (Croat) commander showed us the bodies of 50 of the attackers who died in a suicidal attempt to storm the Croats' trench lines. According to their documents they were Arabs and Iranians. There was not a Bosnian among them. The Mujahedin were also notorious for beheading their Serb and Croat prisoners. The images of these atrocities were used in Serbia as justification for other and reciprocal acts of barbarity, including the Srebrenica massacre. The savagery of the foreign fighters was alien to the Bosnian Muslim tradition.

The Bosnian war ended in November 1995, and most but not all of the Mujahedin moved on. For the Islamic warriors who fought in it, and even for those who wished to fight in it but for one reason or another did not, the perceived indifference of the West to the suffering of Muslims remained a motivating and galvanising force. Bosnia was among their battle honours. It inspired them to further actions including the most lethal of all, the attacks on the World Trade Center and the Pentagon in September 2001.

On the fifth anniversary of 9/11, in September 2006, al-Jazeera television showed a videotape of some of the hijackers preparing for the operation and meeting Osama bin Laden at a training base, probably in Afghanistan. Two of them, Hamza al-Ramdi and Wael el-Shemari, said on camera that their actions were inspired by an urge to avenge the suffering of Muslims in Chechnya and Bosnia. Eight of the hijackers were believed to have fought in Chechnya; and two, Khalid al-Mihdnar and Nawaf al-Hazmi, trained and fought with the Mujahedin forces in Bosnia. Khalid Sheikh Mohammed, described by the 9/11 Commission as 'the principal architect of the 9/11 attacks', also had Bosnian connections and financed some of the Mujahedin operations there. He was arrested in Pakistan and deported to Guantánamo Bay.[3]

Of course there were other forces and influences in play, including the running sore of Palestine, American support for autocratic regimes in the Arab world, and the spread of Islamic Wahibi teaching about the iniquities of the West. But Bosnia also played its part in the incubation of a cult of death and holy war. A chain of events which began with an act of political expediency, the recognition of Croatia in December 1991, ended with an act of extreme mass murder, the most destructive terrorist attack in history.

## THE UNITED NATIONS' WONDERLAND

The first casualty of the conflict in Bosnia was a Serb killed at a wedding party in Sarajevo in March 1992. I attended his funeral in the multi-confessional Titoist cemetery, where there were separate sections for Serbs, Catholics, Muslims and atheists, and wondered how many more would die before it was over. (In a movie travesty of the war, *Welcome to Sarajevo*, he expediently became a Croat.) Whatever happened to our sense of history? This was not the first war in Europe to start with a single shot fired in Sarajevo. It was obvious even at the time that the conflict would have repercussions far beyond Bosnia's borders: it continues to have them to this day. The extent of the war was laid out in the acres of graves. While the fighting was still going on, I reported from the Lion Cemetery in the capital where the war dead lay buried in massed ranks: most of them were Muslims, with green-painted wooden memorials with the names and dates inscribed on them over each earthen mound. Most were in their late teens or early twenties:

This is about more than Bosnia. It is about who we are and how we deal with each other. How we manage the new world disorder – what risks and casualties we are willing to take in the cause of peace. And the stakes could hardly be higher. Just look around here at the death and the tragedy, and you can see the scale of the war in the acres of graves. But the damage extends far beyond here, to our collective security and hopes for a safer world. It is, quite, simply, the most consequential war of our times.[4]

It was even more so than I imagined. Like most people, I was not aware at the time of the full effect of the war in radicalising and even criminalising young Muslims in my own country and others. But I knew of the damage done by and to the United Nations, whose unfinest hour this was, as the historian Brendan Simms has observed, while identifying the British government as the principal culprit. Usually, a UN peace-keeping force arrives in a country after the fighting has begun. This time it was present from even before the beginning. The headquarters of UNPROFOR, the UN Protection Force tasked with policing the ceasefire in Croatia, had been established in Sarajevo. But it was inadequate to the fury that broke around it, bombed out of its accommodation, and forced for a month to retreat to the safety of Belgrade. When it returned, it was with a battalion of Canadian armoured infantry but a soft-ball mandate that required it only to escort aid convoys, not to separate the combatants or try to force a peace. The errors were compounded a year later, in June 1993, with the setting up of five safe areas in which UNPROFOR was mandated to deter aggression and protect the mainly Muslim people, or so the people supposed. The protected enclaves were Srebrenica, Zepa, Gorazde, Sarajevo and Bihac. Herb Okun, the American diplomat who, with Cyrus Vance, negotiated an end to the war in Croatia (and prevented one in Macedonia) described the safe areas as a fiction from the beginning:

> The Security Council has a lot to answer for, and the principal lesson is don't pass resolutions that you're not prepared to back up. Many of these resolutions and presidential statements that now number well over one hundred on former Yugoslavia were Alice in Wonderland productions – just wishing things to happen; and I think the secretariat might have been bolder in saying this to the council members. If the United Nations is sent as a blue fig-leaf it is quickly going to be seen to be that and it will fail.[5]

The most notorious of the safe areas was Srebrenica, where 8,000 men of supposedly military age – although some were as young as sixteen or as old as 60 – were killed in cold blood after the Serbs overran the enclave in July 1995. Bosnia was the base for 30,000 UN soldiers at the time and Srebrenica for more than 300 Dutch UN troops. I have in my files an angry letter from the Dutch Defence Ministry accusing me of reproaching the Dutch for a want of courage. When the true facts were known the Dutch government resigned on the issue. The mass killings could have been prevented by the UN force, but it wasn't willing to risk its own lives to save those of Bosnians: the fault lay as much in its capitals as on the ground. The brutal truth of the time was that Dutch, French and British lives mattered more than Bosnian lives. They were not rated on the same scale of values. A Dutch politician told me: 'If two of our soldiers are killed, the rest will be on the way home.' The Srebrenica massacre was the worst war crime in Europe since 1945: a judge at the Hague tribunal described its effects as 'Scenes from hell, written on the darkest pages of human history'. And on the tenth anniversary of the massacre, in July 2005, at the newly dedicated graveyard in Potocari, where the victims were first rounded up, the British Foreign Secretary Jack Straw made an honest and moving admission of Western guilt, which was to the credit of his government and himself: 'It is to the shame of the international community that this evil took place under our eyes and we did nothing like enough.'[6]

There were other scenes from the Bosnian war that played into the hands of those in the Islamic world who sought to convince their fellow Muslims that the West was not only indifferent to their fate but actively engaged on some kind of crusade against them. One holy war deserved another. These events included the Ahmici massacre in central Bosnia in April 1993, when more than 100 Muslims were burned to death by Croatian paramilitaries in their homes or shot while trying to escape. Images of UN soldiers patrolling the ruins afterwards were used to suggest complicity, as if they had just stood by and let it happen. But the truth was different. The overstretched UN force knew nothing about the killings until two days later, and when it found out, it was anything but indifferent. The British commander of the UN battle-group, Lieutenant Colonel Bob Stewart of the Cheshire Regiment, said: 'I felt ashamed – I felt very ashamed. ... I don't know what we could have done, but my feelings were ... I was in deep shock for three or four days.'[7]

The UN troops saved many lives, including those of a column of Muslim civilians being marched away to an unknown fate by the Croats, and others who camped at the garrison gates for safety. More than 70 French UN soldiers lost their lives on the front line in Sarajevo: the sounds of war were regularly punctuated by the strains of the 'Marseillaise', played for fallen comrades in flag-draped coffins in a hangar at the French headquarters. The United Nations, for all its faults, lost lives to save lives – and it saved 100,000 lives according to Larry Hollingworth of UNHCR, who led the relief efforts at the time.

Nor, after the event, was the UN indifferent to Srebrenica. The massacre led directly to a change of strategy, and the massive use of force against the Serbs on behalf of the Muslims. When the Sarajevo market-place was bombed for the second time at the end of August 1995, NATO war-planes went to work against targets all over the Serbian half of Bosnia – military headquarters, communications networks, arms depots, bridges and even the village where the parents of the Bosnian Serb commander, Ratko Mladic, were buried. 'It was attacked repeatedly,' wrote General Smith, 'in the knowledge that in Mladic's culture a failure to protect the bones of one's ancestors is something of a shameful dereliction of family duty.'[8] Mladic himself knew the game was up. Serbs live their history like no one else (their national legend is of a battle they lost); since the Middle Ages, he said, their history taught them that all

Balkan wars lasted for about four years, and this one was only six months short of that. The demoralised and hard-pressed Bosnian Serb mini-state was one of the few places where force could usefully be applied and military means could achieve a political objective. Within weeks, the war was over.

The lie of Western complicity has had a terrible effect – but it remains what it is, a lie. Western blood and treasure were spent in Bosnia (and later in Kosovo) to help beleaguered Muslim populations. But the hesitations were fatal. From the spring of 1993, the Americans had been pressing for a policy of 'lift and strike' – lift the arms embargo and strike against the Serbs – to help the government forces, which were mostly but not entirely Muslim. The Serbs' military might was greatly over-estimated. No one understood what the long-term consequences of prevarication would be. It is easy now to say that decisive action against the Serbs could and should have been taken much sooner. And actually, it was easy then as well. Most of us knew it – soldiers, aid workers and even journalists. David Rohde of the *Wall Street Journal* wrote this of the Srebrenica massacre which he risked his life to report: 'The fall of Srebrenica did not have to happen. There is no need for thousands of skeletons to be strewn across eastern Bosnia. There is no need for thousands of Muslim children to be raised on stories of their fathers, grandfathers, uncles and brothers slaughtered by Serbs. The fall of Srebrenica could have been prevented.'[9]

It did not have to happen but it did. We stood by transfixed and watched it happen, like a disaster movie on a loop or a monstrous slow-motion car crash. One night in the summer of 1995, I looked out over a city illuminated by tracer fire and wrote from the Holiday Inn in Sarajevo:

'Over the Bosnian years I had felt a whole range of emotions – fear, horror, dismay, sadness, even sometimes hope and exhilaration, but never before such anger; and anger doesn't consort with useful journalism.'[10] It was clearly a local war with global consequences – and we said so, not only myself but Kurt Schork of Reuters, Christiane Amanpour of CNN, Jonathan Randal of the *Washington Post* and Anthony Loyd of *The Times*, but no one was listening. Those of us who made the case for intervention, not polemically but just by showing the realities on the ground, were condemned by our critics at home as 'lap-top warriors', although we were much more in the thick of things than they were, and I never worked from a lap-top from start to finish. And because I tried to show the realities, I was also accused by the high-minded pundit of a broadsheet newspaper of engaging in 'the pornography of violence'. The war in Bosnia could have been prevented – or, if not prevented, brought to an early close – by the timely and determined application of force. That it lasted for as long as it did was a tragedy for the European bystanders as well as the Balkan victims, for in the long run the bystanders joined the ranks of the victims. It allowed the propaganda of the holy warriors to take hold, whose deadly legacy is with us to this day.

## RULES OF ENGAGEMENT

For a nation that sees moderation as a virtue, our foreign policy veers wildly between extremes of action and inaction. We do all or nothing. We see everything as a Munich or a Suez. Iraq and Bosnia provide the end-state examples of these diplomatic mood swings. Either we kick in the door of a stable sovereign state, however tyrannically governed, regardless of the predictable and predicted consequences, including civil war; or else we stand on the sidelines wringing our hands and lamenting what a terrible world it is – which in the case of Bosnia it was, and was made even worse by our inaction. This is not an argument for half-measures, but for taking each case on its merits.

There is no one-size-fits-all formula for the application of force. In Iraq, armed intervention by a so-called coalition (in practice, the Americans and British) turned tyranny into anarchy and led to the deaths of hundreds of thousands of people. In Bosnia it was the long-delayed armed intervention by a real coalition – the flag was the UN's and the force was NATO's – that ended the bloodshed and imposed a settlement which brought the fighting to a rapid end and in time became a peace.

There are certain tests that have to be met for military intervention to be justifiable. First, it must be unambiguously lawful and specifically authorised by a resolution of the United Nations Security Council: unilateral pre-emptive warfare, even on humanitarian grounds, does not qualify. Second, it must be proportionate, with the measure of force employed being sufficient but not excessive for the task: the weapons of shock and awe are futile as well as unlawful in a civilian environment. Third, in a democracy it must be widely supported by the people in whose name it is carried out: the soldiers of the Queen do not sign on to fight unpopular wars on the whim of the Prime Minister. And fourth, it must be doable – Afghanistan provides the example of a conflict where the first three tests can be met but the fourth may not: at this point we still do not know, but the initial signs are discouraging. Bosnia met all these tests. Iraq failed them. The deployment there was not thought through. It incubated terrorism, broke up the state, looted its antiquities and licensed the thieves and murderers in the land of Ali Baba. It is widely acknowledged, even by most of its original supporters, to have been a terrible mistake.

So there is no contradiction in supporting intervention where it is justifiable and feasible and opposing it where it is not. Indeed, it is a necessary function of statesmanship to make that distinction. We expect our politicians to exercise good judgement. It would be hard to find one with a better record on these issues than the Labour MP John Denham, who never belonged to one wing of the party or another, but was a hawk or dove on a case-by-case basis. Early in his career he joined the rebels who opposed the Labour Party's policy of passivity on Bosnia, when its foreign affairs spokesman Jack Cunningham agreed with the government line that the war there was a far-away replay of ancient savageries about which little could be done. Cunningham said: 'Political leaders on all sides of the conflict are willing to continue to wage war. I do not believe that in these circumstances there are any innocents.'[11] Brendan Simms wrote in his book, *Unfinest Hour*, the definitive account of a shameful episode: 'The most striking thing about the parliamentary response to war and ethnic cleansing in Bosnia was the absence of any concerted attack by the opposition on government policy.'[12]

The Labour rebels felt that their party was failing in its duty to oppose an unprincipled policy. They called for sanctions, and if necessary air strikes, against the Serbs; and a lifting of the arms embargo against the government forces. Eleven years later, John Denham recalled this challenge to the leadership of John Smith, when he resigned as Minister of State at the Home Office in protest against the war in Iraq.

I shall never forget the surprised and bemused expression on John Smith's face when some twenty newly elected Labour Members of Parliament went to see him to demand Labour's support for a foreign war. I believe that we should have supported it, and that, had we done so, Balkan history might be different.[13]

John Denham now believes, as I do, that the effects were felt far beyond the Balkans.[14] What goes around comes around. The parliamentary response to the war in Iraq was also notable for the absence of any concerted attack by the opposition on government policy. With a handful of exceptions, the Conservatives just folded. Following the domestic regime change of the 1997 election, the parties were now on different sides of the House; but it made people wonder, on vital issues of war and peace, what oppositions were for. The effects of the policy and the failure to challenge it, in both cases, were in the long run to fuel the flames of Islamic terrorism.

Action has consequences. So does inaction. Some are clear. Others can only be guessed at. We have seen the consequences today, reaching into the heart of our society, of the risk-aversion of the Western democracies, including our own, during the Bosnian war from 1992 to 1995, and of the perceived indifference that left one ethnic and religious group at the mercy of another. Jack Straw's apology was an overdue act of contrition. And our soldiers there were peace-keepers under blue helmets. We have no reason to believe that the effects of the Great Mistake in Iraq, where they were acting as invaders and war-fighters, and for which Mr Straw was a leading apologist, will be any less severe.

## CHAPTER TEN

# ON AFGHANISTAN'S PLAINS

*When you're wounded and left on Afghanistan's plains,*
*An' the women come out to cut up what remains,*
*Just roll on your rifle an' blow out your brains,*
*An' go to your Gawd like a soldier.*

Rudyard Kipling, 'The Young British Soldier'

## THE FOURTH AFGHAN WAR

Apart from Iraq, Afghanistan was the most costly, contro-versial and consequential of all New Labour's expeditionary wars. It was also, morally and legally, easier to justify: the questions about it were practical, logistical and historical. The military commitment to Afghanistan was legal under the UN Charter and international law. It could even be seen as morally imperative and in the national interest. By early 2006, the more-or-less-democratic government of President Karzai was losing ground. It controlled less than half of the national territory. There was a case to be made that the cause was worth fighting for, or rather (for this is the politicians' privilege) getting the armed forces to fight for on their behalf.

The Taliban rebels, so far from being defeated, were burning schools and killing teachers to return the country in a great leap backwards to a state of barbarism, in which (for instance) no songs should be sung, no kites flown and no girls educated except in the Koran. It would be a failed state like Iraq, and a haven and training ground for those who would wage holy war against their own people and the West. As Kabul lost control, the poppy crop increased by 60 per cent in a year; and the production of opium, the only significant export, had reached the point where prices were falling, because supply outstripped demand. But it was wrongly supposed that the time was right for a NATO-led peace-keeping operation to support the central government, encourage post-war development and win the people over.

NATO was operating for the first time in its history beyond its charter and out of its area. It was also, for the first time in its history, fighting a ground war. The plan was born out of the best of intentions, but also out of the slenderest understanding of the terrain, the politics and the history of Afghanistan. Where the Soviet Union had failed with a force of 120,000, how could NATO succeed with a mere 32,000? Where the British army had been checked or defeated in three Afghan wars, including the massacre of a 16,000-strong force in 1842, and the fall of the Kabul Residency in 1879, why should it prevail in a fourth? The misgivings therefore were not about the legality but the *doability* of such a mission in so hazardous an environment. It was another example of what happens when government takes such far-reaching decisions from inside a history-free zone: the sort of war that looks good from a PowerPoint presentation, or the floor of the House of Commons.

Amid high hopes, the NATO force took over in Afghanistan between July and October 2006. Its mission was to establish the rule of law in areas controlled by the re-armed Taliban and by shifting alliances of tribal leaders, drug-traffickers and warlords. The overthrow of the Taliban in 2001, hailed by Donald Rumsfeld at the time as a 'breathtaking accomplishment', did not seem so breathtaking five years later. They had recovered from their early defeats and surged back into Afghanistan on a scale not understood by NATO until its troops started pushing out into the villages, especially in the south. 5,400 British soldiers were deployed, contributing greatly to the overstretch of an army which was under-equipped for the task, as the result – yet again – of a miscalculation by its political masters. The British government, among others, had signed on to peace-keeping but found itself committed instead to intensive war-fighting.

How often the name of John Reid occurs in this chronicle. He was Defence Secretary when the deployment was announced, and expressed the hope that the troops could complete their three-year mission of pacification and reconstruction without a single shot being fired. Instead, they fired 400,000 in the first six weeks and found themselves embroiled in the fiercest combat of any British force since the Korean war. His successor Des Browne admitted they had got it wrong. Dr Reid's prediction gave the British public, and the soldiers who bore the brunt of it, further reason to question the politicians' love affair with expeditionary warfare. (A senior officer said later that he had 'not given the full picture', which was soldierly understatement.) Troops and equipment were being held back from the force in Afghanistan, where they could affect the outcome, by the deployment in Iraq, where they could not. Iraq was the test-bed for insurgent techniques, like roadside bombs and suicide attacks, that were used to deadly effect in Afghanistan. Before 2005, there were no suicide bombings in Afghanistan. By 2006 they were commonplace; and the UN believed that 1,000 volunteers were waiting in line for the privilege of martyrdom by blowing themselves up with their victims. In that way one war impacted on the other. Senior army officers, concerned about the effects of the open-ended Iraq war on recruitment and morale, pressed for a draw-down of forces there so that more could be made available for Afghanistan. The politicians, under American pressure, initially refused; but then gave way to the inevitable.

And we now know from military sources that vital communications equipment was held back from the British army in Afghanistan in March 2002, because *it was already earmarked for the invasion of Iraq a year later.* We also know that badly-needed reinforcements for Afghanistan were withheld early in 2002 in order to prepare for the invasion of Iraq.[1] That was not contingency planning. It was premeditation. The rest was a charade.

Some of the equipment may have been missing, but the quality of troops could not have been higher. They were the very best of those who serve at the sharp end – at the start of the NATO deployment in 2006, 16 Air Assault Brigade from Colchester, including paratroopers, armoured reconnaissance, artillery, special forces and the new Apache attack helicopters to provide close air support. I had taken part with the Brigade a year earlier in a command and control exercise in which the Apaches, flown by the Army Air Corps, were for the first time accredited and integrated into an all-arms fighting force. They were the most versatile killing machines ever deployed by the British army, though I was intrigued to note that the cockpit was unlocked with a key exactly like that of the old Morris Minor. It said a lot about soldiering in the 21st century that the army's only expanding branches were its Air Corps and its Legal Service.

The soldiers were, as ever, consummately professional. They were led by an impressive commander, Brigadier Ed Butler, a veteran of many campaigns and with the medals to show for them (he was ex-SAS). They had already been 'warned off' for an Afghan mission; and though they were unclear exactly what it would be, none of them expected the outcome to be peaceful. They had no problem with that. Soldiers sign on to serve in dangerous places; but more than most people, and for good reasons, they tend to have a limited faith in the wisdom of the politicians who send them there. It was Colchester's finest, and not Westminster's, who would be in the line of fire on the plains of Helmand; and they had known no Defence Secretary with military experience for more than fourteen years. (The last was Tom King, formerly of the King's African Rifles.) When ministers met squaddies, usually on some kind of a fact-finding mission or tour of inspection, they were embarrassingly out of their depth and lost for words: a gulf of incomprehension stood between them. An exchange between soldier and minister, which passed into military legend, went like this:

Soldier: 'Excuse me, sir, but how much do you know about the army?'

Secretary of State: 'Not much, but how much do you know about politics?'

Soldier: 'Not much either, sir, but my friends tell me that I'm a very good liar.'

By their own account, the one politician who had enough

of an affinity with them to talk on their wavelength was John Reid. A battalion commander judged that he would have made an excellent regimental sergeant major – instead of which, he was Secretary of State.

Afghanistan had absolutely no history of non-resistance to military interventions – rather the reverse. More than any other country in the world, it was historically an invader's graveyard, as anyone would know who had read his Kipling. So the hearts-and-minds campaign hardly got started before it was superseded by open warfare. Reconstruction hit the buffers and stayed there. One of the senior officers said: 'We hoped to play the "British not American" card, but it hasn't been easy.'

They had expected a measure of opposition from the Taliban, especially in Helmand province which was the British force's area of responsibility and point of main effort. Outlying posts were established in district centres, sometimes known as 'platoon houses', which became the targets for Taliban attacks of great ferocity. The deployment was controversial, especially when it became difficult for the British to 'unfix' themselves from these outposts without loss of face. The men of 3 Para referred to one of them, Sangin, as 'The Alamo'. A soldier's sign on the wall warned 'Two way firing range'. Instead of the expected guerrilla raids, the Taliban attacked frontally and often suicidally, with wave after wave trying to rush the defences in up to battalion strength. Irregular forces tend to be more innovative than regular forces, to make up in surprise for what they lack in firepower. But the Taliban were fighting like regulars. To stop them the British called in Apaches, A10 tankbusters, Harrier jump-jets, F16s and Mirage 2000s; they dropped 500-, 1,000- and even 2,000-pound bombs; at one point their gunships ran out of missiles. They fired 3,500 mortars and threw 400 hand grenades. It was like Rorke's Drift but with added firepower to give it a better ending. It was time to park reconstruction and hearts-and-minds: even the Sappers don't rebuild a school under fire from rocket-propelled grenades. It was also time for a tactical rethink; and the decision was taken to let the Afghan army take over two of the platoon houses. One of them was in Musa Qala, which was overrun by the Taliban four months later. An American colonel said: 'We've warned there may be soldiers shooting in their villages. I tell them this is the price of peace and freedom.'[2]

In the most intensive phase of the fighting, Operation Medusa in Kandahar, Canadian-led forces including Americans and Danes met fire with fire and revisited places they had flattened before. Some of the combat was within hand grenade range, until the Taliban fell back. Towards the end of Medusa, both the British and Dutch refused to send reinforcements to help the Canadians, on the grounds that to do so would have compromised their operations elsewhere. Kandahar nearly fell. There is a staff college study to be written somewhere on these operations as a textbook example of the perils and pitfalls of multinational soldiering.

In a war among the people, no force, however powerful, can bomb its way to victory. Beyond a certain level of firepower, the more it destroys the less it succeeds. The winner loses and the loser wins. Something like that happened in Vietnam. And more recently in Iraq.

Soldiers always prepare for the worst. But the NATO mission on the ground in Helmand was not the one that the politicians had outlined to them. Brigadier Butler said: 'The fighting is extraordinarily intense. The intensity and ferocity of the fighting is far greater than Iraq on a daily basis.'[3] The Supreme NATO Commander, American General George Jones, called for reinforcements from countries which preferred to leave the fighting to the British and Canadians: 'We should realise that we are a little bit surprised at this level of intensity, and that the opposition in some areas are not relying on hit and run tactics.' And the NATO commander in Afghanistan, Lt General David Richards, added: 'We need to realise that we could fail here.' It was healthy dose of realism which underscored the professional difference between soldiers and politicians: the soldiers saw things as they were, and not as they wished them to be.

In a ten-day period, nineteen British servicemen were killed, including the fourteen-man crew of an RAF Nimrod reconnaissance aircraft which crashed in southern Afghanistan. In this respect, as in every other, the two sides were unevenly matched: NATO's advantage was its firepower and the Taliban's their indifference to the costs that the firepower inflicted. Casualties were of no consequence to them. They were to the NATO forces. And the Taliban knew that. Also, the NATO casualties were under-reported. The more lightly wounded, treated in the field, did not appear on the casualty lists.

The war dead included the first British Muslim soldier to fall in Afghanistan, Lance Corporal Jabron Hashimi, attached to the Royal Signals. He was killed with his comrade-in-arms Corporal Peter Thorpe when their outpost came under mortar fire. The bodies were returned to RAF Lyneham. Although the men were of different faiths, there were not two religious services but one. The bereaved families mourned together. The army's first Imam, Asim Hafiz, read the regimental prayer: 'Grant that we of the Royal Corps of Signals, who speed the word of man to man,

may be swift and sure in sending the message of thy light.'
Day by day the costs of the war were brought home amid
growing disquiet among the people and the armed
services.

The requirement was not only for more boots on the
ground. The force was seriously short of the equipment it
needed to deal with an operational emergency: more
armour, heavy weapons and transport helicopters for re-
supply and casualty evacuation. The British lacked – and
still lack – enough of the heavy Chinooks that can operate
effectively in Afghanistan's heat and height. This was the
result of a chancy decision in the 1990s to buy the less
robust Merlins instead of more Chinooks; while the ageing
Sea Kings lack the capacity to operate 'hot and high'.

The lack of support helicopters was felt most acutely
because it could – and, some believe, did – cost lives.
Supplies were being fought through to the platoon houses,
delivered under fire by battle-groups, because of a lack of
sufficient airlift capacity. After a desperate month, a soldier
complained: 'They still will not give us the helicopters we
have been asking for.' The barrel had already been scraped;
they would scrape it some more. 'We are running hot,' said
the army's new Chief of the General Staff, General Sir
Richard Dannatt, 'certainly running hot. Can we cope? I
pause. I say just.'[4]

There is a saying in the military that no plan survives its
first contact with reality; this one was skewed from the start.
Against the most basic of military principles, it had no
reserves to commit to the fight, because no reserves existed.
The so-called allies decided to stay away and watch from
safer places. Indeed, the improvised NATO force, if it
could have been described as an army, was surely the
most ramshackle ever sent to do battle – or, in most cases,

to avoid doing battle. Twenty-eight nations contributed troops to the International Security Assistance Force, but ISAF's commander had no authority to deploy them as he wished. They were restricted by all sorts of national caveats. Some would not patrol at night. Others would not engage in offensive operations. It was even reported that one contingent refused to go out in the snow and another stayed away because its accommodation was not air-conditioned. Those who were based in the quieter north and west of Afghanistan were forbidden by their govern-ments to send a single soldier to the south and east where the Taliban might be found. The actual fighting was done by the British, Americans, Canadians, Dutch and Danish, with significant but little-known support from the Estonians and Romanians. The rest were, in war-fighting terms, a waste of space. The wonder of it was that ISAF functioned at all.

Like the after-effects of the war in Iraq, the early stages of Britain's fourth Afghan war were under-reported to an extraordinary degree. Maybe it was the general retreat from foreign news. Maybe in the Colosseum of television programming the attractions of *Strictly Come Dancing* were thought to be more compelling than the re-run of an ancient conflict which could have global consequences: there should have been room for both. Maybe it was because, when things are going badly, the press are seldom welcome until a sort of victory can be claimed. Maybe it was the unstoppable rise, on the rolling news networks, of the phenomenon of virtual news or 'newsak', the *talk* about news and the *appearance* of news, with not a shred of the reality. It was cheaper and safer that way, and (if looked at with half an eye) almost as convincing. The reporters weren't actually *there* where they should have been, but standing in front of a video-wall or on a rooftop half a world away. This led to the usual tensions between the media and the military: soldiers complained that too many reporters were embedded with the Taliban, if only by mobile phone. There is also a textbook waiting to be written about the mobile phone as the most potent weapon of the information war.

Parliament was also, as so often in times of crisis, in recess, so there was none of the political fallout or holding to account that there could have been at any other season. Maybe the politicians planned it that way. But I doubt it: everything else that they did proclaimed convincingly that they were not that clever. I think it was a sort of negative serendipity that let them get away with it for a while.

The logistical difficulties and physical dangers were also a deterrent to the kind of free-ranging journalism that we could still practise, for instance, in Bosnia in the 1990s, sometimes with the British army but more often independent of it; and that, after Bosnia, died. Except for the suicidally-minded, free-wheeling in a war zone was no longer an option. In the new world disorder of the early 21st century, reporters and photographers were at risk of being targeted, kidnapped and executed rather than merely being caught in the cross-fire. That left them in Afghanistan with the choice of embedding with the military, staying at home or kicking their heels in a guest house in Kabul. Sometimes it didn't make much difference. The war was among the people. The journalists were not. And even those embedded were (with occasional exceptions) penned back behind the fortifications of the well-named Camp Bastion, the main British base in Helmand. When it took an entire battle-group to relieve a platoon house, and everything that moved was ambushed, the press could hardly expect an armoured escort to go and report the war. And to go unescorted was out of the question. So the only video of this phase of the conflict, which was remarkably graphic, came from a front-line soldier's mobile phone. And the most vivid account of the stress of the moment was conveyed in an email from an officer in 3 Para: 'We are lacking manpower. Desperately in need of more helicopters. Attacks consists of regular rocket, mortar, RPG and small arms on the fire base, plus fairly heavy fire fights out on the ground. The RAF have been utterly, utterly useless. In contrast USAF have been fantastic. I have a couple of soldiers who I have concerns about after some heavy contact.'[5] But the British claimed, despite the inter-service hostilities, to have killed many Taliban mid-level commanders and won a tactical victory. They settled in for the expected winter lull. It never happened. Although the fighting was of a lesser intensity, the Taliban continued their attacks and threatened to lay siege to Kabul and Kandahar.

## 'AGAINST THE ODDS'

When I left Parliament in 2001, I was invited by UNICEF to become one of their goodwill ambassadors. These were usually celebrities like footballers and pop singers, but David Beckham and Robbie Williams were rather too busy and valuable be sent to war zones. So the UN children's fund sent me instead. I asked them to find me my hundredth country, not really expecting palm-fringed beaches and sapphire seas. And of course they chose Afghanistan. It reminded me of an earlier front-line episode when I spotted a Reuters photographer taking pictures of me instead of the fire-fight going on around us.

'Why are you doing that?' I asked.

'In case you get killed,' he said.

The spirit of the Reuters photographer hovered as I flew to Kabul in an elderly Tupolev belonging to one of those airlines that wise men try to avoid. They wouldn't send their shiniest aircraft to Afghanistan, and they didn't. Their in-flight magazine included a section called 'Keep Trusting': 'Keep trusting in the aircraft, the pilots and the cabin crew: this may sometimes seem rather hard to achieve'! Afghanistan was my fifteenth war zone. In the countries I go to, they want to know your blood group before you get on the plane. The RAF asks at check-in: 'Is your baggage lethal?' And when you arrive at the other end the UN hands you a leaflet about what to do if you are taken hostage. The advice is to think happy thoughts, chat with your kidnappers about their families and never ever beg, plead or cry. It always feels good to be in the UN's capable hands.

People wonder what a goodwill ambassador does. I wonder myself sometimes, especially if stranded on an all-night layover in a Soviet-built airport between south Asian mountain ranges. It is not so different to journalism, but better-mannered. It is basically about finding things out and bearing witness; making and listening to speeches; learning from children and their teachers; finding out about the shortages of the basics, like rubber gloves in hospitals, that have to be remedied; being inspired by ordinary people doing extraordinary things; crying a little inside at some of what goes on; seeing other people's children as if they were your own; then taking the opportunity, at home and abroad, to raise funds for child-saving UNICEF projects in the world's most embattled countries. Nowhere is the need greater than in Afghanistan, amid the human and material wreckage of war, where *62 per cent of the people are children under eighteen.* Whoever's fault it is, it isn't theirs, except perhaps when war steals childhoods. In May 2007 the jihadists circulated a video, apparently from one of their camps near the Afghan border, of a prisoner being beheaded by a boy about twelve years old.

We started in Mazar-i-Sharif, the largest city in the north and the first to fall to the Northern Alliance in 2001. Three waves of fighting had swept through it, and more Taliban had died there than anywhere else. It was supposed to be one of the safer places, but nowhere was safe in the sixth year of this war. Seeing something for yourself is always different. I found that TV's obsession with the images of conflict – known in the trade as 'bang-bang' – had blinded me to the other, quieter side, especially the passion of the people for peace and learning.

In a country where men and women lead separate lives in public, Mazar-i-Sharif is what passes for avant-garde. Normally a women's literacy class would be taught privately and within high walls. But this city is special and hospitable. So we had the privilege of seeing hundreds of women, mostly in their twenties and thirties, crowding into a community centre in the winter sunshine and learning to write for the first time in their lives. A few, but not the majority, were still in burqas. Some had been denied education by the Taliban, others by being refugees in Iran. So great was the enthusiasm for learning that there was not enough space for them – and not enough textbooks, provided by UNICEF, which taught practical lessons in survival skills from child-rearing to mine awareness. The theory was persuasive: if you educate a man, you educate a man; but if you educate a woman, you educate a family. One of them said: 'As refugees in Iran we were not allowed to attend school, so for the sake of our children's future we came back to Afghanistan.' And another: 'We come here to read and write. As the saying goes, an illiterate person is a blind person.' And their teacher, Amina Safri, added: 'This programme is unique. It transforms us from darkness to light. Everyone wants education until there are no uneducated people left in Afghanistan.'

We are all the prisoners of our prejudices. One of them is that Afghanistan is an untouchable, beyond-redemption, pre-medieval society. This is not true. It is a deeply traditional and archaically-structured society; but it is also a country of people who, in the direst of circumstances, are struggling heroically to help themselves and each other. One of them, who would identify herself only as Shereena, was a teacher in an ill-equipped school in Sheberghan. The children were kneeling on the floor. They had no desks to work at, but were lucky to have a roof over their heads. In a district where most classes were held in tents or the open air, the whole community was helping to build classrooms in defiance of the Taliban's burning of some girls' schools and intimidating others into closure. Teachers were acting as bricklayers. And the children themselves, wherever possible, paid up to ten cents each into the building fund. Shereena said: 'If they burn schools, the government will build them again. For every school they burn, we will build four more. You see, they are not Muslims. They are enemies of Islam.'

That was the new Afghanistan. The old one challenging it was the war – a war as old as the country's history, but now in a new phase and with a new force in the field. The NATO-led International Security Assistance Force (ISAF) was a weird sort of hybrid which, if it didn't exist, could not have been invented. Now you saw it and now you didn't.

Part of it was real and part was hypothetical. Only a few of its 28 nations were allowed by their governments to take on the resurgent Taliban. The rest of them sheltered behind their caveats. Pity the man who commanded this shambles and had to plead for 'caveat-free' reinforcements.

The man who commanded it was British. General David Richards had just been promoted to full four-star general (since the rank of field marshal was abolished, that is as many stars as, these days, the system allows). And he was one of the most thoughtful and least gung-ho soldiers I ever met – suitable to the theatre of war: the last thing we needed, with our history of failure, was yet another debacle in Afghanistan. General Richards conceded that Kandahar could have fallen in the summer of 2006. The ISAF forces had won a narrow tactical victory against the odds. And it was the first time that NATO in its entire history had launched a ground operation, in brigade strength, against a defended position. Cleverly defended, too, according to General Richards. He had not a shred of respect for the Taliban except as warriors. He described them as a rotten lot, offering a dismal future. But if the government failed, that future might seem more attractive.

By this time, the press had caught up with the war and it was no longer fought in the media blackout of its first phase. The 'embeds' were back, hoping for maximum drama with minimum casualties, which is how the game is played. Air and artillery strikes pounded the edges of settlements in Helmand. The Paras and Marines were doing what they were trained to do, which was when threatened to use every weapon they had and carry the fight to the Taliban. Others could apply the staff college lessons, they would just bash on.

The question that then arose was: how could you win people's hearts and minds by bombing bits out of their villages? General Richards had wondered about that too. His answer was that the Afghans respected force: 'If we had not established in their minds that we were capable of winning militarily, we were not going to secure their hearts and minds. We need their confidence that we can beat a hitherto successful enemy.' But the security situation was still on a knife-edge. It was his assessment that thousands more men would be needed for the next fighting season, including a much-needed strategic reserve, and that these reinforcements would have to be caveat-free. Such a war would not be won by fair-weather soldiers.

A friend in the United Nations, a distinguished army officer from a Commonwealth country, pointed out that part of the problem was rates of pay. If an Afghan army soldier earned $75 a month and a Taliban soldier $300, while both recruited from the same pool of unemployed young men, was it any wonder that the Taliban could attack the NATO force in such strength? A heavy price was being paid for the obsession with Iraq.

There was a symmetry to New Labour's wars of liberation. In Afghanistan as in Iraq, an initial military success led to civil war. It created a power vacuum, which those who competed for power – the warlords, tribal leaders and before long the Taliban themselves – fought to fill. The time-scales were different. It would not trouble the Islamists if it took them 10,000 years, and all the martyrdoms which went with that, to establish their Caliphate. The Taliban had all the time in the world, while the West had only clocks and watches. The former Chief of the General Staff, General Sir Mike Jackson, suggested a 'hundred-day rule' for post-conflict strategy:

You don't have long to get going. There is a sense that you must make a difference within a hundred days, or you will have a lost opportunity. It gives me no pleasure to say that was not the case where Iraq was concerned. And perversely, after a good start in Afghanistan in the winter of 2001–2002, the strategic main effort shifted to Iraq, arguably to the detriment of Afghanistan.[6]

Seen in that light, the ill-considered intervention in Iraq did not doom just that country more than it was already doomed: it may have doomed Afghanistan as well. There may yet be a successful outcome in Afghanistan – the optimists put the chances at above 50 per cent. They would be very much higher but for the Iraqi debacle.

## ENVOI

For a fitting postscript to all this, I am indebted to my friend Robert Fox, who earned his MBE in the Falklands war not only by distinguished reporting for BBC News, but by tending the wounded and being the only man with the British task force with an idea of how to draft an instrument of surrender. He knows more about war not only than any of the politicians, which is not hard to achieve, but than most of the generals too: 'There has to be a pause for serious operational thought. In the UK, a real enquiry has to be held into how we got into this mess, the performance and potential of the forces in both campaigns [Iraq and Afghanistan] and in tackling terrorism – something of the scale of the big enquiries after the Boer War by Lord Esher. Wholesale reform is due. This is beyond the regimes of Bush and Blair, who are out of puff, ideas and time.'[7]

There is a historical parallel here, in the sense that what goes around comes around. The Prime Minister's expeditionary wars, especially the one in Iraq, had no more trenchant critic than Tam Dalyell, Father of the House of Commons until his retirement in 2005. His grandfather, Major Sir James Bruce Wallace Dalyell, who served in the Boer War, went to his personal and political friends including Arthur Balfour, Edward Grey and Henry Campbell-Bannerman, telling them of his experience of the shambles in South Africa and urging the inquiry which was duly held. The Esher Report of 1904 recommended changes to the military command structure that have remained in place to this day.

After more than a century, it is surely time for another re-think – but this time about the political, not the military, command structure. As General Jackson observed, 'risk-free soldiering is a contradiction in terms'. Never again must history be so nonchalantly ignored and military commitments so carelessly entered into.

## CHAPTER ELEVEN

# ETHICAL BOMBING

*The best defence of our security lies in the spread of our values.*

Tony Blair, March 2005

## THE ETHICAL DIMENSION

Labour's break with the past was nowhere more dramatic, at least in terms of presentation, than in the field of foreign affairs. Just ten days after the landslide victory, the Foreign Secretary, Robin Cook, gave the speech that announced a new hand at the wheel. He wrote it himself, having rejected an earlier speechwriter's draft (and fired the speechwriter), and delivered it in the Palmerstonian splendour of one of the great imperial halls at the Foreign Office. But where Lord Palmerston's dictum that 'The furtherance of British interests should be the only object of a British Foreign Secretary' had been quoted with approval by Robin Cook's Conservative predecessor Malcolm Rifkind in his own inaugural address, Cook himself had other ideas. The new politics would reflect the best of the old. The British were allowed to have principles as well as interests. Palmerston was out, and Gladstone was back in fashion.

Robin Cook called his speech 'A new mission statement for the Foreign and Commonwealth Office', as part of the government's contract with the British people. It was widely reported as offering an ethical foreign policy as the way of the future. It did not in fact do that. What it did offer was an *ethical dimension* to foreign policy, which was something different. 'The national interest', he said, 'cannot be defined only by narrow realpolitik.' One of the examples he gave was arms control:

> The global reach of modern weapons creates a clear national interest in preventing proliferation and promoting international control of conventional weapons. The Labour government will give a new momentum to arms control and disarmament. We have already made a start with our joint statement with France and Germany to work for a total ban on landmines.

In fact a total ban on landmines was not on the table. What was being worked for through the Ottawa process, by-passing the UN's cave of winds in Geneva, was a ban on anti-personnel mines, the devices that blow up people rather than tanks. This duly came to pass. But if the credit for it belonged to anyone, it was not to a politician or diplomat, but to Diana, Princess of Wales, the most influential of royals even in a sort of internal exile. She made things happen in a cause and at a pace which, without her, would not have happened. In a celebrated speech at the Royal Geographical Society in the New Labour heyday, two months before her death, she had invoked Shakespeare to define the peculiar curse of the anti-personnel mine: 'The evil that men do lives after them ...'[1]

Clearly, the new man at the top had to get the Foreign Office staff on side throughout the world, from the grandest ambassador to the humblest filing clerk. So at the end of the speech Robin Cook announced that a video would be made, with the help of the film director David Puttnam, and sent to more than 200 posts abroad to explain the new goals and new direction of foreign policy. Great, I thought (for I was in favour with Labour then and one of the MPs present) – the ethical dimension in foreign policy meets *Chariots of Fire*. No looking back now. Roll on the millennium. A bright new day was dawning.

Except that it very soon became overcast, as bright new days tend to. National interest, narrowly defined as the promotion of exports and the protection of jobs, clashed with the ethical dimension, especially in terms of arms sales to Indonesia, Tanzania, Saudi Arabia and Pakistan, among others. The pledge to maintain a strong British defence industry conflicted with the pledge not to sell arms to countries that might use them for internal repression or external aggression. There were also those who wondered why Tanzania, one of the poorest countries in Africa, needed a £28 million military air traffic control system, but they were overruled. Contracts and jobs depended on it.

Some of the incentives and 'sweeteners' in the arms trade, especially in relation to the sale of advanced fighter aircraft to Saudi Arabia, attracted the attention of the Serious Fraud Office. The SFO's investigation was closed down by the Prime Minister in December 2006, on the grounds that to proceed with it would forfeit Saudi co-operation in the so-called 'war on terror'. The Attorney General Lord Goldsmith (the man who changed his mind on the legality of the war in Iraq) said: 'It has been found necessary to balance the rule of law against the wider public interest.'[2] So the rule of law was not absolute. And if it was not absolute on arms sales, why should it be absolute on, for instance, cash-for-peerages? When it was inconvenient it was set aside, as if in a tinpot dictatorship or banana republic. The *Times* columnist Oliver Kamm, generally a Blair supporter, wrote of this decision: 'It is the lowest point in Mr Blair's government, and will be a defining one. It gives cynicism a bad name.'[3]

And there was a pattern to it. It was in line with the creeping advance of realism over idealism whenever the two conflicted, which they were bound to. Time after time New Labour ministers adopted policies in government against which, had they been in opposition, they would have raised a hue and cry. In 2002, the government modified the rules on international arms sales in order, it said, to conform with the 'new reality' of international defence projects. The arms industry by its very nature was more globalised than most. It was also more open to bribery, corruption and no-questions-asked incentives. The new reality was forcing New Labour into some awkward corners.

Throughout its years in office as before them, the British sold arms to rival powers like India and Pakistan. The Prime Minister commented: 'The idea that we should shut down the British defence industry in these circumstances I find bizarre.'[4]

And what of Burma, ruled by one of the most repressive regimes in the world? In March 1998, with the 'ethical dimension' less than a year old, the Burmese opposition leader and Nobel Laureate Aung San Suu Kyi spoke out against the British government's links with an oil company which planned to build a pipeline through Burmese territory into Thailand. She asked: 'Why is the British government pursuing one policy and British companies another? There are some who think the government is not altogether sincere if it permits its companies to invest in the present regime.'[5]

It is in the nature of politics that parties will advocate measures in opposition which, in government, are quietly discarded for practical or electoral reasons. Freedom of information is one. Disarmament is another. There will always be compromises between what is ethically right and what is practically expedient. The arms trade will inevitably throw up some of the most acute dilemmas. This is the real, not the ideal, world; and no one can blame a government for trying to navigate a course through those rapids. But there was one disarmament issue on which no dilemma existed. New Labour could have taken the lead on it from the outset, or even in midstream, without any electoral or political cost, but with a mighty benefit to its reputation as showing the ethical dimension in action and practising a new and different sort of politics. The issue was cluster bombs. For more than nine years, before a welcome and overdue change of mind, it looked the other way.

## CLUSTER BOMBS

As fate would have it, I grew up among cluster bombs. During the war I was evacuated from east Suffolk to Westmorland; and returning before the war was over (for I remember the searchlights) I found the lanes around the family home in Redisham festooned with tin signs, nailed onto oak trees and telegraph poles, warning of the dangers of butterfly bombs. From Guernica onwards, the Luftwaffe (with the RAF not far behind) had been pioneers in the technology of aerial warfare, from incendiary to butterfly bombs and other inventions, like ballistic missiles, which are with us to this day. The German prototype of the cluster bomb, also known as the SD2 or *Sprengebombe Dickwandig 2kg*, was the first to be used operationally. As a seven-year-old, I found the threat from these bombs immensely exciting. The war zone had arrived in our own back garden. My self-appointed mission was to be ground crew and bomb-spotter for Biggles, a fictional fighter pilot much admired by kids of my age. I had given up on unmasking spies, but looking for bombs in the ditches and hedgerows was definitely my part in the war effort. I should have thanked the German pilots, who on their way home from their targets in the Midlands dumped their unused ordnance on what they believed to be, because of the black-out, a deserted part of East Anglia. They didn't want to kill me, and (speaking as a seven-year-old) I didn't really want to kill them, although the story books show that Biggles had other ideas. Some of the crews of RAF Bomber Command reciprocated over apparently empty corners of Germany. Since I was never in favour of death and destruction, I saw them as knights of the skies. And I still do. There is an unofficial history to be written somewhere about the bombs that were deliberately dropped to cause no casualties.

The butterfly bomb, like the modern cluster bomb, was designed to be released from a casing in mid-air and scatter across the target area. And like the modern cluster bomb, its effect was not only to kill and to maim, but also to terrorise. Its most telling use was against civilians. Jack Dixon, who served in the Royal Navy, gave this account of an attack on Grimsby:

> The bombs that were dropped that night were later to be known as 'butterfly bombs'. ... Some exploded

on impact with the ground, others landed in the trees and were suspended by their 'wings' on the branches of trees, others caught on guttering, telephone wires, chimney stacks. It was dangerous to touch them. A young naval officer was seriously injured that night after kicking one of these bombs just outside the hostel. ... There was complete terror among the population of the town for many months as these bombs turned up in the most unexpected places.[6]

Cluster munitions are used in just the same way today to attack military targets and – inevitably – to terrorise civilians. They are dropped by aircraft or fired by artillery. It isn't necessary to wade through the alphabet soup of the different types and acronyms. But it is useful, to understand what they do, to distinguish the bomb from the bomblets. The air-delivered cluster bomb, like the British-made BL755, is a casing holding 147 sub-munitions, the bomblets, which fall to the ground over an area, known as its footprint, roughly the size of two or three football fields. On detonation, the bomblet blasts a jet of molten copper, a ball of fire and 2,000 steel fragments all around it. Thanks to the advances in ballistic science, the twelve-tube multi-launch rocket system (a development of the Soviet 'Stalin organ') can saturate a target with 7,728 of these engines of death in less than five minutes. It is a weapon of area bombing, whose purpose differs from its effect. Its purpose is to kill enemy forces and deny territory to them, although its variants can also be used against tanks, fortified positions and runways. Its effect is to terrorise people.

That is because many of the bomblets fail to explode. For bombs dropped from the air, the Ministry of Defence estimates a 5 per cent failure rate under test conditions at a low level, falling to 1 per cent at a medium level. (If replicated by artillery, even that would mean 77 unexploded bomblets for each volley by the multi-launch rocket system.) In the campaign in Kosovo in 1999, NATO forces dropped 2,000 cluster munitions containing more than 380,000 bomblets over the landscape. And these were not test conditions: as the terrain was mountainous, the failure rate was high. After the conflict and while I was still an MP, I visited Kosovo for Landmine Action, the organisation which campaigns against land mines. From evidence gathered on the ground by professional de-mining agencies like the Mines Advisory Group, it was clear that the proportion of bomblets which did not explode was actually in the order of 10 to 15 per cent. And according to the International Red Cross, cluster bombs and anti-personnel mines accounted for 73 per cent of all the post-conflict casualties. In the Falklands in 1982, the failure rate was at a minimum 9.5 per cent; but because of the smaller population the casualties were much lower, except among sheep.[7]

Statistics for the war in Iraq and its casualties are (perhaps deliberately) unavailable, but cluster munitions were widely used by the British against military targets in built-up and populated areas. 930,000 pieces of unexploded ordnance cleared from the battlefield in the British sector included 5,800 cluster bomblets, suggesting a high rate of failure.[8] After studying all known cases of death and injury from cluster bombs, Handicap International concluded that 98 per cent of their victims were civilians. These were not estimates or extrapolations, but people who were confirmed to have actually been killed or wounded.

The ethically-nuanced British government claims to

deploy cluster bombs 'only rarely'. In that case the 78,000 sub-munitions used in Kosovo and the 98,000 used in Iraq make an interesting definition of 'rarely'. 'Frequently' would be something like Armageddon.

The case made against anti-personnel mines by Diana, Princess of Wales in her speech in June 1997 applies with equal force to cluster bombs:

> For the mine is a stealthy killer. Long after conflict is ended, its innocent victims die or are wounded singly, in countries of which we hear little. ... And so, it seems to me, there rests a certain obligation on the rest of us.[9]

This is the scandal of it. The casualties don't end when the war does. And they are seldom military. The manufacture, use and export of anti-personnel mines were banned under the Ottawa Treaty of 1999. Cluster munitions are still legal weapons of war. *Yet they have exactly the same characteristics.* A cluster bomblet is, in effect, an aerially-sown anti-personnel mine. It blows people up just the same, whether they are wearing a uniform or jeans and a T-shirt – and usually, they are not wearing uniform. The victims are overwhelmingly civilians. Among the civilians, two groups of people stand out as being especially vulnerable – farmers and children. The farmers, trying to reclaim their land, are often the first to encounter unexploded ordnance. And the children, playing and exploring as children do, will be put in harm's way by their sheer energy and curiosity. The small size, bright colour (usually yellow) and toy-like appearance of a bomblet makes it dangerously attractive to the young. An American general described it as 'unfortunate' that it was the same colour as air-dropped food parcels.

Cluster munitions are of limited military value. A distinguished former Adjutant General, Lord Ramsbotham, told the House of Lords: 'I can find no justification for the deployment of these weapons in any activity the British Army has been involved with since the end of the Cold War.'[10] For the hundreds of thousands of bomblets dropped on Kosovo, the reckoning at the time was that a mere seven Serbian tanks were disabled. I saw one of them. It was not even badly damaged. And when the Serbs returned with their armour across the border, they did not look like a depleted force, but an undefeated army rolling home. It was the civilians of Kosovo, both Serbs and Albanians, who were left to face the consequences.

It is hard to escape the irony that a government which took office on the promise of a moral dimension to its foreign policy was the same government which for too long defended the use by its armed forces of a weapon which had the effect of targeting and killing children. *This also undermined trust in public life.*

## A RECORD OF INCONSISTENCY

When it came to power, the Labour government had the wind in its sails on arms control. The Ottawa Treaty on anti-personnel mines was being prepared and was ready for signature at the United Nations from 5 December 1997. Britain was, at least rhetorically, an enthusiastic supporter. Even so, Labour's business managers in the Commons had difficulty finding parliamentary time for the enabling legislation in the summer of 1998. Other measures, like Scottish and Welsh devolution, had priority. I was an MP at the time, and suggested to the Defence Secretary, George Robertson, that if the time could not be found for it we should call MPs back from their recess and vote for it on 31 August, the first anniversary of Princess Diana's death. The parliamentary obstacles melted away as if by magic, and the treaty came into force on 1 March 1999.

Sometimes good things happen. Since that date, the countries which signed on to the treaty have destroyed more than 39 million anti-personnel mines. But sometimes also good things are prevented from happening. The major powers with the largest armed forces – the United States, China and the Russian Federation – have not signed on to it; nor have more than 30 other states, following their example.

This leads to the conclusion that there are two sorts of national foot-soldier on these life-and-death issues – countries who put their best feet forward and countries who drag their feet. The British government has moved from one camp to the other, and maybe half the way back. The United Kingdom was part of the best-foot-forward brigade on anti-personnel mines, but for nine years a foot-dragger on cluster bombs. As the evidence accumulated against these weapons, from the civilian casualties they inflicted in Kosovo, Iraq, Lebanon and elsewhere, government ministers continued to insist that their use was consistent with international humanitarian law; and that, whatever the collateral damage, they were a legitimate weapon of war like any other. On 30 October 2006 the Minister for the Armed Forces, Adam Ingram, presented the case aggressively in answer to a question by the Liberal Democrats' Tim Farron:

> The matter is constantly reviewed. The honourable gentleman is saying that we should take a capability out of the hands of our forces that could result in a

situation in which, if they were deployed, British soldiers' lives could be lost. If that is what he is advocating and we ban such weapons, what is the next thing that he will want us to ban? Will he want our soldiers to have no weapons at all?[11]

The government even maintained that the use of cluster bombs was more humane than the alternative, which was to blast an area with larger quantities of conventional high explosive, causing 'excessive damage to buildings, land and people' (and it is interesting to note the order of priorities subconsciously set out there).[12]

But the government's position by this time was barely sustainable. Pressure was growing on it not only from public and parliamentary opinion, but even from within the Cabinet. The first to break ranks was Hilary Benn, the highly respected International Development Secretary, who sent a letter to his colleagues calling for a worldwide ban on the use of cluster bombs. He wrote:

> The high failure rate of many cluster munitions, and the failure of many militaries round the world to use these munitions in a targeted way, means that cluster munitions have a very serious humanitarian impact, pushing at the boundaries of international law … it is difficult to see how we can hold so prominent a position against landmines, yet somehow continue to advocate that use of cluster munitions is acceptable.[13]

Momentum was building for a ban, both nationally and internationally. At a review of conventional weapons in the Geneva Disarmament Conference in November 2006, a number of smaller states, led by Norway, tried to force cluster bombs onto the agenda. They were blocked by the usual suspects – the United States, China and Russia – and the United Kingdom appeared, alarmingly, to be on the side of the usual suspects. The smaller states vowed to go it alone, bypassing Geneva, as they had done with anti-personnel mines.

At this point, the British were persuaded into a change of policy. It happened as a result of Hilary Benn's letter, and was a remarkable example of the effect that a principled intervention can have, if made by the right man at the right time. The government distinguished for the first time between 'dumb' and 'smart' cluster bombs. 'Dumb' cluster bombs are those without an ability to discriminate between targets or to self-destruct; 'smart' cluster bombs, with these characteristics, are supposed to have a lower failure rate. There is no international understanding on these definitions, and different countries construe them in different ways; but the proposal introduced at Geneva let the British claim to be leading the way in pressing for a ban, rather than just keeping bad company. So the British ambassador to the Geneva Conference, John Duncan, set out the new policy:

> The United Kingdom agrees on the need to withdraw dumb cluster munitions from service … withdrawing dumb cluster munitions from service would not only have a humanitarian benefit but also a politico-military one as subsequent operations, including stabilisation operations, would not be hampered by them.[14]

A distant date, 2015, was given for the phasing out of these weapons. But only four months later the British government completed its volte-face and announced the immediate withdrawal of the most notorious of the 'dumb' clusters, the air-dropped BL755 and the artillery-fired M26. They kept the Israeli-made M85, which is, however, not as 'smart' as it thinks it is – many of its bomblets fired into Lebanon failed to self-destruct. It is only a matter of time before that goes too.

The about-turn on cluster bombs was matched by a remarkable change in policy on the arms trade. The United Kingdom was one of seven co-authors of an Arms Trade Treaty, which gathered 153 votes in the United Nations in December 2006 and would for the first time bind all countries to a responsible arms transfer policy – no weapons to be sold or moved across borders except for self-defence, collective security and other legitimate purposes; and none to violators of human rights. (Hopelessly idealistic? Perhaps; but it was the first such treaty ever proposed to curb the arms trade free-for-all, and anything was surely better than nothing.) Only one country, the United States, voted against. So it happened that in March 2007, and rather to my surprise, I found myself speaking in support of the British government at the UN in Geneva.

It is one of my character flaws, consistent over 40 years, that diplomats drive me crazy. They live and work so remotely from the issues they deal with. They exchange civilities, debate agendas and sip their *vins d'honneur*; and, with a few exceptions, seem to have as much sense of urgency as a hibernating hedgehog. For all the difference that they make they might as well relocate to Disneyworld. Their Geneva Disarmament Conference had been stalled *for ten years* while the wars of the world took an ever higher toll of civilian victims. So I challenged them: what did they want the year to be remembered for – real progress on limiting the arms trade, or the 60th anniversary of Mikhail Kalashnikov's remarkable invention? Mr Kalashnikov is the greatest gunsmith of his time, or probably any other. 100 million of his rifles are in service around the word. He is still going strong in his mid-80s. He says he would rather have invented the lawnmower.

But the major policy change was on cluster bombs; and for that, the Israelis were at least partly responsible.

## A WAR THAT FAILED

The war between Israel and Hizbollah was the first in the history of Arab–Israeli conflict that was a war of bombardment rather than manoeuvre. It was also the first that the Israelis, who are masters of manoeuvre, failed to win. Cluster munitions were their weapon of choice. Some were fired by artillery, including 1,800 US-supplied cluster rockets. Others were dropped by air. Sixty per cent of the targets were around towns and villages. The deadly legacy of the war includes up to a million unexploded bomblets, mostly in southern Lebanon. Thirty-five per cent of the casualties were children.[15]

Hizbollah also used cluster bombs, but on a much smaller scale. Human Rights Watch confirmed that two Chinese-made Type 21 missiles had been fired into Israel, each carrying 39 bomblets made of ball-bearings wrapped around a core of high explosive. The Israelis said they had been targeted by 113 such missiles.[16]

What was truly extraordinary was the scale of the Israelis' parting barrage. In the last three days of the war they carpeted Lebanon with up to 1.2 million sub-munitions from rocket fire. These figures did not include air-dropped cluster bombs. Their use was controversial in Israel itself. An officer of the Israeli Defence Force (IDF) described the attacks as 'insane and monstrous'.[17] A reservist told the Israeli newspaper *Haaretz*:

> In the last 72 hours we fired everything we had, we didn't even alter the direction of the gun. Friends of mine in the battalion told me they also fired everything in the last three days – ordinary shells, clusters, whatever they had.[18]

The newspaper quoted the commander of a multi-launch rocket system:

> According to the commander, in order to compensate for the rockets' imprecision, the order was to 'flood' the area with them. 'We have no option of striking an isolated target, and the commanders know this very well,' he said. … The reserve soldiers were surprised by the use of MLRS rockets, because during their regular army service they were told that these were the IDF's 'judgement day' weapons and intended for use in a full-scale war.[19]

These rockets were hardly ever fired in practice, for fear that the number of duds would turn the training ground into a minefield.

So Lebanon, especially southern Lebanon, was turned into a minefield instead. The damage was done, and is still being done, by both 'smart' and 'dumb' cluster bomblets that failed to explode on impact but will continue to kill and maim for years to come. The claim that these faulty weapons can be used in a precise or surgical way is demonstrably false. They have contaminated the ground. They kill the innocent. They have prevented the reaping of one harvest and the sowing of another. They contravene the Geneva Conventions. There is no case for keeping them in the arsenal of a law-abiding nation.

The United Kingdom was a signatory to Additional Protocol II of the Geneva Conventions adopted on 8 June 1977, and is still bound by that commitment. Article 13 of Part IV states:

> The civilian population as such, as well as individual civilians, shall not be the object of attack. Acts or threats of violence the primary purpose of which is to spread terror among the civilian population are prohibited.

For nine years the government claimed that the weapons used by its armed forces were internationally lawful. Then in the tenth year it admitted, in effect, that two of them were not. This was an extraordinary change and a welcome one – both for itself and for the break with Washington that it represented. The reasons for it came from all points of the compass. One was the failure and human cost of the Israelis' bombardment of Lebanon. Another was the proven record of cluster bombs as a weapon whose victims are almost entirely civilian. A third was the declining authority of the Prime Minister. And a fourth was the dynamic of the struggle for succession for deputy leader, if not leader, of the Labour Party.

The mystery left for future historians is: what on earth took them so long?

## CHAPTER TWELVE

# MEMORY LOSS

*They shall not return to us, the resolute, the young,*
*The eager and whole-hearted whom we gave:*
*But the men who left them thriftily to die in their own dung,*
*Shall they come with years and honour to the grave?*
Rudyard Kipling, 'Mesopotamia'

## THE OLD LIE

I have pointed up the part played by military inexperience in making it easier than it used to be for politicians to send the armed forces to war. Not only have they not been there and known the realities, but they may also relish the adventure of embarking on wars that others will have to fight: it is the *Boy's Own Paper* dimension of contemporary politics. The illusion persists that the glory might rub off on them. That applies not only to the Prime Minister who single-handedly selects the military option (Tony Blair revealingly described the war in Iraq as 'the action that I ordered'), but to the Cabinet and Parliament which can question the decision or rubber-stamp it; and on Iraq they chose the rubber stamp. We are historically a war-fighting people. The empire on which the sun never set was secured not by traders and missionaries, but by regiments which carry its place names as their battle honours. They are lessons in imperial history and geography. Those of my own, the 12th of Foot, include Minden and Dettingen, South Africa (twice), Seringapatam, Gallipoli and Imphal among dozens of others: defeats as well as victories, including the greatest defeat of all, at Singapore. Afghanistan and Mesopotamia are especially prominent on regimental colours. We have fought there before and are fighting there still. Our history binds us together. At the dedication of a war cemetery in Flanders in 1922, King George V observed: 'We can truly say that the whole circuit of the earth is girdled with the graves of our dead.'

Yet today the flags are furled and forgotten outside the regiments. The sacrifices are of another age, and remembered ritually for two minutes once a year. We live in a demilitarised society, with a smaller standing army than at any time since the 1830s. That should make it harder for our leaders to take the warpath; in fact it makes it easier.

That is not only their fault. It has to do with the laid-back, self-indulgent, privileged and take-everything-for-granted culture in which we live. We have gone absent without leave from our history. We British, whose war graves girdle the earth, are no longer the war-fighting people that we once were. And for that we must be thankful. We no longer pick quarrels with our neighbours, despatch armies to the continent in the fighting season, seek to colour the map red by force of arms, or embark on suicide missions in flat-bottomed boats. But the years of peace since 1945 have paradoxically endangered us. Our armed conflicts have been limited, expeditionary and fought a long way from home. In deciding which courses of action to take, those who lead us have lost the sense – a restraining, sobering, life-saving sense – of the horror and pity of war and the lives routinely lost in it. It no longer touches us as it used to, or carries the weight that it should in the balance of decision-making. We ignore it at our peril. We should know that we have been there before. Kipling wrote of the politicians of his time, who had presided over an earlier debacle in Iraq:

*How softly and how swiftly have they sidled back to power*
*By the favour and contrivance of their kind?*

'Mesopotamia', 1917

I was asked to deliver the annual speech of the Glasgow Chamber of Commerce. Since I love Glasgow as one of the great cities of Europe, I agreed. I asked them 'Who has heard of the Glasgow Commercials?' Very few of them had. The Glasgow Commercials were a battalion of infantry raised by the Chamber of Commerce for Kitchener's New Army in 1915. Alongside them – and the recruiting bases were in the names – were formed two other battalions, the Glasgow Tramways and the Glasgow Boys' Brigade. Together they became the 15th, 16th and 17th Battalions of the Highland Light Infantry. It reflected the patriotic ardour of the times that a single regiment could raise so many battalions. These three were part of the 32nd Infantry Division which went over the top in the battle of the Somme on 1 July 1916, the most disastrous day in the history of the British Army. 19,000 men died not just in one day but mostly in one hour, between 7.30 and 8.30 in the morning. Another 38,000 were wounded, missing, or taken prisoner. The 32nd, including its new Glasgow battalions, lost 3,939 men, more than half its fighting strength. And next to it, the 34th Infantry Division was all but wiped out. The

211

battalion orders of the Cambridgeshires, who were part of the ill-fated 34th, included the following: 'The use of the word "Retire" is forbidden'; 'Assisting a wounded man to the rear is a court martial offence'; and 'Too much credence should not be given to the opinions of wounded men.'[1] Major General Montagu Stuart-Wortley, whose 46th North Midland Division suffered the lightest casualties, 2,455 men, was promptly relieved of his command for not having sacrificed more.[2]

Many of the men who fought on the Somme had expressed concern that the war would have run its course before they played their part in it. In August 1914 some of them even believed that it would be over by Christmas. But it wasn't over by that Christmas or the next three. Even so, the carnage of the Somme was presented at the time as a good day's work, and even a kind of victory. This was partly because the accredited war correspondents, who with their green tabs were almost as despised in the trenches as the staff officers with their red ones, either did not know or would not report the truth of what was happening. They did most of their work, such as it was, closer to the chateaux than to the front lines. Philip Gibbs of the *Daily Chronicle* wrote: 'It is on balance a good day for England and France. It is a day of promise in the war.' Others, like William Beach Thomas of *The Mail*, were later to acknowledge their part in the great deception: 'I was thoroughly and deeply ashamed of what I had written, for the good reason that it was untrue; the vulgarity of the enormous headlines and the enormity of one's own name did not lessen the shame.'[3]

The fiction of victory was not sustainable. The truth came out in other ways – in the death notices in local newspapers, through word of mouth by the wounded and survivors on home leave, and through another group of witnesses who saw the war from the front lines as the official correspondents did not. These were the soldier poets, nearly all of them junior officers in infantry regiments of the line: Wilfred Owen of the 6th Manchesters, Edmund Blunden of the 11th Royal Sussex and Siegfried Sassoon and Robert Graves of the 1st and 2nd Royal Welch Fusiliers. Graves was so badly wounded on the Somme that he was reported as having died, and later read his own obituary in *The Times*.

Revisionist historians have sought to diminish them by claiming that they were unrepresentative of the broad mass of Great War soldiers. Of course they were unrepresentative. They were poets and the rest were not. But they did not write to be typical; they wrote to be truthful, and they were not all of one mind. Edmund Blunden, author of the epic *Undertones of War*, was as patriotic as anyone in the trenches, a good soldier and volunteer who served longer at the front than any of the others. But in later life he became increasingly bitter about the useless waste of young lives, including the sacrifice of half his battalion on the Somme in November 1916: 'But still we were a good battalion and deserving of a battle, not a massacre.' And Wilfred Owen, well aware that he was in a minority, challenged the blind nationalism of the time. One of his most enduring pieces was addressed to a fashionable poetess who was urging the young, some of them little more than children, to sign on for the war. He described the blood-curdling effects of a gas attack – 'bitter as the cud / Of vile, incurable sores on innocent tongues' – on the young soldiers. If you had seen them, he told her,

*My friend, you would not tell with such high zest*
*To children ardent for some desperate glory,*
*The old lie: Dulce et decorum est*
*Pro patria mori.*

The tag from Horace was engraved on monuments to the war dead: Wilfred Owen's refutation was not. Yet his work was itself one of the war's most enduring memorials.

As striking as the contrast in their views of the war was the contrast in the treatment given to these two select groups of witnesses to it. The six principal accredited correspondents all received knighthoods, and the proprietors of their newspapers were rewarded with peerages for supporting the war effort with their despatches and editorials, for being 'on side' from start to finish – and, ultimately, for misrepresenting the truth. Of the poets, Wilfred Owen was killed on a canal crossing a week before the signing of the armistice. And Siegfried Sassoon was narrowly saved from a court martial by his brother officer Robert Graves of the Royal Welch Fusiliers.

Yet it was the poets, not so well known then as they are now, who won the day historically and culturally. Not only was their account of the conflict the one that prevailed *because it was true,* but its message of the horror and pity of war entered the national bloodstream and stayed there, with the most powerful consequences, until quite recent times. One of those consequences was that war would no longer be regarded as it had been in 1914 by many of those who ordered it as a policy option, and by many of those who fought it as an adventure. There were many reasons for the outbreak of that war, ranging from imperial ambitions to railway timetables, but it did not have to be fought when it was and for the reasons advanced for it.

That should have been the end of the illusion, for our time as well as for theirs. But it is one of the tragedies of these past years that, after nearly a century, the ideas of war as an adventure and a policy option are making an unwelcome comeback.

They have to be challenged, but we lack an Owen or Sassoon – or indeed a George Orwell – to challenge them.

## THE GLORIOUS DEAD

The consciousness of the reality of war remained unchanged, as part of the shared national experience, throughout the terrible events of the Second World War. The generals then, who had been no more than majors in the Great War, were much more sparing of their soldiers' lives. With a few exceptions, like the Dieppe raid and (arguably) Arnhem, they did not employ the sacrificial strategies of their predecessors. But in all our history, the British losses by land, sea and air were second only to those of the Great War – with the added dimension of a home front opened up, with tens of thousands of civilian casualties, by the bombing of British cities. In the matter of bombing, the British inflicted more casualties than they suffered; and the policy of area bombing will remain, as Churchill noted after the destruction of Dresden, a question mark against the Allied conduct of the war. But the battlefield included most of the continent, from Norway to Sicily and from France to Russia; so that by 1945 all of its peoples, winners and losers, were left with few illusions about the great adventure of warfare.

One of the most alarming trends since then has been the accelerating *civilianisation* of the effects of armed conflict. It has continued apace with the wars of the collapsed states of the late 20th and early 21st centuries, from Rwanda to Iraq and from Bosnia to the Democratic Republic of the Congo. Today's ratio of 90 per cent civilian to 10 per cent military casualties is the reverse of what it was in the Great War: the figures are approximate, but they are in accordance with what I have observed and with the experience of most of today's war-zone witnesses. And civilians are increasingly not only the accidental, but deliberate, victims of armed conflict. In Sarajevo in 1992 the UN commander, Major General Lewis MacKenzie, accused both sides of targeting their own people in order to appear on the world stage as the victims rather than the aggressors. These were among the special effects of war in the media age.

The best ambassadors for peace are the soldiers who have witnessed and survived the alternative and lost whatever faith they ever had in it. So it was that at the Thiepval monument on the 80th anniversary of the battle of the Somme, on 1 July 1996, I met a 103-year-old survivor of the Great War, who had been a captain in the Royal Field Artillery and who seemed to speak for them all. 'War', he said, 'is a complete waste of time and a waste of lives. Let us have no more of it.' The old soldier understood what those who came after seem to have forgotten: that in today's high-intensity warfare, even more than in the trenches of 1916, there are no winners but only losers. The weapons themselves are more destructive than ever and not necessarily more accurate. The precision-guided missiles are not so precise as to distinguish between military and civilian targets, but can kill more people over a shorter period than any previously deployed in conventional warfare. The British Army's multi-launch rocket system (MLRS), which made its debut in the first Gulf War in Iraq in 1991, is capable of bringing down a more intensive bombardment on enemy positions than any battlefield weapon in British military history. The first man to order its use was a soldier of conscience, Brigadier Patrick Cordingley, who commanded 7th Armoured Brigade. He now concludes: 'I do now wonder whether it was entirely necessary. My commanders and myself wondered how to stop killing people. We were killing people quite unnecessarily.'[4] The hoped-for strategic outcome, the overthrow of Saddam Hussein, was not achieved. And even when it was achieved twelve years later, it led to anarchy, mass murder and civil war on a scale that exceeded the gloomiest predictions. The campaign in 2003 will stand for years as an object lesson in how not to fight a war. Again, there were no winners but only losers.

Only the living speak of the glorious dead, who themselves have no say in the matter. 'To The Glorious Dead' is the inscription on the Cenotaph in Whitehall, and I am not suggesting that it should be changed, but it belongs to an age of primitive industrial warfare. It seems inappropriate to the conflicts of the 21st century; and it offers no comfort to the families of those who have fallen in the optional and ill-considered wars of these past years. I stood there at the season of remembrance, with a field of poppies around the monument, in the company of Reg Keys, who had lost his boy in one of those wars and who saw the familiar phrase in a different light. 'I never for a moment imagined', he said, 'that my son Tom would be one of the Glorious Dead.'

It is not that there is a pro-war mood among the people. Rather the reverse. After all that has happened, their attitude is more questioning and critical. Recent decisions to go to war, and the supporting propaganda campaigns, have shaken their faith in the institutions of government.

They still see the decision to wage war as justifiable, if ever, only as a last resort and in the most extreme circumstances. Even then it must be backed by solid evidence and a consistent legal ruling. This did not happen in 2003. In the following year, when I stood as an Independent for the European Parliament in the Eastern Region of England, I spoke to voters as various as the Colchester Pensioners' Action Group, the farmers of Newmarket, community activists in Stevenage and a grand Tory dinner club in north Norfolk (Tories don't come grander than in north Norfolk). Among them there was no one – *not a single soul* – who supported the war in Iraq on the grounds on which it was fought, because the grounds on which it was fought were utterly false. The chasm between government and people has grown even wider since. For a government to be trusted, it first has to show itself to be trustworthy. This one has not.

In matters of war and peace, the British people have not been afflicted by the same memory loss as the political class. But it is the political class that sends the armed forces to war, without paying much attention to the will of the people. The most striking expression of this is to be found in David Blunkett's diaries, the only account that we have of meetings of the War Cabinet in the crucial months before and during the war in Iraq. His entry for 15 February 2003 is about the million anti-war protesters who took to the streets in the largest peacetime demonstration in British history: 'I think Tony has stood up very well to the enormous turn-out – frighteningly intimidatory, and people so bellicose.' The following month, on the Prime Minister's orders, the weapons of shock and awe were let loose; the Royal Artillery alone fired 22,500 shells in southern Iraq at targets where civilian casualties were inevitable. Yet for a Blair loyalist it was the people at home who were seen as threatening and bellicose. There could be no clearer example of the corruption of language and thought that sustained the New Labour project in the most extreme of its ventures. *This too undermined trust in public life.*

## THE ROAD FROM MANDALAY

In August 2005, the 60th anniversary of VJ Day, the bemedalled veterans of the Second World War gathered at the Cenotaph for the last of their great parades. The men of the Burma Star Association were led by Viscount Slim, General Bill Slim's son, who had been just old enough to serve on his father's staff in 1944. They were joined by some of the few surviving Far East prisoners of war. Places of honour were reserved for Arthur Titherington and Syd Tavender, the redoubtable leaders of the Japanese Labour Camp Survivors' Association, who had campaigned for half a century for restitution, and a real apology, by the Japanese for the inhuman treatment of their captives. The band of the Gurkhas gave a stirring performance of 'The Road to Mandalay' as a quick march, which put a spring into the step of the old soldiers as they limped away to a reception in the Great Hall of Westminster. All who saw them applauded them, some with tears in their eyes, for we knew we were in the presence of something special which we would not see again.

It was not a view, apparently, that everyone shared; for it was interesting to note, at the official level, who was present and who was not. The chiefs of staff of the three armed services were on parade, resplendent in their uniforms and whether or not they had had to break into their holidays to be there. It was less of a priority for the Prime Minister, who was represented by his deputy John Prescott, and for the Secretary of State for Defence, John Reid, whose place was taken by the Minister for the Armed Forces, Adam Ingram. The veterans noted their absence, but hadn't really expected anything else. Nothing had changed in 60 years. They were still the forgotten army.

A government aiming to change the very nature of politics will have little time for military commemorations. They are necessarily steeped in tradition and backward-looking. That is the point of them. They have no place in the Downing Street 'grid' in which the political schemes of the moment are promoted. Yet they serve a purpose and teach lessons about the costs of war that the politicians ignore at their own peril and everyone else's. Those lessons, unfortunately, are fading away with the last of the Second World War veterans. Every one of them, as he passes off parade, takes his own store of memories with him.

At the outbreak of the Second World War, Norman Winchester chose the 2nd Cameronians, also known as the Scottish Rifles, because he was up for a fight and felt that they were war-like: he was certainly right about that. He served with them as a machine-gunner from Dunkirk to the invasion of Sicily in 1943. He was a good machine-gunner, he recalled. More than 50 years later, in his eighties and with the help of a professional musician, he composed a remarkable piece of music for string quartet and narrator called *Memory Like Shells Bursting*. On Remembrance Day 2002 I introduced a performance of it at the Imperial War Museum. He used the words and music to express his wartime exhilaration in Sicily and the remorse that he felt, so long afterwards, about the taking of other men's lives – men whom he killed with his Bren gun and saw dying. He wrote: 'This memory stinks a bit ... The joy it gave me was intense, we really were a killing people then.' Warfare is seldom glorified by the men who know it. And those with the most nightmarish memories seldom talk about them, except near the end of their lives. We really were a killing people then: and we girdled the earth with our graves.

Like most of his contemporaries, Norman Winchester is no longer on parade. One effect of their passing is the collective amnesia that grips the political classes. It has allowed the government to slip the safety catch and resort to force when other means are available, especially in those corners of the world where force has seldom succeeded. Baroness Kennedy – a Labour appointee to the House of Lords, but one of her party's critical friends and free spirits – has described 10 Downing Street in these years as 'a history free zone'. Look at Iraq, look at Afghanistan ... it is the truth of her reproach that makes it so powerful. Whoever taught the young Tony Blair history at Fettes, if anyone did, would seem to have much to answer for.

In this respect it is possible to see a triple link between Blair's wars and those in the Balkans. The first link is that one of them, the intervention in Kosovo in 1999, was actually in the Balkans. The second link is that the Prime Minister's interventionist policies, set out in his Chicago speech in April 1999, were driven to a considerable extent by the consequences of the previous government's failures over Bosnia between 1992 and 1995. The third link is generational. The glue that held Tito's Yugoslavia together was not just the dictator's ruthlessness, but the folk memory of the horrors of the Second World War, in which the Serbs suffered disproportionately. It was ironic that some of the first battles of the war in Croatia in 1991 were fought on the 'highway of brotherhood and unity', the motorway that ran north to south across ancient frontiers and bound the republics together. Under the pressures of nationalism, brotherhood and unity were not enough to save the federation. National flags and songs and allegiances, long suppressed, came out of hiding. In Slovenia, Croatia, Bosnia and Serbia there was a new generation of men in power, not only politicians but soldiers and paramilitaries, who had in some cases been marked by war (General Ratko Mladic, commander of the Bosnian Serb army, was himself a war orphan) but who had not themselves fired a shot in anger, and who saw in the application of force a means of advancing and protecting the interests of their peoples. The wars were then justified, to themselves and to others, as wars for the survival of those peoples. But the men who embarked on them were no longer restrained by the collective memory of what had gone before.

For them as for the British – and for others as far away as Iraq – that memory loss has had catastrophic consequences. Generational historians like Arnold Toynbee and William Strauss have argued persuasively that global conflict occurs in predictable cycles, and politicians born after one great war will tend to lead their countries into another. So it is with the post-war 'baby boomer' generation now in power. Bill Clinton said he wished he had been president at a time of great national crisis. His contemporary George W. Bush saw himself as a wartime leader – even dressing up as one, which real soldier presidents like Eisenhower never did – and leading the charge on everything from a rhetorical 'war on terror' to a very real war in Iraq. It is a seductive fallacy that war is for statesmen and peace is for politicians.

In this respect, I blame Winston Churchill. It was not his blunders, from Gallipoli to Singapore, that did the damage to later generations. It was his triumphs. Britain's greatest war leader has had the most baleful influence, creating a myth that seduced too many of his successors. His rallying of the nation after the years of appeasement has been cited by successive prime ministers – Anthony Eden, Margaret Thatcher and Tony Blair – to justify sending the armed forces to war in very different circumstances. Margaret Thatcher succeeded. The other two failed.

Very occasionally, when national survival is at stake, we need a war leader to inspire us. 1939 was one of those times. 1997 was not. Most of the time we fare better under prime ministers like Clement Attlee, Churchill's unspectacular but effective successor, who work for peace and build on it.

The lesson for our future leaders, of whichever party, is that the Attlees are as heroic as the Churchills. And they tend to do less damage.

## Chapter Thirteen

# BROKEN SOLDIERS

*Such as have adventured their lives and lost their limbs or
disabled their bodies, in defence and service of Her Majesty
and the State, should at their return be relieved and rewarded
to the end that they may reap the fruit of their good deservings,
and others may be encouraged to perform the like endeavours.*
Act for the Relief of Soldiers, 1593

A measure of the health of a country, the strength of its
people and the good sense of its government is the way in
which it treats its soldiers, and especially its casualties of
war. By that standard, ours has performed on the whole
well and creditably over more than four centuries since the
reigns of Elizabeth I and Charles II. But lately it has fallen
into ill-health and disrepute. The hospital that Charles II
founded in Chelsea 'For the care and succour of soldiers
broken by age and war' was a retirement home as well as a
medical centre for old soldiers. It was the first of our
permanent military hospitals. As a result of budget-driven
political decisions, it is also now the last. We have gone
from a system that served the soldiers to one that fails them.
The consequences have been shameful and severe.

When the Cold War ended, the much-vaunted 'peace dividend' included the savings made possible by the reduction in size of all three armed services. It was unwisely supposed that the money saved would be better spent on other, peacetime projects. Under 'Options for Change', the euphemism for the cutbacks, the forces were reduced to the point where they were losing the critical mass at which they could operate efficiently, or indeed at all, over their full range of functions. They were suitable for dealing with civil emergencies, for UN peace-keeping and for medium-sized expeditionary operations conducted one at a time. But that was the limit. They were at risk of becoming an armed gendarmerie with a seaborne, amphibious and airborne capability, but without enough back-up in men and equipment for high-intensity warfare. If the politicians continued down that road, a point would be reached where the soldiers especially, as the front-line force, would be too few to fight and too many to die.

MPs with no experience of the military – which was all but a handful – were happy enough to agree to the cuts. Regiments were disbanded, warships mothballed and RAF bases decommissioned. The service hospitals were also closed, on the grounds that there was no longer a large enough military population to sustain them. Despite vociferous protests by MPs in the constituencies affected, like Sir Peter Viggers in Gosport, it was not at the time an issue of great contention between the parties. The process was begun by a Conservative government and continued by a Labour one.

And then the Labour government embarked on its wars. The limited excursions in Kosovo and Sierra Leone could be accommodated easily enough within the new order of things. There was no ground combat in Kosovo and casualties were light in Sierra Leone. But Iraq and Afghanistan were simultaneous combat operations on an entirely different scale. The casualties ran into hundreds – thousands including those treated at aid posts and field hospitals – and the home-based military hospitals no longer existed. Instead, a partly military wing was established within the NHS hospital at Selly Oak in Birmingham. But civilians as well as soldiers were treated there. The report of a wounded soldier at the hospital being abused by an anti-war civilian was seen as sign of the breakdown in the covenant between the services and the nation. The story was never verified but widely believed by the military.

It was, again, the new army chief, General Sir Richard Dannatt, who sounded the alarm where others had stayed silent. He said: 'It is not acceptable for our casualties to be in mixed wards with civilians. I was outraged at the story of someone saying: "Take your uniform off." Our people need the privacy of recovering in a military environment.'

Similar concerns were expressed as far back as the 1991 Gulf War. Although the casualties turned out to be light, NHS hospitals were ordered to prepare wards for the wounded and to ensure the safety of patients 'should they be attacked by disaffected members of the public'.

The Military Covenant lies at the heart of the matter. It is the contract that recruits sign on to when they join the army. They agree to forgo certain rights, like the rights to engage in political action or join a trade union, and to be willing to make certain sacrifices – including the ultimate sacrifice – in the service of the nation. They put their lives at risk so that the rest of us should be safer. The nation, for its part of the bargain, undertakes to sustain, reward and provide for them and their families and to treat them fairly: 'This mutual obligation forms the Military Covenant between the nation, the army and the individual soldier; an unbreakable common bond of identity, loyalty and responsibility which has sustained the army throughout its history.' The contract is presumed to apply to the other services, but the army provides the prime example, since it is the largest of the three, fights at the closest quarters and usually sustains the highest casualties.[1]

I made a television documentary about the covenant early in 2007. We wanted to call it *Broken Soldiers*, after the inscription on the colonnade at the Royal Hospital; but that was vetoed by the Ministry of Defence in the course of some legal wrangle with Channel 4. So we called it *Britain's Throwaway Soldiers* instead. The medical care for those who are serving seldom falls below a certain standard. But for those who have served it is something else; and all too often they find the covenant broken.

Wounded soldiers first treated in military hospitals now depend, like everyone else, on the NHS; and some will need special care for all their days. John Moore was a nineteen-year-old rifleman serving with the Royal Green Jackets when he was paralysed by a sniper's bullet in South Armagh in 1981. He was well looked after in the military hospital at Woolwich. A generation later, and still confined to a wheelchair, he cannot get the physiotherapy he needs from the NHS; it is paid for instead by a charity. He accepts the principle of equality of treatment in the state system, and the waiting lists that go with it, but still he wonders about depending on charity and whether the covenant he signed on to has any real meaning.

'If your country has asked you to serve, they rely on you to serve so when you leave the army you should be able to rely on your country to look after you.'

'And does that happen these days?'
'Not much.'[2]

Support Company of 3 Para defended the Sangin outpost in Helmand for the first six months of Britain's fourth Afghan war. (If you ask who won the other three – we didn't.) They lost three dead in close-quarter fighting, using not only assault rifles but hand grenades and cannon fire to throw the Taliban back from the perimeter of their compound. Their ammunition ran low, and a lesser force could well have been overrun. Under terms implicit in the Military Covenant, they should then have had two years before deploying to another combat zone. But the contract between the nation and its soldiers is breaking down. Instead, they were 'warned off' for another tour of duty in Afghanistan within eighteen months. They had hardly recovered from one tour before they were in training for the next. It said a lot for the morale of the Paras that they were looking forward to it. One of the reasons they were doing so was that they were professional war-fighters and liked doing what they trained for. Another was that they would be as far away as possible from the Ministry of Defence. Having dealt with the MoD's bureaucracy, I understood their feelings.

There is a real danger that, as the Afghan deployment continues, and deficiencies in reinforcement, equipment and re-supply continue with it, an outpost or convoy may be overwhelmed and prisoners taken, with human and political consequences that both the army and the Taliban understand very well. In recent years British military personnel have been captured by hostile forces in Sierra Leone, briefly in Iraq, and humiliatingly in the Persian Gulf. There are never wars without prisoners of war, unless the prisoners are killed. I know of no reason why Afghanistan should turn out to be an exception.

The Persian Gulf incident, in which a naval boarding party was captured by the Iranians and then released in un-heroic circumstances, had all the armed services, including the navy, seething with indignation. It also exacerbated inter-service rivalries. An army ditty of the time, set to the tune of 'We Are Sailing', included the following:

*We were captured,*
*We were crying,*
*On the telly,*
*On the news.*

There was an exodus of veterans from the Parachute Regiment after the Falklands War, in which the 2nd and 3rd Battalions lost 40 men. There has been no mass demobilisation this time, at least so far. Corporal Guy 'Posh' Roberts ('Posh' because he has officers in his family) was hit by a sniper's bullet in the shoulder, at the start of a hard battle outside the Sangin perimeter. Three months later, he was back with 3 Para in Colchester training for the next tour. He said that he loved 99 per cent of his time in the outpost. It was only the remaining 1 per cent, being wounded, that he could have done without. Such are the kind of people that soldiers are. They live in the moment. They show courage and resilience beyond civilian under-standing. They call it 'cracking on'. They can also crack up.

## COMBAT STRESS

The military live separately from the rest of us. They face hardships and dangers that we in our comfortable lives can hardly imagine. When they become casualties they need to be treated separately as well. The victim of a roadside bomb in Basra, if he survives, will commonly know nothing more about it until, heavily sedated, he wakes up in a hospital ward in Selly Oak. There he may find that bits of him are missing. He needs and expects the care of army doctors and nurses, so far as possible, and the company of other soldiers in the ward around him. This applies not only to the physically wounded, but to those whose injuries are not so obvious but may be long-term. And long-term can mean for the rest of a man's life.

What used to be described as shell-shock has been most commonly diagnosed, since 1980, as post-traumatic stress disorder (PTSD). The army didn't want it to exist and pretended for a long time that it didn't, not recognising it until more than ten years later. It is an illness on a time fuse. Often its effects are not immediately obvious even to its victims. Soldiers will be in denial about them, not only to their comrades-in-arms but most of all to themselves. There is nothing wrong with them, they will say, that a couple of drinks won't put right; and hard drinking has always been part of the military culture. So they may drink to excess to blank out the symptoms – nightmares, flashbacks and loss of physical control as the nervous system breaks down. Personal lives will spiral downwards. Marriages will collapse, sometimes violently. There is also a stigma attached – a sense of shame and guilt at being seen as a hero, yet having broken when others have not. All this makes it hard to seek treatment. The average time delay was twelve to fifteen years for Falklands veterans, but much shorter for the victims of more recent wars. The first 140 casualties of the 2003 Iraq war are coming through the system already, and some from Afghanistan. They are the bow wave of a predictable flood. The toughest of the tough are not exempt, but are more at risk than most. Combat Stress, the armed services' mental health society, has a high proportion of Paras and Marines coming to it for help. These are the men from the spearhead battalions, who fought more and saw more than most, and who therefore suffer more in later life.

The result is a surge of unparalleled proportions in what is supposed to be peacetime. Combat Stress calls these victims of war its clients. In eight years their average age has fallen from 71 to 47, and their numbers have risen sharply. It has 8,000 men on its books – a few women, but mostly men – at the three residential centres where the clients stay for two weeks three times a year. Another 1,000 seek treatment every year. The waiting lists are growing. There aren't enough beds or staff or centres to cope with them all. And because most of them were discharged from the army with a clean bill of health – the symptoms did not afflict them until later – they then have to prove that their illness is combat-related. The onus is on them, often ill-prepared, to do so. That is itself stressful and adds to a sense of alienation and lack of self-worth.

As a paratrooper, Jim Russell was among the toughest of the tough. He was a section commander in A Company of 2 Para in the battle for Goose Green in the Falklands in May 1982. He led his ten men in an attack on a well-defended Argentine position on Darwin Ridge. They called it 'gutter fighting'. They killed or wounded an entire platoon in taking it, and then went on to storm the next position. Two of Jim's NCOs were killed and he was wounded. He didn't know it at the time, but he was hurt in the mind as well as the body, and the physical wounds were the easier ones to deal with. He soldiered on for another three years, but was already starting, as the army puts it, to go 'wobbly'. He spoke to a captain in his battalion about the symptoms: 'He told me in no uncertain terms that if I was to mention that to any one else in the army rank-wise that my career would rapidly come to end, because they didn't like that sort of talk.'

Michael Iddon, known as 'Iddy', was a young army medic on the *Sir Galahad* when it was bombed in Bluff Cove by the Argentine air force. One fifth of all the British deaths in the war were caused by that attack. Iddy survived, at least physically, and was discharged from the service soon afterwards through the psychiatric unit at Woolwich, which no longer exists. He wandered around for fifteen years as a lost soul, using drugs and alcohol to try to control the memories and spasms, before Combat Stress and the British Legion found him. With their support, he played the inevitable percentage game. He was offered 14 per cent of a full war pension – as a sort of 'bung' he says, to go away and stop rocking the boat. He went to a tribunal, which he remembers as a sort of trial where he had to prove that he was innocent, and that his injuries were real and war-related. The offer was raised to 50 per cent and accepted, because it was just enough to pay for the care he needs. He says: 'I would never treat my worst enemy like that. You know, I wouldn't treat one of the Argentinians that bombed us on the *Galahad* as they treated me, and the boys like me.'[3]

Neither Jim nor Iddy were what the army calls skivers or scrimshankers. They were good soldiers who became casualties of war, just as surely as if they had been burned on the *Galahad* or machine-gunned at Goose Green. Today, these broken soldiers are referred to NHS hospitals, which through no fault of their own are ill-prepared to treat the psychiatric cases. The NHS doesn't understand them. Collective therapy doesn't work in a mixed group of soldiers and civilians. A soldier will sit in such a group, says Toby Elliott of Combat Stress, with the victims of traffic accidents and such, and be asked to talk about his experience: 'He says, "I can't talk about it. I can't talk about my best mate whose brains I wore down the front of my uniform to anyone who doesn't understand." … It's so different from the experiences the others have had.'

Perhaps a confession is in order. Keeping the company of these wonderful men made me reflect that I might one day become a candidate for the kind of treatment that keeps their demons at bay, if I am not already. These things affect different people at different times and in different ways. There is no knowing when or how. (My nightmares even now are about television, which I found more stressful than war.) My front-line coping mechanisms were an unlimited amount of comradeship and a limited measure of whisky. Towards the end of my war-zone days, I would work only with people I not only trusted but loved, and that applied as much to the cameramen Nigel and Carl as to the producer Anamarija: and at curfew time we would drink to our survival, whatever had happened during that day, at least until the next. It doesn't work to think too deeply. You take it one day at a time. You will never be the same as you were before. Everyone who has been close to war is in some sense changed by it, usually but not always for the worse.

## THE MILITARY COVENANT

The treatment of our soldiers is an issue of trust because, in the opinion of many best placed to know, the government cannot be trusted, on behalf of the nation, to keep its side of the bargain. Lt Col Tim Collins was the army's most prominent field commander in the Iraq war of 2003, because of his remarkable eve-of-battle speech to the Royal Irish. He was the politicians' darling for a while. Now he is among their harshest critics. 'The politicians, those in government, have never dared to serve their nation. They've never understood what it is to put their lives on the line and to selflessly stand up for their country and be prepared to make the ultimate sacrifice. The attitude of the government is ... we have an all-volunteer army – you don't have to be there, and if you don't like it, leave.'[4]

Another admired veteran is Simon Weston of the Welsh Guards, badly burned in the bombing of the *Sir Galahad* in the Falklands in 1982. His recovery under the circumstances was so extraordinary that he became a national symbol of courage and endurance – and also of the special care available to the badly wounded in the now closed military hospitals. His view too is that the covenant no longer has the meaning that it had when he signed on:

> Quite simply, we've lost care and concern. These men and women who have signed up to serve have done it honourably; and yet the government still gives so little service to them and they come out with their platitudes and excuses and say 'Yes, we're looking into it, we know we should do more, we will do more', and no they don't.

I wondered: 'What would you say to a young man who wants to join the army today?'

> Years ago I would have said go and enjoy it. I would have difficulty saying that hand on heart now.[5]

It is an irony of warfare that as the weapons of war become more destructive, there is a higher proportion of wounded to dead among the military than when they were more primitive. Survival rates are higher, partly because the soldiers are wearing body armour, and partly because of medical and surgical advances. The cost of these advances also makes the re-opening of the military hospitals highly unlikely. The clinical care of wounded soldiers is as good as it ever was. At Selly Oak hospital, Shane Willoughby of the 2nd Rifles, badly injured by rocket fire in Basra in January 2007, paid tribute to the skill of the surgeons and 'the very good mix of military and civilian nurses' looking after him. But the *aftercare* of the wounded, especially those who have left the service, is not less than a national scandal. For those who serve, the Military Covenant may still mean something. For those who have served, it does not. And for the mentally injured, it might as well not exist.

At the heart of the covenant is the idea that those who risk their lives for the nation must be treated as special people: 'The army differs from all other institutions, and must be sustained and provided for accordingly by the nation.' Yet it was only a matter of time before the government's military inexperience would coincide with its need to save money, and wounded soldiers would be treated like victims of an industrial accident. That time arrived with the introduction of the Armed Forces Compensation Scheme in 2005. It removed the benefit of the doubt previously given to soldiers and required them to prove, on the balance of probabilities, that their injury or illness was caused by their military service. For the physically wounded, that was not a problem. The likes of Simon Weston of the Welsh Guards or John Moore of the Royal Green Jackets would be as entitled to a full war pension now as they ever were. But for the mentally injured, it was the start of a long ordeal before tribunals in which they would be forced to play the percentage game.

The more I heard from the old soldiers, and the more I learned about their plight, the more I was convinced of the case for a British equivalent of the American GI Bill. This was enacted after the Second World War, to protect those who serve and have served in the armed forces. As a result of recent emergencies – more than 20,000 wounded in Iraq alone – the Americans are moving to strengthen its provisions still further. The British are going backwards. We have only the Military Covenant, which would be fine if it were observed, but it is not. It is as shot through with holes as an old regimental colour. I was not the only one to see this. So the Royal British Legion, the leading veterans' organisation, prepared a campaign to follow the American example and turn the covenant into the law of the land, applicable across all three services. As the Legion's national chairman John Hawthornthwaite put it, the case was unanswerable by anything other than a change in the law: 'The serviceman is the only employee who says to his employer, I will go out there and die for you – if necessary. And they are doing. They are dying. We feel that that sort of person should have special treatment afterwards as a civilian when he comes out, because he has given his life contract to the country and the country owes it to him to look after him when he comes out. And they're not doing so.'[6]

When the New Labour project is laid prematurely to rest, after so promising a beginning, it will have one word and one only on its tombstone: Iraq. The decision to go to war changed many things: one of them was the military's relationship with the government. Without it, senior commanders below the level of chiefs of staff would not have been so critical of the politicians' judgement. Without it, resources that were needed for two armed conflicts could have been concentrated on one; and the army would not have been deployed in Afghanistan so late, so under-equipped, and with so precarious a chance of long-term success. Without it, the substitution of NHS for military hospitals would not have been an issue of such widespread concern. And without it, it would not have been necessary for the Military Covenant to become the law of the land.

In the Britain that I grew up in, the military were embedded in the community. Every county had its regiment: some had several. The people understood that and played their part. As a soldier in battledress, I could hitch-hike home across Suffolk almost as quickly as if I had driven myself. Fifty years on, the armed forces are remote, behind the wire and just not sufficiently valued for securing the peace and freedom that we take for granted. We have lost more than we know, because we have forgotten that we had it.

I flew home from Basra just before Christmas 2006 in a civilian aircraft chartered by the Ministry of Defence. It had 200 soldiers on it, and was scheduled to land at Teesside, the airport nearest to the Catterick garrison. Because of fog, it was diverted to Newcastle, where the authorities went into a mode of obstruction and denial. They seemed embarrassed by the uniforms, and couldn't cope with the encased weapons, certified as unloaded and without ammunition, that the soldiers had in their checked baggage. In vain did the senior officer, a full colonel, point out that under the law of the land our military have the right to bear arms. They were kept waiting for hours as flight after flight of holiday-makers and businessmen came and went, looking the other way: as if men in combat fatigues had no place in an arrivals lounge, or maybe they had blundered into the set of an SAS movie. The soldiers bore it with patience. They were used to being treated like second-class citizens, and anything else would surprise them. I made a fuss in the local media, as a result of which Newcastle airport put out an oleaginous statement congratulating itself on the integrity of its 'no weapons' regime. It was a small incident, but indicative of the way that we as a people fail to give even equal treatment to those who risk their lives on our behalf.

The issue is one of a national debt. It is time that we paid what we owe.

## Chapter Fourteen

# REGIME CHANGE

*They that stand high have many blasts to shake them,*
*And if they fall, they dash themselves to pieces.*
William Shakespeare, *Richard III*, Act I, scene 3

### Shakespearean Echoes

Shakespeare was the poet of regime change. If he had written a soap opera – which, in his way, he sometimes did – he would have found in New Labour's power struggles a wealth of material for the pen that never blotted a line. The metaphors most often used to describe them, of daggers and crowns and the trappings of power, were altogether Shakespearean. The bloodshed was figurative, but the plots were as complex and the hostilities as deep as those of the Wars of the Roses. In this case there was only one rose to be fought for, the symbol of the supposedly fraternal people's party, whose protagonists were tearing it and each other apart. The two main characters were the Prime Minister and the Chancellor, or the King and the Pretender, with a supporting cast of dukes, earls, marshals, grave-diggers, messengers, fools and shady characters with an eye on the main chance. It was ever thus. Politics is about power, and those who hold it will always be outnumbered and threatened by those who seek it; nor will they surrender it without a struggle, any more in our day than in Shakespeare's.

Like all good soap operas, this one plays itself out in daily instalments with an omnibus edition on Sunday. The scriptwriter works to a formula: each edition ends with a cliff-hanger written into the script to hook the audience into the next episode; they must be left wondering – can it be as compelling as what has gone before? In this case a stellar and larger-than-life cast never failed to deliver. The narrative veered wildly between *Richard II*, *Richard III*, *Macbeth*, *Coriolanus* and *Julius Caesar*. Shakespeare should have been living at this hour. Or perhaps in some mysterious way he was. They surely couldn't have done this by themselves.

*On Tuesday, there are stirrings of a conspiracy against the King, provoked by his apparent intention to reign for ever. Through a leaked parchment one of his courtiers sets out a plan, in the unlikely event of an abdication, for a grand royal progress through the kingdom to receive the applause of the ever-grateful people and leave them clamouring for more. This is too much for some of the ever-grateful people to take. So on Wednesday a group of minor office-holders of the King's Party, led by the little-known Baron of West Bromwich, send a message to the King, threatening to leave his service unless he takes himself off or falls on his sword. The Baron of West Bromwich, said to be close to the Pretender and to have plotted with him on a blasted heath in Scotland, resigns before he is exiled or sent to the Tower. The King accuses him of treachery. The Pretender denies any part in the affair; but voices are rumoured to have been raised at an encounter, or joust, in the royal palace. On Thursday, the King delivers an emotional address promising to relinquish the crown within a year, but insists that the timing will remain within his prerogative for the good of the kingdom, which is his sole concern; the Pretender admits only to having asked him certain questions at their meeting the day before. On Friday the Pretender calls on the King to name him as heir apparent. The King refuses. The Duke of Norwich, out of favour with the King but also a long-time foe of the Pretender, accuses the Pretender of having acted unwisely and not shown the necessary king-like qualities.*

*On Saturday, the Duke of Norwich returns to the fray and in coded language questions the Pretender's balance of mind. Courtiers on the Pretender's side allege that the Duke's outburst was the result of too much red wine in the afternoon, consumed in the company of an attractive lady scrivener, the Mistress McElvoy. On Sunday, in the omnibus edition, the plot thickens. The King's soothsayers accuse the Pretender of mendacity. The Pretender's position is weakened when it is made known that he has held a private meeting with the Baron of West Bromwich, which the Baron explains as a courtesy call to deliver a present for the Pretender's new-born son. The Pretender still looks forward to his coronation and promises to lead a court of all the talents, including even those of the Duke of Norwich, such as they are. But the consensus of the ink-stained wretches who dance attendance on both courts is that he has damaged his chances and his accession to the throne may be challenged by one of the Scottish barons. There is blood all over the battlefield. And this is just the end of the first act.*

Such, more or less, were the intrigues in the upper reaches of the Labour Party in the first week of September 2006. For nine years in office its leading figures, mindful of the wilderness into which their predecessors cast them, had gritted their teeth and pretended to like each other even when they didn't. No one's teeth were more permanently gritted than those of the Chancellor, Gordon Brown, who was well placed to inherit the crown when it had last fallen vacant in 1994, but it went to another in disputed circumstances. He gritted them especially in the presence of the man who took it, a politician whom he disliked, distrusted and yet helped to rescue from defeat in 2005. He spoke of the partnership and friendship between them, and even shared a campaign ice cream to show it; but it was a tense and difficult relationship. After a previous rift, he was said to have told the Prime Minister: 'I can never believe a word that you say'.

Then there was Charles Clarke, MP for Norwich South and a leading player in the Shakespearean soap opera. He wrote to *The Independent* in April 2006: 'It is perhaps worth remembering that my relationship with the Chancellor is extremely cordial.'[1] Yet this was the same man whom he now called absolutely stupid and psychologically flawed. The settling of old scores damaged the party but entertained the nation. As an Independent I value honesty and like it when politicians say what they think, especially about each other. But there are limits to what is allowable under the party system. In the war of the Labour succession, these limits were regularly overstepped, handing whole bandoliers of ammunition to the party's opponents for use at the next election. Other names were being canvassed by the anyone-but-Gordon faction: John Reid, David Miliband and the hitherto little-known Alan Johnson. The interesting question, for the party that claimed to have learned the lessons of disunity, was why it allowed open warfare to break out. Whatever possessed it that it formed itself, as the Conservatives had done ten years earlier, into a circular firing squad? From my experience of politics, brief but intense, I have developed a number of theories.

For the first, I am indebted to Sir Thomas Browne from Charles Clarke's adopted city of Norwich: 'The iniquity of oblivion blindly scattereth her poppy.' Time passes and people forget. The MPs who signed the letter calling on the Prime Minister to step down – one junior minister and five parliamentary private secretaries – were all of the intake of 2001 or thereafter. They took their seats when New Labour's wave was still cresting. They had not been there in the wilderness years. They had no experience of the grim and grinding adversity of opposition. Tony Blair, however, had. He arrived in the Commons in 1983, with Labour demoralised by its crushing post-Falklands defeat, Margaret Thatcher triumphant – and no one could triumph as mercilessly as she did – and his party committed to a leadership and to policies that made it unelectable for the foreseeable future. Imagine the indignity of it, facing an eternity on the losers' side of the House – for that's how an opposition sees its role, as a loyal waste of time – and of being barracked by the likes of Neil Hamilton, the Tory MP for Tatton, who was also first elected in 1983. Whatever the MP for Sedgefield could have been accused of when he started out in politics, it certainly was not opportunism. It took nine years of hard Labour, in every sense, to end the blood-letting, change the leadership, frame sensible policies and mount a serious challenge: five more years after that, and two changes of leadership, to become the party of government.

But the past is the poorest guide to the future, because the nature of politics has changed. For a start, it is now more professional than it ever was – not in the positive sense that those who practise it take it more seriously, but

in the negative sense that so many of them do not have –
and never have had – what most people think of as a proper
job to go back to. After leaving university, where they have
nursed their political ambitions in student activism (both
Jack Straw and Charles Clarke took this route), they join
the party of their choice as volunteers, interns, researchers
or speech-writers – whatever it takes to gain a foot-hold on
the bottom rung of the ladder. Those with the talent for it
and the best connections will enter the ranks of special
advisers in a minister's private office at an improbably
young age (the route taken by David Cameron and George
Osborne among others). They are clever, articulate and
swift as sharks to spot an opportunity. It may take them as
little as five years from working the photocopier to a seat
on the front bench. But outside the precincts of Whitehall
and Westminster they can actually *know* very little by doing
it, because they haven't done it. This is not to criticise them,
for many excellent MPs came in this way (and George
Osborne, my successor in Tatton, is one of them), but just
to explain how things are.

They were not always so. The great A.P. Herbert,
Independent MP for Oxford University, said this of a
more experienced House of Commons: 'You could hardly
mention any subject without some Member shyly coming
forward and confessing that he knows all about it, whether
it is the battle of Waterloo, the keeping of hens, the
geography of Malaya, or the running of a coal mine. For
many years you may have maintained without much
contradiction (in clubs and pubs) that all cows have five
legs. But when you rise to make the same assertion in the
House of Commons, you have to realise that there are 638
other Members, each one of whom may rise, politely or
not, to say that he knows more about cows than you do.'[2]

There is no need here to glamorise the past. There never was a golden age of democracy, although some were undoubtedly less worse than others, and ours belongs at the lower end of the range. A.P. Herbert himself described the Parliament of 1945, his last, as 'the rude Parliament', and quoted a Tory surveying the rising tide of new Labour MPs pouring into it: 'They look like a lot of damned constituents!'[3] I would like to be proved wrong, but I have a feeling that, 60 years on, today's Parliament will be seen to have surpassed the rude Parliament and to have plumbed new depths of ruthlessness and frenzy – and just as much within parties as between them. It has certainly plumbed new depths of disrepute. That is because the professional politicians who represent us will do whatever it takes to keep their seats. They will vote for measures that they privately oppose, or against measures that they privately support, placate the whips at all costs, and even urge unity while conspiring against the leadership if they feel their majorities threatened – for if they lose their seats they will be literally unemployable. The dole queue awaits them, or at best an ill-paid sinecure on a think-tank. The MPs of 1945 had jobs to go back to if the voters turned against them. Their heirs and successors do not.

It is no accident that the free spirits within the political parties, who will risk their careers by speaking their minds, do not have to depend on politics to earn a living. Examples on the Tory side are Richard Shepherd (one of John Major's 'bastards'), whose family runs a successful business, and on the Labour side Bob Marshall-Andrews, a barrister who has used his position in Parliament to call repeatedly for his leader's resignation. He also had the distinction, in the general election of 2005, of conceding defeat in his Medway constituency before it actually happened – and it never did happen; for he beat his opponent, whose name was Reckless, by 213 votes. Mr Marshall-Andrews was so out of favour with his own party that the seat he held was the only one which it wouldn't have minded losing.

The new politics is not only more professional than the old, but increasingly drained of ideology and in some cases even belief. In 1945, government and opposition were divided by more than the two swords'-length of carpet between them. They represented labour against capital, socialism against free enterprise, reform against the status quo – whichever way you put it, there were real and tribal political differences between them. Most of today's Labour MPs are no longer socialist. Most of today's Tories have no intention of dismantling the welfare state. The differences between the parties, with the exception of the Scottish and Welsh nationalists, are more managerial than doctrinal. (I except Northern Ireland, which was and always will be a political law unto itself.) Elections are fought over a narrower middle ground, of the level of taxation, the delivery of public services, immigration, the European question, the protection of the people from a variety of threats ranging from terrorism to global warming, and occasionally the wisdom of embarking on foreign wars. Of course, there are still opinionated people in Parliament, believing passionately in their unique ability to contribute to the common good and the irreparable harm that will be done by the party opposite. In their view, against all evidence to the contrary, one party has the monopoly of wisdom and the others the monopoly of folly. That is the way the game has always been played. But, rather as in the 18th century, it is now about power, patronage and personality. This doesn't diminish the mock hostilities of the Commons or what one MP described as 'a concerto of nastiness and imbecile yelling'. It does mean that what most MPs want in a party leader is not the champion of a particular point of view, still less a class warrior, but a vote-winner able to help them secure their seats. It came as no surprise, therefore, that it was not a group of disaffected Labour Cabinet ministers but second-term 'young Turks' who tried to bring down the most electorally successful leader in their party's history.

There is a further creeping tendency in today's politics which was not present in yesterday's: the growing power and isolation of the premiership. Partly it was something done *by* prime ministers, from Margaret Thatcher onwards, and partly it was something done *to* them. In Tony Blair's case, a faith-based foreign policy proved to be highly combustible, when poured into the crucible of a Downing Street cut off from the real world by the ring of steel that, literally and figuratively, surrounds a prime minister whether waking, sleeping or travelling, and whether he wants it or not. Even his weekly visit to the Commons becomes an exercise in heavily-armed and armoured close protection. And an election campaign is run on a secret schedule. Before ever the 'war on terror' was launched, the IRA campaign included a mortar attack on Downing Street launched from a pick-up truck just off Whitehall. The security gates and road blocks went up. Long gone are the days when ordinary citizens could stand in the street at the heart of their government, or the prime minister could travel in an ordinary railway carriage with just a policeman and a secretary for company, and not so much as a spin doctor along for the ride. Today he enjoys power without freedom. He is institutionally remote and separate, denied everyday contact with normal people more than anyone else in the country except the royal family, who have at least got each other to talk to. It is virtually impossible for a 21st-century prime minister not to be out of touch both physically and politically.

As a former Downing Street adviser explained it: 'The world stage is an intoxicating place and performing on it becomes much more absorbing than the domestic agenda. It is at that point that the political fingertips that got you to the top begin to lose their sensitivity.' The rise and fall of Tony Blair, our Plantagenet prime minister, were the extreme example of this.

I once spoke to a former holder of the office who admitted to knowing more about the state of the world after leaving 10 Downing Street than actually while living there. Forget that stuff about all political careers ending in tears: politics is the only profession in which success can be a burden and failure a liberation. I certainly felt happier as a candidate in defeat than in victory. Imagine the sense of relief, at the level of prime minister, when the ordeal is over. The close protection regime for former premiers is moderate: Ted Heath's bodyguards used to keep him company at the pub. There is time to reflect; no troublesome back-benchers to win over; no rubber chicken dinners to attend (except for a very substantial fee); no standing ovations to be milked from a reluctant conference; no hateful headlines or cruel cartoons; no need to reason with people you don't give a damn for; no need to stand at the despatch box ever again. The doors of world leaders are still open, the welcomes are as warm as ever for a former member of the club, but without an agenda, a dispute to settle, a deadline to meet, a communiqué to agree, a state-ment to make to the House of Commons or the next morning's *Daily Beast* to worry about.

One explanation for the disappointments of New

Labour's first decade was that the Prime Minister, isolated and under all these pressures, was driven back onto his inner circle and his battery of unsupported convictions. His former foreign policy adviser, Sir Stephen Wall, wrote this of his predicament at the time of the fighting in Lebanon in the summer of 2006:

> In their bunker, leaders become isolated from the world. Pressure, isolation and fatigue undermine good judgement. But the over-riding reason for Blair's loss of moral authority is Blair's conviction that he has to hitch the United Kingdom to the chariot of the United States president. 'What kind of ceasefire?' Blair asks. One that stopped the horror, even for 24 hours, would be a start.[4]

His self-belief, and his mastery of politics as a performing art, also made him an extraordinarily difficult man to dislodge. He was in his way as great a communicator as Ronald Reagan. The difference was that he ran the government that bore his name and Ronald Reagan did not: for eight years in Washington I observed a curious reversal of the law of diminishing returns – the less Reagan did, the more successful he was. (The exception was the inattention that led to the Iran–Contra scandal in his second term.) Tony Blair's communication skills, by contrast, were both the making and the unmaking of him. They propelled him to the highest office but kept him there too long. An astute observer was Britain's former ambassador to Moscow, Sir Rodric Braithwaite:

> In spite of the disasters he has wreaked abroad, in spite of the growing scandal and incoherence of his

performance at home, Mr Blair is still a consummate politician. How else can one explain the failure of his party to do the decent thing and get rid of him? How else does it still appear as though he alone controls the timing and circumstances of his departure?[5]

He wished of course to control them both. And so the soap opera resumed.

*As the time for his abdication approached, the King grew ever more reluctant that the Pretender should succeed him. So he cast around among his courtiers for one who might make the challenge. His eye fell upon the Marquis of Miliband, an aspiring and capable young baron, who was thought to entertain royal ambitions for some time in the future. The King's friends let it be known through divers messengers that if the Marquis were to enter the fray now, he (the King) would be by no means displeased, but believed that with the summoning up of the blood and straining of every sinew, the Marquis might find the Crown within his reach. Plots were laid to blacken the Pretender's reputation and question his management of the Privy Purse. The conspiracy was supported by the rabble of scribes and soothsayers, who in the nature of their murky trade preferred clashes to coronations. The Duke of Norwich re-entered the fray, also urging a challenger to step forward. The Pretender wearily gathered his clans around him. He wondered if there could be any end to the perfidy of the King.*

## TRANSITION TIME

Then the people spoke and the insubstantial pageant faded. The soap opera ended suddenly and abruptly, shunted off the schedules by the news – and the news was of an implosion of Labour support. The New Labour project lasted for ten years almost to the day. Its dawn was 2 May 1997, when it carried all before it – remember that time of 'hope beyond ordinary imagining'? Its dusk was the evening of 4 May 2007, when it lost the Scottish election to the SNP. Its nightfall was the end of the Blair premiership on 27 June 2007. The party's weakness strengthened the Chancellor's claim to the succession. With the ship going down, the crew stopped fighting each other. So deep was the crisis and so troubled the party that no one dared challenge Gordon Brown for its leadership, except two no-hope candidates of the left who lacked enough supporters to enter the contest. David Miliband was not to be persuaded. Charles Clarke decided against standing. So did John Reid, no friend of the Chancellor, who resigned as Home Secretary on Tony Blair's departure.

The electoral landscape that the new prime minister looked out on was not quite the no man's land that faced the Conservatives after their defeat ten years earlier, but the prospects it offered were not much more hopeful either. In the elections of 2007 the Labour vote, at 26 per cent, was down to its bedrock. This was beyond the usual mid-term blues. The party shed council seats like autumn leaves. It was no longer the dominant force in Wales. And it lost Scotland for the first time in 50 years. The victory of the SNP in the Scottish parliamentary election was a vote not for independence but for honest politics. According to every available measure of opinion, most people north of the border still did not favour the break-up of the United Kingdom: two-thirds of them voted for parties that opposed it. But on the driving issues of public trust in public life – the Iraq war and the sale of peerages – the Scottish Nationalists had a better record than any of the mainstream parties. Labour's defeat was entirely self-inflicted. They could easily have averted it if they had paid due attention to the promise – 'We will clean up politics' – that brought them to power in the first place. But they did not. Politics remained conspicuously uncleansed. And the events of this transition time raised serious questions about the state of British democracy.

The first had to do with the handover of power in Downing Street. The prime minister is no longer first among equals, but more like the king of a court. The Americans have checks and balances – not always successful in time of war – to rein in the monarchical tendencies of their head of government. The British do not. As the Great Mistake on Iraq showed so clearly, when the prime minister is determined to have his way, the House of Commons retreats before him; the Cabinet bends to his will; even the law is adjusted to conform to his interpretation of it. So great is the concentration of power in Downing Street that its transfer in the summer of 2007 was not just from one man but from one government to another. It was regime change. The people at large were not consulted, not even the small proportion of them who were Labour supporters and members of a shrunken and unpopular political party. A decision of great political consequence was taken rather in the manner of the election of a pope, with MPs in the place of cardinals. It was dramatic, historic and managerially effective because the pulse of government never skipped a beat. Nor were the Conservatives well placed to object (although they tried), because they had done the same in 1990 when they ousted one prime minister and installed another without consulting anyone but themselves. But it was not in any real sense democratic. It was something done to the people rather than by them.

The transfer of power behind closed doors, however

undemocratic, was at least traditional: it was the way politicians did things. Much more alarming was the scandal of the miscounting of votes in the elections to the Scottish Parliament. More than 100,000 of them, 9 per cent of those cast, were declared invalid. There were a number of reasons for this. One was the confusing nature of the ballot papers themselves: people had to understand three different voting systems (two for the Parliament and one for local councils) in the same polling booth. Tens of thousands of postal votes were delayed or went missing. Computers crashed. The electronic counting of votes failed spectacularly. And unlike the old hand counting of votes, the computers' decisions could not be overridden, in the presence of the returning officer, by a common-sense agreement between the parties. In Edinburgh Central 1,501 papers were rejected by the machinery, in Glasgow Baillieston the total was 1,850 and in Glasgow Shettleston it was 2,035. In some constituencies the number of spoiled papers exceeded the winning candidate's majority, in others it was greater than those cast for established political parties. The outcome was a disgrace and a humiliation. If it had happened in a third-world country, international observers might well have concluded that the election had been fraudulent or stolen. We expect it in Harare and Lagos, but not in Edinburgh and Glasgow. After the Scottish experience, Robert Mugabe's offer to send observers to the British general election of 2005 did not seem quite so fanciful.

Before we preach democracy to others we could at least try it ourselves.

## CHAPTER FIFTEEN

# RESTORING TRUST

*It was our fault, and a very great fault – and now we must
put it to use.*
*There were forty million reasons for failure, and not a single
excuse.*

Rudyard Kipling, 'The Lesson'

### 'TIME TO MOVE ON'

The normal mistakes that governments make can be
corrected with a ministerial shuffle, a touch on the rudder,
a discreet U-turn or an announcement that circumstances
have changed and policies must change with them. But the
decision to go to war in Iraq was not a normal mistake. It
was a blunder of epic and historical proportions. The
gravity of its consequences does not diminish, but increases,
with the passage of time. It will continue to increase for at
least as long as those responsible remain in a state of denial.
Iraq is in ruins, but our own democracy is also damaged.

Richard Horton, the editor of *The Lancet*, which estimated the true scale of the Iraqi casualties as accurately as
they could be estimated, observed: 'The best hope we can
have from our terrible misadventure is that a new political

and social movement will grow to overturn the politics of humiliation.' He said that on the same day that General Peter Schoomaker, the US Army Chief of Staff, announced that there would be no reduction in American force levels in Iraq for at least three years: 'This is not a prediction that things are going poorly or better. It's just that I have to have enough ammo in the magazine that I can continue to shoot as long as they want us to shoot.'[1] And then the Americans decided to send another 21,500 soldiers, as if Vietnam held no lessons for them. To go on shooting is the strategy that failed. It achieved nothing in the past but to separate us from our friends and embolden our enemies. There is no mystery to this: it is what happens in a war among the people. High explosive does not change minds. And reinforcing failure is never an option.

One of the British government's catchphrases, as invasion turned to civil war, was that it was time in our domestic politics to draw a line under it and move on. But lines don't just draw themselves. They have to be drawn *with* something. The obvious instruments would be an inquiry or an apology. For years it ruled out an inquiry: there were too many reputations at stake – indeed, an entire legacy – but there will have to be one in the end. And only twice did it even hint at the shadow of an apology. Once was in Tony Blair's resignation speech in May 2007, when he admitted to mistakes without specifying them. The other time was in his address to the US Congress in July 2003, thanking his hosts for the Congressional Medal of Honour, which for one reason and another he never actually collected while he was still in office: 'If we were wrong, we will have destroyed a threat that, at the least, is responsible for inhuman carnage and suffering. That is something that I am confident history will forgive.'[2] It was a good time to be talking of forgiveness. That was the day when the government scientist Dr David Kelly was hounded to death in one way or another.

Along with the change of leader there will come, because it has to come, a change in the style of leadership. Government by one-man-band is profoundly dangerous. David Blunkett's diaries tell us that there were heated discussions in the Cabinet before and during the war in Iraq (although others dispute that – 'wouldn't say boo to a goose' was one insider's characterisation of the Cabinet); and that the Prime Minister's judgement was called into question to the point where he protested: 'Look, the management hasn't lost its marbles. We do know these things. We are not going to rush in.' But the language he used was revealing. He was the management, his colleagues were the workforce on the shop floor, and the decision to go to war was entirely his. He had not taken it with the Cabinet in 2003, but privately in March or April the year before. The likeliest date was March 2002, when military equipment earmarked for Iraq was held back from Afghanistan. *This also undermined trust in public life.*

After a mistake of that magnitude, the new leaders of both main political parties are bound to adopt a more collegial style. They are aware of the loss of trust that resulted from the stampede to war; because, whatever was said at the time, the British and Americans did rush in. No conceivable British government in the future will park its foreign policy so unconditionally up the Potomac. The former Home Secretary admitted in his diaries that the government misjudged the mood of the nation: actually, it paid no attention to the mood of the nation. David Cameron and Gordon Brown were reluctant supporters of the war; and according to Mr Blunkett's account, Gordon

Brown signed on to it only in the week before it began; if he had not, he would have been ousted from the Treasury. He complained of being kept in the dark and said that he learned more from the press than from meetings of the War Cabinet. That's no way to run a business, never mind a war.[3]

Political failures can be so calamitous as to become, in time, self-correcting. As Robin Cook observed after his resignation from the Cabinet over the war, the next time it happens the case for war will be more thoroughly tested by a more sceptical Commons. Indeed, he wrote his own epitaph, in words engraved on his tombstone in Edinburgh: 'I may not have succeeded in halting the war, but I did secure the right of Parliament to decide on war.'

There are encouraging signs too of a change of politicians' attitudes to the military. I have set down what I know from personal experience, and from what those in the front lines have told me: the feelings of the armed forces, from Iraq to Afghanistan and beyond, of being over-committed and over-stretched, under-valued and under-equipped, ill-directed and ill-used. These people are not pacifists or barrack room lawyers. They are as far from the awkward squad as it is normally possible to be. Their natural instinct is to bash on regardless and make the best of things, even when the resources, as in Afghanistan, are perilously inadequate for the task. If you meet them, you are aware of keeping the company of the best of British – as you are not, for instance, on the floor of the House of Commons.

So it is not enough for our leaders to lay wreaths at the Cenotaph or to stand at the despatch box and praise the courage of the men and women who serve in the armed forces. That is easy and costs nothing. The serving men and women see through it in our time just as Kipling did in his:

'But it's "thin red line of 'eroes" when the drums begin to roll.' In the matter of being a forgotten army, Bill Slim's 14th Army in Burma in the Second World War has had its multiple heirs and successors in the British armed forces of the late 20th and early 21st centuries. The deployments to Basra in Iraq and Helmand in Afghanistan have been their hardest tours of duty in a generation, because of shortages of equipment as well as failures of policy. The scandal of the war in Iraq was not only that it was fought on a falsehood, but that having been fought on a falsehood, the means with which to fight it never fully caught up with those at the sharp end who had to do the fighting. The cheese-paring procurement policy of 'just enough just in time' cost lives. The fiction was maintained that the decision to go to war was taken almost on the eve of battle in March 2003. In fact it was taken long before. So for political reasons the troops were deployed and the ships were loaded after they should have been. Most of the war-fighting platforms, the armour and artillery, arrived in time, but not the ancillary equipment that should have gone with them. This applied especially to body armour, which really can make the difference between life and death. In 1991, in the first Gulf War, it was delivered to the troops the day before it was needed. (And not very efficiently: we were 'embedded' with the Irish Hussars at the time and the BBC's cameraman Nigel Bateson, who was a heavyweight South African, had to make do with a bantamweight's flak jacket, which was the only one on offer.) In the second Gulf War, some of the armour arrived after the fighting began. Lives were unnecessarily lost as a result.

The first British soldier to die in March 2003 was Sergeant Steve Roberts of the 2nd Royal Tank Regiment. Because he served in an armoured unit he was ordered, on the eve of battle, to hand his flak jacket over to an infantryman. But the tank did not protect him outside its turret, when he tried to quell a demonstration near Basra and was killed by 'friendly fire'. His wife Samantha brought a legal action for negligence against the Ministry of Defence, which ended three-and-a-half years later in an out-of-court settlement. 'It's horrible to put a price on someone's life,' she said, 'but sometimes money is the only language people listen to.'[4] At the inquest on his death, in December 2006, the coroner Andrew Walker concluded:

> To send soldiers into a combat zone without the appropriate basic equipment is, in my view, unforgivable and inexcusable and represents a breach of trust the soldiers have in those in government.

And it got worse. The inquest was told that an emergency request for 37,000 sets of body armour, submitted by a defence logistics team in September 2002, was not acted on by the Ministry of Defence for fear of telegraphing that Britain was preparing for war in Iraq while appearing to negotiate for peace at the United Nations. Sergeant Roberts was a casualty of that deception.[5]

All that was in the past. Too late for some, the government learned to deal better with the armed forces. In October 2006, under the pressure of relentlessly bad publicity, including desperate emails from the troops in southern Afghanistan, it announced a tax-free bonus of £2,240 for soldiers serving a six-month tour of duty in Iraq, Afghanistan and the Balkans. The money was no more than they would need to pay their tax bills when they were as far away from taxable territory as anywhere on the planet, but it was the gesture that mattered and that made a world of difference to those whose lives were on the line. They could begin to believe, for the first time in years, that they would no longer be taken for granted. Unlike the missing body armour, the bonus was just enough and just in time. It had a significant impact on morale.

There has also been an important changing of the guard at the level of the chiefs of staff of the armed services. Unlike so many of their predecessors, they are not out-and-out cold warriors. They have not, or at least not recently, played war games through the Fulda Gap in a still-divided Germany. They have not commanded the blue forces against the red in an army staff college that was crumbling then and now no longer exists. They are not (we must hope) 'safe pairs of hands' who have put 'all the ticks in boxes'; these were the qualities which used to be required for peacetime promotion. They have served in and around the collapsed states of the new world disorder, and have the medals to show for it. They know the world as the service chiefs of an earlier generation, and the politicians of today, do not. They have learned from the past and are not of a mind to allow a debacle on their watch. They have seen for themselves the disastrous results of attempting too much with too little. If presented for a second time with a dodgy dossier or shifting legal grounds for an illegal war, it is probable that at least one of them, and maybe all of them, would resign rather than comply. My favoured candidate for this distinction – and I picked him long before he embarrassed the politicians over Iraq – would be the Chief of the General Staff, Sir Richard Dannatt, formerly of the Green Howards, a thoughtful Christian soldier and good officer. When he was a brigadier in Bosnia in 1995, I once described him as 'the grand master of smoke and mirrors' for rushing his troops around the country so as to make a small force seem like a large one. But as the most senior commander of the British Army, over-committed in Iraq and Afghanistan, he was in a situation where smoke and mirrors would not work any more; and he knew that better than most.

General Dannatt's call for the withdrawal of British forces from Iraq 'sometime soon' sent shock waves through the political establishment but had his own soldiers cheering him on. Here was a general who dared to speak his mind: 'Honesty is what it is about. The truth will out. We have got to speak the truth. Leaking and spinning, at the end of the day, are not helpful.'[6] The army was breaking under the strain; its most senior officer had a duty to make this known; and the government of the day, having turned a deaf ear to his warnings, and those of his predecessors, did not dare to dismiss him when he uttered them in public. Instead, he was asked to wind his neck in, which is military parlance for desisting and staying silent. He gave fewer interviews, but within the Ministry his neck remained unwound. He went on campaigning to keep the welfare of his soldiers at the top of the agenda.

What Dannatt did, as an infantryman, was to take a hill – and then, having taken it, to find that he had to take another beyond it. He took that too, in the face of some opposition, and could not be dislodged. His soldiers knew that, and admired him all the more.

A senior officer in Iraq, a strong supporter of General Dannatt, traced the malaise back to the crucial period between the turn of the century and the war in Iraq. The top brass on watch then had let everyone down. In his bullet-scarred headquarters in the desert he told me: 'Four or five years ago was the time for someone at the top of the chain of command to fall on his sword. Not only did he not fall on it, he did not even draw it out of the sheath. We are where we are today because of that.'

## TIME FOR REFORM

One thing remains constant. In all our politics, reform follows scandal as surely as day follows night. If there is any point in scandals it is to create the necessary conditions for reform. Without them, nothing happens. Only after things have got worse do they get better. The scandals of the Tory years led to the formation of the Committee on Standards in Public Life, a code of conduct for MPs and a new attempt to persuade the Commons to set its own house in order. Although it was initially frustrated by the poison of partisanship, that is no reason not to keep trying. The scandals of the Labour years cry out for a new season of reform, and there are signs that the politicians themselves are coming to understand that. They do not enjoy being held in lower esteem than journalists and estate agents. They would like to enjoy a measure of respect from those who vote for them, and even from those who don't.

Once in my parliamentary days, when I was doing the rounds of the Tatton constituency, a man came up to me in the street with a mystified expression on his face. He thought that he knew me from somewhere.

'Weren't you that TV war reporter once?' he asked. I had to admit that I was.

'So what are you doing now?'

'Actually I'm your Member of Parliament', I answered.

'I'm so sorry,' he said, 'I didn't know that you were out of a job.'

The otherness of politics baffles people. So does the perceived mendacity of it.

The new leaders are paying serious attention to the advice of the Committee on Standards. The old ones not only ignored it but attacked it through their placemen and planned to demolish it. Sir Alistair Graham had to endure a back-bench campaign against him similar to the ordeal by tea-room gossip that undermined Elizabeth Filkin. The parties' own musketeers do them more damage than any outside regulator, and they still don't understand it. Surely by now they should have learned from past mistakes. But they have not. Clever people are so often more stupid than stupid people; and that certainly applies in politics.

1605 was a year that speaks to us directly across the centuries. It was not only the year when Shakespeare made an unanswerable case, in *Henry V*, about where the blame lies for casualties in an unjustified war – 'Now if these men do not die well, it will be a black matter for the King that led them to it'[7]; the black matter of the time was an unpopular expeditionary war in Ireland. It was also the year when the House of Commons passed a resolution making it a high crime for an MP to accept money for the 'promotion of any matter whatsoever'. The standards of conduct have risen and fallen since then. Over the past twenty years they have fallen shamefully. Now the time has come for them to rise again. Reform is not only due but overdue. It is also inevitable, because politics is self-correcting and we cannot go on as we have been. This is the political pendulum that matters: swinging not between right and left but between the politicians who can be trusted and those who cannot. The two main parties in the 21st century contain striking examples of both. But we have reached a point where the scope for improvement, in the conduct and reputation of MPs, is surely greater than at any time since 1832.

The reform will come from two directions. One is bottom up from the people, demanding from their MPs that they perform their duties in an honest and straightforward way, and punishing those who fail to do that with de-selection or defeat at the polls: this is much more possible at a time of weaker allegiances than it was in the age of mass political parties. Dr Richard Taylor in Wyre Forest and Peter Law and Dai Davies in Blaenau Gwent have shown what can be done when the people lose their faith in party politics and those who represent it. They turn elsewhere, to someone they can trust. When the parties fail, the Independents have an occasional, but vital, part to play.

The other direction of pressure is from the top down. MPs and ministers are obliged to set an example. That is why leadership is one of the seven principles they sign on to: 'Holders of public office should promote and support these principles by leadership and example.' It is hard to do that when we have slithered in ten years from cash-for-questions to cash-for-peerages; when veteran MPs campaign for a 22 per cent pay increase, to be voted for, of course, by themselves, bringing them into disrepute and widening still further the gap between them and their constituents; when, to escape public scrutiny, they cynically and disgracefully try to exempt themselves from the Freedom of Information Act; when their salaries and expenses cost the taxpayers an average of £200,000 each; when they charge 20 pence a mile for riding a bicycle; when they spend up to £25,000 in postage in a single year, most of it in self-promotion, and then vote themselves a £10,000 'communications allowance' on top of that; when the parties expect the public to fund their activities on an ever more lavish scale; when party conferences take on the aspect of a trade fair; when ministers in grace and favour homes still enjoy the extra benefits of the parliamentary housing allowance for their London lodgings; when expense claims go virtually unchecked; when the MPs' gold-plated pension scheme is protected against the chill winds of the market-place; when there is absolutely no penalty to be paid for idleness; or when the holders of public office, at the highest level, take their holidays in the overseas villas of millionaires – especially where the hosts might have a financial interest in winning the favour of 10 Downing Street, in a matter of copyright law or media regulation or whatever the advantage may be. As I once observed in the House of Commons, to an unappreciative audience, the appearance of impropriety can do almost as much damage to public trust as the impropriety itself.

It doesn't even *look* like the sort of place where honest people do business. The House of Commons, the elected end of the Palace of Westminster, has taken on the aspect of a fortress. This is partly the effect of the unsightly concrete blocks that have been put in place to protect it against car bombs, and the thick glass barrier that seals off the public gallery to save MPs from missile-throwers. They may feel safer, but they are also more remote. And Parliament is a fortress in a wider sense. Its members guard their privileges jealously. Its private areas are a sanctuary where they are safe from public view. Liveried servants give it the air of an 18th-century gentleman's club, a stronghold of wealth and power safe from the mob. It is easy enough for an MP in this comfort zone to regard himself as no end of a fellow, and his constituents as frankly a distraction and a bit of a nuisance. The diaries of Alan Clark attest to this: 'The sheer hell of being an MP.'[8] (Which did not stop him from seeking and winning re-election.) There is nowhere in London, except perhaps Buckingham Palace, more totally cut off from the real world. Maybe that was why Alan Clark, who lived in a castle, enjoyed it so much. And, appropriately for a fortress, its symbol is a portcullis.

## THE POWER OF PENITENCE

We are adrift in mid-river among swirling currents with rapids ahead, and in the most dangerous times since 1945, with the possible exception of the Cuban missile crisis of 1962. We are threatened by the unprecedented perils of the 21st century: global warming, nuclear proliferation, Islamic terrorism and – no less dangerous than these – the rise to power of the professional politician and the illusion that disputes between countries, and within them, can be resolved by armed conflict at an acceptable cost. Sometimes that happened in the past and sometimes it did not. Those times are over. The old panaceas no longer apply. The politicians live in a dreamland of their own, like Disney-world with gun turrets. The option of 'Give war a chance' has been tried and has not worked. The Americans are still trying it and it is still not working. The greater the reinforcement, the greater the failure. They haven't got the message yet, but it is coming at them loud and clear from wherever they put boots on the ground: even their super-power is limited and warfare no longer delivers the results that they expect of it. The rules of the war game have changed.

Upstream of us lie events that have shaped the world we live in; they have led to avoidable consequences and were not well dealt with by those who governed us. Downstream of us, if we negotiate the rapids, will lie other events which we cannot control but can influence and move towards peace rather than war, or a better rather than a worse outcome, according to our manner of dealing with them. There is no magic in this. It is just common sense. If the New Labour years have taught us anything, it is that experience is a better guide than instinct, that faith-based policy-making is a recipe for disaster, that the denial of evident truth is an offence against democracy, and that we cannot afford a future like our past.

The politicians themselves have recognised this. Of course we have been promised a new politics before, most notoriously in 1997, and it turned out to be the old politics redecorated with bells and whistles and Cool Britannia and glittering promises and surfeits of spin and a great cascade of peerages. They promised a clean-up. This time they have to mean it. Gordon Brown has pledged that 'The executive will be more humble about the power it has in future' – including, specifically, its power of patronage. That means taking the granting of peerages – if any peers are to be appointed in a reformed House of Lords – out of the hands of the prime minister and other party leaders. It means a return to cabinet government and parliamentary account-ability. It means the prime minister showing up in the House more than once a week, and sometimes even voting. It means reining in the suffocating power of the whips. It means separating the Attorney General's political and judicial functions. It means respecting or reinventing the Committee on Standards in Public Life. It means appoint-ing an independent figure to investigate allegations of misconduct by government ministers. It means renouncing the doctrine of pre-emptive warfare. It means forswearing the notion that the prime minister is also de facto commander-in-chief. It means visiting the wounded and paying attention to the chiefs of staff of the armed forces.

It means enacting the Military Covenant. It means (in point of symbolism) living cheerfully but frugally, dealing with people equally and keeping the oligarchs, both domestic and foreign, as much at arm's length as possible. It means wiping the slate and starting all over again.

In all the Abrahamic faiths there is a special place for the confession and forgiveness of sins. In Christianity and Judaism it lies at the heart of man's relationship with God. To Muslims, Allah the All-merciful has the power to forgive the sins of the truly penitent. Yet whoever heard of a penitent politician? They are a rare breed and very few of them ever exercised real power. A reluctance to confess even to ordinary human error is one of the least attractive features of the political animal. Tony Blair has shown it to an extreme degree. Yet there is a precedent for it. The post-apartheid South Africans needed their Truth and Reconciliation Commission to help their new society to make a new start. So did the Bosnian Serbs with their recognition of the reality of the Srebrenica massacre in 1995. It took them nine years, but they got there. 'We have reached historic perceptions,' said the head of their investigating commission, 'and we will have to face ourselves.'[9] In both cases, a reckoning was necessary.

So why should the British and Americans also not face themselves? When the error was on the scale of the war in Iraq, *and still not admitted,* then the ordinary voters turned away in despair. The political process had failed them. They knew from the start that the war was illegal. They knew it was waged on dubious grounds and against their wishes. They turned out a million strong and were ignored. They guessed – because every expert prediction told them – that it would end in limitless bloodshed and destruction. As in Kipling's time, there were forty million reasons for failure and not a single excuse. The outcome deserves an epitaph:

*Here lies the fame of Tony Blair,*
*Who sent his soldiers everywhere.*
*His exercise of power was regal;*
*The war, however, was illegal.*

The former Prime Minister, who dominated British politics for ten years, has an opportunity now which, were he to grasp it, would secure his reputation as not just the most successful vote-winner in his party's history but also a great and good man. It is to admit the magnitude of the mistake; to track back along the trail of decision-making from 9/11 to the invasion of Iraq; to explain why the military option was chosen when others were still available; and to express at least a measure of contrition. Most politicians' memoirs are exercises in self-justification. If his, by contrast, were to be among other things an act of atonement, they would soften the harshness of history's verdict and allow a clearer view of his real achievements, especially in Northern Ireland. It was his great misfortune that his time in office coincided with that of a blinkered, baffled and undistinguished American president who believed that the wars he embarked on were the fulfilment of God's will; and who should have been challenged, but wasn't. No one was better placed to challenge him than the British prime minister. On the third anniversary of the war in Iraq, the theologian Paul Oestreicher wrote to Tony Blair along these lines:

It is not sufficient to say the obvious, that history and God will judge you. ... You can still save your honour and your credibility, by admitting to an error of huge

proportions, although made with good intent. ...
Penitence, also the mark of a Christian, is something
both private and profound.[10]

What a prime minister cannot do, an ex-prime minister
can at least consider doing. It would be a waste and a
tragedy if a man of such gifts, leaving office at the height of
his powers, were to spend the remainder of his years
justifying the unjustifiable and in some sense embroidering
a falsehood and living a lie. He has it in him, with grace
and courage, to do so much more than that.

Did anyone ever do so? Yes, Robert McNamara did. He
was Defence Secretary to Presidents Kennedy and Johnson
and the principal architect of the Vietnam war. He was the
Donald Rumsfeld of his time. The parallels are eerily exact.
He served for a presidential term and a half. He was a hard-
charging technocrat who thought he knew more than his
generals about winning a war. He never grasped the gravity
of the task or the nature of the enemy. He never knew how
much he didn't know – what Rumsfeld described as the
'unknown unknowns' (and Rumsfeld did not invent them:
they are actually called the 'unk-unks' by the Pentagon's
deep thinkers). He threw in reinforcements, division by
division and year after year, especially in 1965, because he
believed that a military solution was possible in war just as a
management solution was possible in the motor industry.
(He was a former president of the Ford Motor Company.)
And he failed, because it wasn't.

Then 30 years later he wrote a book explaining the
failure – a book that he found it extremely painful to write.
*In Retrospect* was an act of expiation. 'How did it happen?'
he asked. 'What lessons can be drawn from our experience?
... We were wrong, terribly wrong. We owe it to future

generations to explain why.' Some of the mistakes resound with special force today, for they were step by step and surge by surge the same as those made 40 years later in Iraq:

> If we had asked more questions back then, if only we had looked at more options, if only we had raised the discussion to a higher level, perhaps there would be fewer names on the memorial wall today.[11]

There is not yet a memorial wall to those who have died in Iraq. It is still too soon. The book is still open. The numbers of the fallen continue to rise. We have no idea of the size of wall we shall need. Iraq's post-war prospects are immeasurably darker than Vietnam's. There isn't even a post-war yet. We too owe it to future generations to explain why. We cannot do so without a full accounting by those responsible. There is no other way.

# OPENING A FURROW

Shortly after this book was published, I received a letter from an ex-soldier in Suffolk who had been given it as an 83rd birthday present. He had fought in Normandy as a Bren gunner with the 1st/6th Queen's Royal Regiment, and like so many survivors of the campaign had been badly wounded and brought home on a stretcher. He knew the costs of war, having borne them himself. He wrote: 'You have put your hand to the plough and opened a furrow.' He continued ominously: 'There may be a price to pay!' I cannot judge the straightness of the furrow. I lined up the markers as best I could, as my father did before me. It is as true a furrow as I could open.

Towards the end of the first edition, I wrote of the importance of the admission of error in restoring public trust in public life. But now I must confess to my own mistake: I hoped too much. After all we had been through, I really believed in the possibility of a new beginning, in which the political parties would not continue as they had been, but understand that if they lost trust they lost legitimacy and that they would therefore pay serious attention to their reputations and to their watchdog, the Committee on Standards in Public Life. I was wrong about that. After Sir

Alistair Graham was let go because, like Elizabeth Filkin before him, he had dared to be a champion of honest politics, his committee was set adrift for seven months before a new chairman was appointed. Also, after the years of frauds and falsehoods that had brought the whole process into disrepute, it was reasonable to suppose that New Labour had learned its lesson from the donor scandals from which it had suffered, all the way from Bernie Ecclestone to cash-for-peerages, that the intersection of cash and politics is always dangerous ground. It should have done, but it didn't. The scandals rolled on relentlessly one after the other, some of them involving senior ministers who had themselves been propelled into office by Tory sleaze.

In November 2007 it emerged that Labour's third-largest donor was David Abrahams, a property developer from Tyneside. There was nothing wrong with that – property developers tend to have an interest in local government and can be as generous and public-spirited as anyone. Mr Abrahams was so well regarded in Labour circles that he was rewarded with a front-row seat at Tony Blair's farewell to his Sedgefield constituency in June 2007. The proximity to power has an allure all of its own. What was wrong – indeed, strictly speaking, illegal – was that his donations of £663,975 over four years had been channelled through friends, associates and their families: a builder, a lawyer and two others, one of whom said that she voted Conservative. The identity of the donor was hidden from view, which was outside the spirit and the letter of the Political Parties, Elections and Referendums Act of 2000. Once again, the government was hung out to dry by the reforms it had introduced. One of those irreparably damaged was Peter Hain, who failed to register £103,000 in donations for his campaign for the Labour Party's deputy leadership, a position that would have been overpriced if he had paid a fiver for it. Some of these contributions were channelled through a mysterious think tank, the Progressive Policies Forum, which apparently existed for no other purpose. It neither thought nor tanked. For all his fundraising, Mr Hain came fifth out of six candidates. And then the police were called in and he had to resign.

Nor were the scandals confined to the Labour Party. In January 2008, the Conservatives offered us déjà vu all over again, when Derek Conway, Ted Heath's successor as MP for Sidcup and Old Bexley, was found to have paid his two sons more than £40,000 of public money while they were full-time students, with no evidence that they did any work for it. If he had been on the payroll of a public corporation or private company he would have been out on the street immediately. But the House of Commons, as usual, took a more lenient view and protected one of its own. He was reprimanded and suspended for a mere ten days. He even remained for a while on the Speaker's Panel of senior MPs who preside over parliamentary business. The usual apologists offered the usual excuses. Mr Conway himself was one of them: 'I still believe I have done nothing wrong', he said. Other abuses thudded onto the doormat almost daily with the morning papers. MPs had used the taxpayers' money to improve their kitchens. They had acquired extra properties for rent. They had paid their children unearned income as a means of dodging inheritance tax. They had pushed every available allowance to the limit. They had done whatever was do-able and then some more. Among the worst offenders were MPs so senior that they set the rules, and so wealthy that they hardly needed their salaries to live on, let alone their expenses.

The racketeering was not exceptional but widespread and routine. The 'few rotten apples' defence was no longer available. The rotten apples were to be found in abundance on both sides of the House. When I spoke out against this, I was quite properly asked whether I had ever employed members of my own family. The answer was yes, that I had. My daughter Melissa was my press officer and my nephew Oliver my policy adviser during the Tatton campaign of 1997. But neither of them was paid a penny. Oliver, who later became a blogger of note and a *Times* columnist and disagrees with me on just about everything under the sun, was among the apologists. He wrote: 'The British polity is far from corrupt.' I found this hard to reconcile with the skimming off of millions of pounds in parliamentary allowances by so-called Honourable Members.

By every available indicator, the public were up in arms against the unabated looting of taxpayers' money. And the Speaker, who had himself employed family members, ordered a 'root and branch review' of parliamentary allowances by a few hand-picked backbenchers. These included MPs of the old guard who were notorious for their creative accounting and their resistance to reform. One had claimed a quad bike as a parliamentary expense. Another had played a part in dismissing the Commissioner for Standards who had made them all uncomfortable. Poachers and gamekeepers slid back and forth through the same revolving door. This raised the question: what had the politicians learned since the scandals of cash-for-questions more than ten years earlier? About as much as I know about quantum physics, so far as I could see. At the Lord Eldon pub in Knutsford, where a focus group formed itself over a glass of something, I found that these voters of Tatton, who had more experience of sleaze than most, believed that things were even worse than when their MP fell from grace in the 1990s. Some were angry. Others just shrugged their shoulders and turned away.

The cash-for-peerages scandal ended with a verdict of 'not provable'. The Crown Prosecution Service, advised by a government-paid lawyer, concluded that charges could not be brought with a reasonable prospect of securing a conviction. But that was in the nature of the trade. No contracts existed. The thing was done, as it always had been, by whispers and winks in neo-Gothic nooks and crannies: the parties would reward their benefactors, as they always had, in direct proportion to the size of the gift or loan. No rate card could be produced in a court of law: it didn't exist because it didn't need to. Those who aspired to a seat in the Lords could work it out for themselves. The Pugin Room, the red-carpeted frontier between Lords and Commons, was the stock exchange of these deals.

When the dust had settled, Assistant Commissioner Yates appeared before the House of Commons Public Admin-istration Committee. Asked whether he thought there was a trade in honours, he replied with an eloquent pause and a refusal to comment, except to point out that by their very nature these things were difficult to prove: 'They are bargains made in secret, both parties have an absolute interest in making sure those secrets don't come out.'[1] The House of Commons Public Accounts Committee conduc-ted its own inquiry, and recommended that the award of peerages should be taken outside the hands of political parties. Its chairman, Tony Wright, observed that that lack of a prosecution 'has not diminished the damage done to trust in public life'.[2]

It was like a court case without a conviction or acquittal, but ending with a hung jury and a tainted adjournment.

The fix was in. At home and abroad, politics generally slid into disrepute. The government claimed to have been vindicated on cash-for-peerages, just as it had after the Hutton and Butler inquiries on Iraq. Its protestations were not widely believed.

The more we know of the ill-considered decision to go to war in Iraq, the more it appears as the result not just of an individual failure of judgement but of a collective failure of government. Those who could and should have challenged it in the Cabinet, 10 Downing Street, the Foreign Office and the Ministry of Defence, mysteriously failed to do so. The entire system short-circuited. In his generally sympathetic chronicle of the Blair years, Anthony Seldon quotes from an interview with a senior diplomat: 'There was a collective failure of the Chiefs of Staff and the Foreign Office to present a coherent case that would make Blair think again.' The court biographer was especially baffled by the role of Foreign Secretary Jack Straw, whose written reservations seemed to have been entered only for the record: 'To some, his failure to speak out in Cabinet was weak; to others it was a fine demonstration of service.'[3]

In September 2007 the British completed their withdrawal from Basra City, secretly and in the middle of the night, having secured safe passage by agreeing to the release of certain Iraqi prisoners. The operation was planned and executed by the force commander, Major General Graham Binns, who was a practised hand in such matters. He had done something similar once before, as a company commander with the Prince of Wales's Own Regiment of Yorkshire in Gornji Vakuf in Bosnia in 1993. He was forever telling me how they would hold on in their forward operating base – until the moment when they decided not to. He should write a staff college manual on how to escape from untenable positions without casualties or too much loss of face. Whatever else this was, it wasn't a victory. And as usual in this tragic story, the Iraqis suffered disproportionately. In the months after the British left Basra, to be replaced by Shia militias under the rule of the gun, the police chief reported that 42 young women had been executed for 'immoral behaviour': some of them were shot in front of their children.[4]

Further north, in and around Baghdad, the Americans veered between defeat and deadlock. The surge in troop levels under a new commander delivered some initial and welcome successes. Aided by astute deal-making with Sunni leaders opposed to the foreign fighters in their midst, and a general war weariness (most wars tend to lose momentum after about four years), long-term enemies backed off from the carnage and the country was divided along the lines of a soft partition. Only in Iraq would a reduction of sectarian killings from 1,800 to 600 a month be saluted as a 'success story' by the pro-war press. More than 24,000 Iraqis were known to have died in the violence of 2007.[5] If this was success, you had to wonder what on earth failure would look like.

Lt General Ricardo Sanchez, who commanded American troops in Iraq for a year from mid-2003, took advantage of his retirement in 2007 to speak out and describe the Americans' outcome in Iraq as like living a nightmare with no end in sight. He put the blame on US political leaders, whom he called incompetent and corrupted, and said that if they had been in the military they would have faced court martial for dereliction of duty.[6] He named no names. By then he did not need to. And as time went by, the destructive consequences of the invasion spread far beyond the borders of Iraq, recruiting and emboldening jihadists across the region from Algeria to Afghanistan.

Afghanistan also experienced a soft partition along ethnic lines. The central government weakened. The Taliban grew stronger in the Pashtun areas, controlling most of the countryside and engaging the NATO-led forces in pitched battles. Tajiks, Uzbeks and others looked to their traditional leaders and warlords to protect them. I returned to Afghanistan to write a report for UNICEF on the plight of its children – a report that ruffled feathers in some quarters, because it showed things as they were rather than as certain well-intentioned people wished them to be. Children were not only the victims of suicide bombs, but in a few appalling cases tricked into becoming suicide bombers themselves. They were killed for going to school or intimidated into staying away from it. They also suffered on a large scale from the allied bombing campaign. Overstretch led to overkill. Because the British, Canadians and others did not have enough troops on the ground, they were dangerously dependent on air power to hold what they had. The Afghanistan Independent Human Rights Commission documented a battle in Helmand province in June 2007 in which the British and the Taliban fought each other for 48 hours. When it was over, there were no known military casualties on either side, but 27 civilians were killed, including seventeen children.

None of this was reported in the mainstream media. Despite a few brave ventures by individual journalists, Afghanistan like Iraq offered no foothold for free-ranging and independent news-gathering. The embedded coverage of troops in the front line, vivid as it was, was so restricted in scope and necessarily one-sided that it came over as little more than a recruiting movie. It was a tiny, postage stamp-sized image in an otherwise blank big screen. And it enabled the governments concerned to claim they were making progress when in fact they were not. A smokescreen of falsehood settled over the battlefield.

The fundamental problem here, as much in the fighting of unwinnable wars as in the conduct of the MPs who vote for them, is the widening of the gulf dividing Them from Us: not only the government from the governed but, since the miscreants come from both sides of the House, the political class from the people. They (the political class) still don't get it. Listening only to their inner voices, they seem incapable of holding up a mirror and seeing themselves as others see them. The younger MPs, in my view, are even more to blame than the older ones. They should be eager to challenge the customs and practices of the Westminster club. Instead, they seem to be driven by ambition rather than principle. They are inexperienced and untouched by hardship or even a serious exposure to the world outside Westminster. They know nothing of warfare. They are children of their time, which in the emergencies of the early 21st century we can reasonably describe as a comfortable and take-it-all-for-granted time. They have no granite in them, no hinterland or substance or anchorage. They should have lived some more before they represented us. But it is too late now. They made our politics what it is, and sent those soldiers to fight those wars, and some of the blame must be ours because we let them do it. If we want such people to run our lives, all we have to do is nothing, and they are happy to oblige. They are already in place on the back and even the front benches. You don't have to take my word for it. The best witnesses are the Honourable Members themselves – or at least the good apples, the independent-minded who dare to tell the truth about the bad. One of the very best is Gwyneth Dunwoody, MP for Crewe and Nantwich. In December 2007 she denounced a political stitch-up, presented as a local government reform in Cheshire, in terms that shook the rafters of the Westminster village:

> I have been in the House long enough to see the coming and going of many inadequate personalities. I have seen those on both sides of the House who have been promoted for various reasons. I have seen the crawlers. I have seen those who have used sex – there are so many it would take too long to name them. ... I have seen those who demonstrated a great commitment to their own interests, irrespective of the political parties they were supposed to represent. But I have rarely seen a decision such as this [the proposed local government reform] taken with such cynicism and so little respect for the interests of the average voter.[7]

And she was surely right. The damage done to Parliament's reputation is largely self-inflicted, from Neil Hamilton to Derek Conway, and countless others before and after.

Everything connects. As well as the obvious and unprecedented threats out there – of nuclear proliferation, terrorism, climate change, regional wars and the mass migration of peoples – there are three separate and relatively new forces at work in our own society. Each of them would probably be manageable on its own, but together they interact in a peculiarly dangerous and malignant way and threaten all our futures. One is the *stupidification* of the news agenda: foreign news-gathering is dangerous and expensive, so the media retreat into a comfort zone of health scares, celebrity tittle-tattle, 'news you can use' and crime stories – especially the growing phenomenon of necro-news, an obsession with the death or disappearance of girls and young women; splashing around in the froth of this stuff, we do not see the tsunami until it is upon us. Another is the rise of the political class, insouciant to a fault, who seem to believe in nothing much but their own advancement and will do whatever it takes to stay in positions supported by all those lucrative allowances. The third, abetted by the media's myopia and with the political class at its leading edge, is a creeping ignorance about the world beyond the garden fence: the more dangerous it gets, the less we know about it. Hence the easy resort to the military option, the adoption of a *Boy's Own Paper* view of the glory of war and the use of justifying euphemisms like 'hard power', which actually means killing people and blowing things up. The scale of the self-deception is staggering. We are literally fighting blind.

These forces have to be checked and challenged. If they are not, we are sleep-walking towards a catastrophe to which the war in Iraq will have been the merest prelude. And no one else will have done this to us. We shall have done it to ourselves.

# NOTES

**CHAPTER ONE**
1   Speech introducing the Annual Report of the Committee on Standards, 27 March 2007.
2   Labour Party manifesto, 1997.
3   *The Lancet*, 11 October 2006.
4   *The Guardian*, 24 April 2007.

**CHAPTER TWO**
1   Committee on Standards and Privileges Second Report, 21 December 2000.
2   Eighth Report of the Wicks Committee on Standards in Public Life, November 2002.
3   Ibid.
4   *Hansard*, 31 October 2001.
5   *The Guardian*, 14 January 2000.
6   BBC News, 2 March 2006.
7   Downing Street briefing, 23 March 2006.
8   Quoted by Peter Hennessy in *The Guardian*, 28 February 2005.

**CHAPTER THREE**
1   Labour Party manifesto, 1997.
2   *Electoral Reform for Westminster*, by the Electoral Reform Society, 2006.
3   Report of the Commission on Candidate Selection, 2003.

4  *The Times*, 2 September 2005.
5  BBC News, 17 November 2006.
6  *The Guardian*, 'Comment is Free', 17 November 2006.
7  Report of the Commission on Candidate Selection, 2003.
8  *The Guardian*, 1 November 2006.
9  *The Guardian*, 23 April 2007.


**CHAPTER FOUR**
1  *Hansard*, 7 February 2001.
2  BBC News, 18 March 2006.
3  *The Mail on Sunday*, 3 December 2006.
4  *Daily Telegraph*, 18 July 2006.
5  *The Guardian*, 16 January 2007.
6  *Daily Mail*, 15 September 2006.


**CHAPTER FIVE**
1  *Hansard*, 16 February 2000.
2  *The Independent*, 8 April 2006.
3  *The Independent*, 17 July 2006.
4  Dissenting opinion in *Olmstead v. United States*, 1928.
5  *The Times*, 20 March 2006.
6  *The Guardian*, 'Comment is Free', 17 March 2006.
7  Published by HarperPress, 2006.
8  *The Independent*, 19 December 2006.
9  *The Independent*, 16 July 2006.
10 *New Statesman*, 18 December 2006.
11 Eleventh report of the Committee on Standards in Public Life, 18 January 2007.
12 24 January 2006.


**CHAPTER SIX**
1  *Sunday Times*, 22 August 1920.
2  *Hansard*, 24 September 2002.
3  *Hansard*, 22 October 2003.
4  *Hansard*, 22 February 2007.
5  *Hansard*, 18 March 2003.
6  *The Guardian*, 20 October 2005.

7   *Iraq: the Futility of War,* Channel 4, 13 January 2006.

8   *Daily Mail,* 13 October 2006.

9   BBC Dimbleby Lecture, 6 December 2006.

10  *Notes of Conversations with the Duke of Wellington,* by the Earl of Stanhope, 1888.

11  *Somme,* by Martin Gilbert (John Murray, 2006), p. 189.

12  *Mail on Sunday,* 8 January 2006.

13  *The Independent,* 6 December 2006.

14  BBC News website, 27 December 2006.

15  *T.E. Lawrence In War And Peace* (Greenhill Books, 2007).

### CHAPTER SEVEN

1   Press conference in Baghdad, 28 August 2006.

2   *Hansard,* 18 March 2003.

3   Speech prepared for delivery, 18 March 2003.

4   John Wilson, *Sir Henry Campbell-Bannerman,* 1973.

5   Letter to Hilda Chamberlain, 25 June 1938.

6   *The Guardian,* 20 December 2006.

7   Speech at UC Berkeley, 11 October 2004.

8   *The Independent,* 6 December 2006.

9   *Independent on Sunday,* 13 August 2006.

10  *Guardian* ICM poll, August 2006.

11  *The Utility of Force* (Penguin, 2006), p. 398.

12  *The Guardian,* 2 June 2007.

### CHAPTER EIGHT

1   *The Guardian,* 28 February 2005.

2   Evidence by Carne Ross to the Butler Inquiry, 9 June 2004.

3   *Financial Times,* 3 August 2006.

4   *The Observer,* 28 August 2005.

5   *The Guardian,* 20 June 2005.

6   Evidence to the House of Commons Foreign Affairs Committee, 8 December 2006.

7   Evidence by Carne Ross to the Butler Inquiry, 9 June 2004.

8   Ibid.

9   *Independent Diplomat* (Hurst & Company, 2007), p. 14.

10  *The Guardian,* 20 June 2005.

11  *Independent Diplomat,* p. 15.

12 *The Guardian*, 20 June 2005.

13 Evidence to the House of Commons Foreign Affairs Committee, 8 December 2006.

14 Speech in the Foreign Office, 28 March 2006.

15 Evidence to the House of Commons Foreign Affairs Committee, 8 December 2006.

16 Ibid.

17 *DC Confidential* (Weidenfeld & Nicolson, 2005), p. 202.

18 *Independent Diplomat*, p. 137.

19 Evidence to the House of Commons Foreign Affairs Committee, 8 December 2006.

**CHAPTER NINE**

1 Letter to the European Council of Ministers, December 1991.

2 Depositions to the International Criminal Tribunal for ex-Yugoslavia, 29 December 1995 and 6–7 February 1996.

3 *New Statesman*, 2 August 2004.

4 BBC *Newsnight*, September 1995.

5 BBC *Newsnight*, September 1995.

6 Speech at the Srebrenica memorial, 11 July 2005.

7 BBC *Newsnight*, September 1995.

8 *The Utility of Force*.

9 *A Safe Area* (Pocket Books, 1997).

10 *In Harm's Way* (Penguin, 1996).

11 *Hansard*, 29 April 1993.

12 *Unfinest Hour: Britain and the Destruction of Bosnia* (Penguin, 2002), p. 297.

13 *Hansard*, 18 March 2003.

14 Letter to the author, 15 December 2006.

**CHAPTER TEN**

1 Evidence by Carne Ross to the House of Commons Foreign Affairs Committee, 15 December 2006.

2 *The Times*, 16 September 2006.

3 *The Independent*, 9 September 2006.

4 *The Guardian*, 4 September 2006.

5 Sky News, 22 September 2006.

6    BBC Dimbleby Lecture, 6 December 2006.
7    *The Guardian*, 'Comment is Free', 7 September 2006.

**CHAPTER ELEVEN**
1    Speech at the Royal Geographical Society, 12 June 1997.
2    *Hansard*, 15 December 2006.
3    *The Times*, 16 December 2006.
4    *The Scotsman*, 8 July 2002.
5    The Burma Campaign website, 30 March 1998.
6    *My Life in the Royal Navy in the Second World War*, by Jack Dixon.
7    *Out of Balance*, by Landmine Action, November 2005.
8    *Hansard*, 5 May 2004.
9    Speech at the RGS, 12 June 1997.
10   *Hansard*, 16 December 2006.
11   *Hansard*, 30 October 2006.
12   Speech by ambassador John Duncan to the Geneva Conference, 13 November 2006.
13   BBC News, 5 November 2006.
14   Speech to the Conference on Disarmament, 13 November 2006.
15   *Foreseeable Harm*, by Landmine Action, 2006.
16   *Daily Telegraph* Online, 20 October 2006.
17   *Haaretz*, 12 September 2006.
18   *Haaretz*, 7 September 2006.
19   *Haaretz*, September 2006.

**CHAPTER TWELVE**
1    Regimental diary of the 11th (Cambridgeshire) Battalion The Suffolk Regiment.
2    Martin Middlebrook, *The First Day on the Somme* (Penguin, 1971).
3    Philip Knightley, *The First Casualty* (André Deutsch, 1975).
4    Channel 4 documentary, *The Futility of Force*, 13 January 2006.

**CHAPTER THIRTEEN**
1    Army Doctrine Publication Volume 5, February 2000.

2   *Britain's Throwaway Soldiers*, Channel 4, 30 March 2007.
3   Ibid.
4   Ibid.
5   Ibid.
6   Ibid.

#### CHAPTER FOURTEEN
1   *The Independent*, 11 September 2006.
2   *Independent Member* (Methuen, 1950).
3   Ibid.
4   *The Guardian*, 28 July 2006.
5   *Financial Times*, 3 August 2006.

#### CHAPTER FIFTEEN
1   *The Guardian*, 12 October 2006.
2   Speech to a joint session of the US Congress, 17 July 2003.
3   *The Guardian*, 11 October 2006.
4   *The Guardian*, 24 September 2006.
5   *The Independent*, 19 December 2006.
6   *Daily Mail*, 13 October 2006.
7   *Henry V*, Act IV, scene 1.
8   *Diaries* (Phoenix, 1993), p. 111.
9   BBC News, 11 June 2004.
10  *The Guardian*, 'Comment is Free', 15 March 2006.
11  *In Retrospect* (Random House, 1995).

#### POSTSCRIPT
1   *The Times*, 24 October 2007.
2   BBC News, 19 December 2007.
3   *Blair Unbound* (Simon & Schuster, 2007), p. 169.
4   BBC World Service, 15 November 2007.
5   'Iraq Body Count', *The Independent*, 7 January 2008.
6   BBC News, 13 October 2007.
7   *Hansard*, 18 December 2007.

# INDEX